OFFICIAL
BLUE BOOK OF UNITED STATES COINS ®

1984 HANDBOOK OF UNITED STATES COINS

With Premium List

By R. S. YEOMAN

★

FORTY-FIRST EDITION

Edited by Kenneth Bressett

Containing mint records and prices paid by dealers for all U.S. coins from 1616 to the present time, including Colonials, Regular Issues, Commemoratives, Territorials, Gold, Proof Sets, and Mint Sets. Information on collecting coins—how coins are produced—mints and mint marks—grading of coins—location of mint marks—preserving and cleaning coins—starting a collection—history of mints and interesting descriptions of all U.S. copper, nickel, silver and gold coins. Fully illustrated.

 Whitman Coin Products

Copyright © 1983 by
WESTERN PUBLISHING COMPANY, INC.
RACINE, WISCONSIN 53404

WHITMAN and OFFICIAL BLUE BOOK OF UNITED STATES COINS are registered trademarks of Western Publishing Company, Inc.

9050-84　　　ISBN: 0-307-01984-5　　　Printed in U.S.A.

Important Notice

THIS BOOK IS *NOT A RETAIL PRICE LIST*

Premium prices are the average amount dealers will pay for coins (according to condition) if required for their stock. (See page 11)

Current *retail* valuations of all U.S. coins are listed in Whitman's A GUIDE BOOK OF UNITED STATES COINS by R. S. Yeoman, Western Publishing Company, Inc., Racine, Wisconsin ($5.95)

Brief guides to grading are placed before each major coin type in this book. For those readers who desire more detailed descriptions of all coin grades, we recommend OFFICIAL A.N.A. GRADING STANDARDS FOR UNITED STATES COINS, Western Publishing Company, Inc., Racine, Wisconsin ($6.95).

Foreword

Since 1941, annually revised editions of this Handbook have aided thousands of people who have coins to sell or are actively engaged in collecting United States coins. The popular coin folder method of collecting by date has created ever-changing premium values, based on the supply and demand of each date and mint. Through its panel of contributors the Handbook has, over the years, reported these changing values. It also serves as a source of general numismatic information to all levels of interest in the hobby.

The premium list gives representative prices paid by dealers for various United States coins. These are averages of prices assembled from many widely separated sources. On some issues slight differences in price among dealers may result from proximity to the various mints or heavily populated centers. Other factors, such as local supply and demand or dealers' stock conditions, may also tend to cause deviations from the prices listed. While many coins bring no premium when circulated, they usually bring premium prices in Uncirculated and Proof condition.

The publisher of this book does not deal in coins; therefore, the values shown here are not offers to purchase (or sell) but are included only as general information.

IF YOU HAVE COINS TO SELL

The publishers are not engaged in the rare coin business; however, the chances are that the dealer from whom you purchased this book is engaged in the buying and selling of rare coins—contact him first. In the event that you purchased this book from a source other than a numismatic establishment, consult your local telephone directory for the names of coin dealers (they will be found sometimes under the heading of "Stamp and Coin Dealers"). If you live in a city or town that does not have any coin dealers, it is suggested that you obtain a copy of one of the trade publications in order to obtain the names and addresses of many of the country's leading dealers.

The following numismatic magazines are obtainable by subscription. They are published monthly or as indicated below. Information or sample copies may be obtained by writing to the individual publisher.

COINage Magazine
17337 Ventura Boulevard
Encino, California 91316

Hobbies Magazine
1006 S. Michigan Ave.
Chicago, Ill. 60605
(Has a coin section)

Coins Magazine
Iola, Wisconsin 54990

Numismatic News Weekly
Iola, Wisconsin 54990

Coin World
P.O. Box 150
Sidney, Ohio 45367

The Numismatist
P.O. Box 2366
Colorado Springs, Colorado 80901
(Published monthly by American Numismatic Assn.)

CONTRIBUTORS

Lee F. Hewitt, the former editor and publisher of the NUMISMATIC SCRAPBOOK MAGAZINE, was an early contributor, having supplied many of the historical references and explanations which appear throughout this book.

Charles E. Green gave valuable counsel when the first edition of the HANDBOOK was undertaken. He supplied most of the original mint data and was a regular contributor to each revised edition until his death in 1955.

CONTRIBUTORS TO THE FORTY-FIRST EDITION

Dolores Toll — *Project Coordinator*

Burl Armstrong
B & M Coins
802 Avenue G, Suite 3
Fort Madison, IA 52627

Michael Aron
Michael Aron Coin Auctions
P.O. Box 33166
Granada Hills, CA 91344

Richard A. Bagg
Bowers and Merena Galleries
P.O. Box 2745
Boston, MA 02208

Robert F. Batchelder
Robert F. Batchelder Company
1 West Butler Avenue
Ambler, PA 19002

Gerald L. Bauman
Manfra, Tordella & Brookes, Inc.
59 West 49th Street
New York, NY 10112

Aubrey E. Bebee
Bebee's, Inc.
4514 North 30th Street
Omaha, NE 68111

Lee J. Bellisario
Bellisario Rare Coin Gallery
121 Mount Vernon Street
Boston, MA 02108

George H. Blenker
Lincoln Yellow, Inc.
Box 56
Blenker, WI 54415

Brad Bohnert
Superior Stamp & Coin Co., Inc.
9301 Wilshire Blvd.
Beverly Hills, CA 90210

Q. David Bowers
Bowers and Merena Galleries, Inc.
P.O. Box 1224
Wolfeboro, NH 03894

Phil Bressett
Viking Coin & Currency
1210 North Green Bay Road
Racine, WI 53406

Hy Brown
Hy Brown, Inc.
P.O. Box 111
Painesville, OH 44077

Judy Cahn
Judy Cahn & Associates
P.O. Box 49824
Los Angeles, CA 90049

Bill Causey
American Gold & Silver Corp.
985 West Foothill Blvd.
Claremont, CA 91711

J. H. Cline
Cline's Rare Coins
4421 Salem Avenue
Dayton, OH 45416

Kurt E. Eckstein
31 North Clark St.
Chicago, IL 60602

Chuck Furjanic
Chuck Furjanic Rare Coins
P.O. Box 8739
Pittsburgh, PA 15221

Dorothy Gershenson
Dorothy Gershenson, Inc.
P.O. Box 395
Bala Cynwyd, PA 19004

Harry M. Gittelson

Ira M. Goldberg
Lawrence S. Goldberg
Superior Stamp & Coin Co., Inc.
9301 Wilshire Blvd.
Beverly Hills, CA 90210

Kenneth M. Goldman
Kenneth Goldman, Inc.
P.O. Box 1477
Boston, MA 02104

David J. Hendrickson
Leon E. Hendrickson
Silver Towne Coin
P.O. Box 424
Winchester, IN 47394

C. Edward Hipps
Ed Hipps' Gallery
9100 North Central Expressway, #143
Dallas, TX 75231

Karl D. Hirtzinger
Bowers & Merena Galleries, Inc.
P.O. Box 1224
Wolfeboro, NH 03894

Ron Howard
Kagin's Numismatic Investment Corp.
1000 Insurance Exchange Bldg.
Des Moines, IA 50309

John Hunter
Hunter Numismatics
P.O. Box 508
Winchester, IN 47394

Robert H. Jacobs
Jake's Marketplace, Inc.
2955 North Central Avenue
Chicago, IL 60634

Floyd O. Janney
Universal Numismatics Corp.
P.O. Box 469
Richland Center, WI 53581

James J. Jelinski
Essex Numismatics, Inc.
Eight Cannon Road
Wilton, CT 06897

A. M. Kagin
Donald H. Kagin
Kagin's Numismatic Investment Corp.
1000 Insurance Exchange Bldg.
Des Moines, IA 50309

Paul S. Kagin

Stanley Kesselman

Edwin Leventhal
J. J. Teaparty
43 Bromfield Street
Boston, MA 02108

Stuart Levine
J. J. Teaparty
43 Bromfield Street
Boston, MA 02108

Denis W. Loring

Robert T. McIntire
McIntire Rare Coins & Auctions
P.O. Box 546
Jacksonville, AR 72076

Bill Mertes
1206 North 11th Avenue
St. Cloud, MN 56301

Sylvia Novack
P.O. Box 729
San Bernardino, CA 92402

Sidney L. Nusbaum
Arch City Supply Co.
P.O. Box 10956
St. Louis, MO 63135

Robert M. Paul
William P. Paul
American Heritage Minting, Inc.
Benjamin Fox Pavilion, Suite 510
Box 1008
Jenkintown, PA 19046

Joe Person
Joe Person & Co., Inc.
Bank of Florida Bldg., Suite 2
1101 Pasadena Avenue, South
St. Petersburg, FL 33707

Joel D. Rettew
Rare Coin Galleries, Inc.
201 North Indian Avenue
Palm Springs, CA 92262

Maurice Rosen
Numismatic Counseling, Inc.
P.O. Box 231
East Meadow, NY 11554

Robert R. Shaw

Maurice A. Storck, Sr.
P.O. Box 644
Portland, ME 04104-0644

Charles Surasky
Essex Numismatics, Inc.
Eight Cannon Road
Wilton, CT 06897

Gary L. Young
Gary L. Young, Numismatist
P.O. Box 9
Manton, CA 96059

COLLECTING COINS

Numismatics or coin collecting is one of the world's oldest hobbies, dating back several centuries. Coin collecting in America did not develop to any extent until about 1840, as our pioneer forefathers were too busy carving a country out of wilderness to afford the luxury of a hobby. The discontinuance of the large-sized cent in 1857 caused many persons to attempt to accumulate a complete set of the pieces while they were still in circulation. One of the first groups of collectors to band together for the study of numismatics was the Numismatic and Antiquarian Society of Philadelphia, organized on January 1, 1858. Lack of an economical method to house a collection held the number of devotees of coin collecting to a few thousand until the Whitman Publishing Company and other manufacturers placed the low-priced coin boards and folders on the market some years ago. Since that time the number of Americans collecting coins has increased many-fold.

The Production of Coins

To collect coins intelligently it is necessary to have some knowledge of the manner in which our coins are produced. They are made in factories called "mints." The Mint of the United States was established at Philadelphia by a resolution of Congress dated April 2, 1792. The Act also provided for the coinage of gold eagles ($10), half-eagles and quarter-eagles, the silver dollar, half-dollar, quarter-dollar, dime (originally spelled "disme") and the half-disme or half-dime; the copper cent and half cent. According to the Treasury Department, the first coins struck were one-cent and half-cent pieces, in March of 1793 on a hand-operated press. Most numismatic authorities consider the half-disme of 1792 as the first United States coinage, quoting the words of George Washington as their authority. Washington, in his annual address, November 6, 1792, having said, "There has been a small beginning in the coining of the Half-Dimes, the want of small coins in circulation calling the first attention to them." In the new Philadelphia Mint are exhibited a number of implements, etc., from the original mint, and some coins discovered when the old building was wrecked. These coins included half-dismes, and the placard identifying them states that Washington furnished the silver and gave the coined pieces to his friends as souvenirs.

Prior to the adoption of the Constitution, the Continental Congress arranged for the issuance of copper coins under private contract. These are known as the "Fugio cents" from the design of the piece, which shows a sundial and the Latin word "fugio"—"I Fly" or, in connection with the sundial, "Time Flies." The ever appropriate motto. "Mind Your Business," is also on the coin.

In the manufacture of a given coin the first step is the cutting of the "die." Prior to the latter part of the nineteenth century dies for United States coins were "cut by hand." Briefly this method is as follows: The design having been determined, a drawing the exact size of the coin is made. A tracing is made from this drawing. A piece of steel is smoothed and coated with transfer wax, and the tracing impressed into the wax. The engraver then tools out the steel where the relief or raised effect is required. If the design is such that it can all be produced by cutting away steel, the die is hardened and ready for use. Some dies are not brought to a finished state, as some part of the design can perhaps be done better in relief. In that case, when all that can be accomplished to advantage in the die is completed, it is hardened, a soft-steel impression is taken from it, and the unfinished parts are then completed. This piece of steel is in turn hardened and, by a press, driven into another piece of soft-steel, thus making a die which, when hardened, is ready for the making of coins.

This hand method of cutting dies accounts for the many die varieties of early United States coins. Where the amount of coinage of a given year was large enough to wear out several dies, each new die placed in the coining press created another die variety of that year. The dies being cut by hand, no two were exactly alike in every detail, even though some of the major elements (head, wreath, etc.) were sunk into the die by individual master punches. Of the cents dated 1794, over sixty different die varieties have been discovered.

Hundreds of dies are now used by the mints of the United States each year, but they are all made from one master die, which is produced in the following manner:

After the design is settled upon, the plaster of paris or wax model is prepared several times the actual size of the coin. When this model is finished an electrotype (an exact duplicate in metal) is made and prepared for the reducing lathe. The reducing lathe is a machine, working on the principle of the pantograph, only in this case the one point traces or follows the form of the model while another and much smaller point in the form of a drill cuts away the steel and produces a reduced size die of the model. The die is finished and details are sharpened or worked over by an engraver with chisel and graver. The master die is used to make duplicates in soft-steel which are then hardened and ready for the coining press. To harden dies, they are placed in cast-iron boxes packed with carbon to exclude the air, and when heated to a bright red are cooled suddenly with water.

In the coinage operations the first step is to prepare the metal. The alloys used are: silver coins, 90% silver and 10% copper; five-cent pieces, 75% copper and 25% nickel; one-cent pieces, 95% copper and 5% zinc. (The 1943 cent consists of steel coated with zinc; and the five-cent piece 1942-1945 contains 35% silver, 56% copper and 9% manganese.) Under the Coinage Act of 1965, the composition of dimes, quarters and half dollars was changed to eliminate or reduce the silver content of these coins. The copper-nickel "clad" dimes, quarters, halves and dollars are composed of an outer layer of copper-nickel (75% copper and 25% nickel) bonded to an inner core of pure copper. The silver clad half dollar and dollar have an outer layer of 80% silver bonded to an inner core of 21% silver, with a total content of 40% silver.

Alloys are melted in crucibles and poured into molds to form ingots. The ingots are in the form of thin bars and vary in size according to the denomination of the coin. The width is sufficient to allow three or more coins to be cut from the strips.

The ingots are next put through rolling mills to reduce the thickness to required limits. The strips are then fed into cutting presses which cut circular blanks (planchets) of the approximate size of the finished coin. The blanks are run through annealing furnaces to soften them; next through tumbling barrels, rotating cyclinders containing cleaning solutions which clean and burnish the metal, and finally into centrifugal drying machines.

The blanks are next fed into a milling machine which produces the raised or upset rim. The blank is now ready for the coining press.

The blank is held firmly by a collar, as it is struck under heavy pressure varying from 40 tons for the one-cent pieces and dimes to 170 tons for silver dollars. Upper and lower dies impress the design on both sides of the coin. The pressure is sufficient to produce a raised surface level with that of the milled rim. The collar holding the blank for silver or clad coins is grooved. The pressure forces the metal into the grooves of the collar, producing the "reeding" on the finished coin.

How a Proof Coin Is Made

Selected dies are inspected for perfection and are highly polished and cleaned. They are again wiped clean or polished after every 15 to 25 impressions and are replaced frequently to avoid imperfections from worn dies. Coinage blanks are polished and cleaned to assure high quality in striking. They are then hand fed into the coinage press one at a time, each blank receiving two blows from the dies to bring up sharp, high relief details. The coinage operation is done at slow speed with extra pressure. Finished proofs are individually inspected and are handled by gloves or tongs. They also receive a final inspection by packers before being sonically sealed in special plastic cases.

Certain coins, including Lincoln cents, Buffalo nickels, Quarter Eagles, Half Eagles, Eagles and Double Eagles, between the years 1908 and 1916 were made with a matte or sandblast surface. Matte proofs have a dull frosted surface which was either applied to the dies, or produced by special treatment after striking.

Mints and Mint Marks

In addition to the Philadelphia Mint, the U.S. Government has from time to time established branch mints in various parts of the country. At the present time a branch mint operates in Denver. Starting in 1968, proof sets and some of the regular coins are produced at the San Francisco Assay Office. The Denver Mint has operated since 1906. A mint was operated at New Orleans from 1838 to 1861 and again from 1879 to 1909. Mints were also in service at Carson City, Nevada, from 1870 to 1893; at Charlotte, North Carolina, from 1838 to 1861; at Dahlonega, Georgia, from 1838 to 1861; and at San Francisco since 1854.

Coins struck at Philadelphia before 1979 (except 1942 to 1945 five-cent pieces) do not carry a mint mark. The mint mark is found only on coins struck at the branch mints. It is a small letter, usually found on the reverse side. The Lincoln cent is one exception to the rule. All coins minted after 1967 have the mint mark on the obverse. The letters to signify the various mints are as follows:

"C" for Charlotte, North Carolina (on gold coins only).
"CC" for Carson City, Nevada.
"D" for Dahlonega, Georgia (gold coins only, 1838 to 1861).
"D" For Denver, Colorado (from 1906 to date).
"O" for New Orleans, Louisiana.
"P" for Philadelphia, Pennsylvania.
"S" for San Francisco, California.

The mint mark is of utmost importance to collectors due to the fact that the coinage at the branch mints has usually been much smaller than at Philadelphia and many of the branch mint pieces are very scarce.

DISTINGUISHING MARKS

The illustrations and explanations in this section will help the collector to identify certain well-known varieties.

HALF CENTS OF
1795-1796
SHOWING LOCATION OF
POLE TO CAP

The end of the staff or pole lies parallel with the line of the bust, which is pointed. The die-maker, probably through error, omitted the pole on some of the dies of 1795 and 1796.

Pole to Cap

No Pole to Cap

Stemless Wreath

Stems to Wreath

STEMLESS WREATH VARIETY OF HALF CENTS AND LARGE CENTS
Observe the reverse side for this variety. Illustrations at left show both stemless and stems to wreath types for each comparison—stemless wreath found on 1804, 1805, 1806, Half cents. 1797, 1802, 1803 Large cents.

1804 HALF CENT PROTRUDING
TONGUE OR SPIKED CHIN VARIETY

DISTINGUISHING MARKS

Details showing differences in 1804 plain 4 and crosslet 4. Note serif on horizontal bar of figure 4 as shown at right.

Plain 4

Crosslet 4

THE 1856 FLYING EAGLE CENT

Collectors are advised to inspect any 1856 Flying Eagle cent carefully.

A few tests will aid in establishing genuineness of this cent, as follows:

THE DATE

The 6 in the date should be as illustrated. If the lower half is thick, it is probably an altered 1858. A magnifying glass will often reveal poor workmanship.

The figure 5 slants slightly to the right on a genuine 1856. The vertical bar points to the center of the ball just beneath. On the 1858, this bar points *outside* the ball. (Compare the two illustrations.)

THE LEGEND

The center of the O in OF is crude and almost squared on the genuine 1856, but on the large letter 1858 it is rounded.

The letters A and M in America are joined in both the 1856 and large letter 1858, but they join at a slight angle on the 1856, while the bottom of the letters form a smooth curve on the 1858 large letter cent.

1858 FLYING EAGLE CENT

Large Letters

Letters A and M in the word AMERICA are joined on the LARGE LETTER variety. They are separated on the SMALL LETTER variety.

Small Letters

1864 BRONZE INDIAN HEAD CENT WITH "L" ON RIBBON

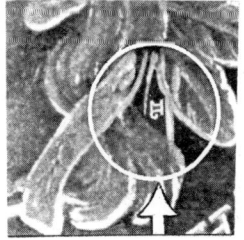

A small "L," the initial of the designer Longacre, was added to the Indian design late in 1864 and was continued through 1909. For coins in less than fine condition, this small letter will often be worn away. The point of the bust is rounded on the 1864 variety without "L"; pointed on the variety with "L." The initial must be visible, however, for the 1864 variety to bring the higher premium. If the coin is turned slightly so that the Indian faces the observer, the highlighted details will usually appear to better advantage.

DISTINGUISHING MARKS

During 1909 initials appeared on reverse. Starting in 1918 they appear below the shoulder.

1918-S Quarter
8 Over 7
A variety of this kind is rarely found in coinage of the twentieth century.

1938D over S Nickel Variety

1942 Dime with 2 over 1

1955 Cent Error
"Doubled Die" Obverse

Large Date Cent
1960

Small Date Cent
1960

Large Date Cent
1982

Small Date Cent
1982

CONDITION OF COINS
Essential elements of the A.N.A. grading system

PROOF — A specially made coin distinguished by sharpness of detail and usually with a brilliant mirrorlike surface. Proof refers to the method of manufacture and is not a condition, but normally the term implies perfect mint state unless otherwise noted and graded as below. See page 42 for details.

MINT STATE — The terms Mint State (MS) and Uncirculated (Unc.) are interchangeably used to describe coins showing no trace of wear. Such coins may vary to some degree because of blemishes, toning or slight imperfections as described in the following subdivisions.

PERFECT UNCIRCULATED (MS-70) — Perfect new condition, showing no trace of wear. The finest quality possible, with no evidence of scratches, handling or contact with other coins. Very few regular issue coins are ever found in this condition.

CHOICE UNCIRCULATED (MS-65) — An above average Uncirculated coin which may be brilliant or lightly toned and has very few contact marks on the surface or rim. MS-67 or MS-63 indicates a slightly higher or lower grade of preservation.

UNCIRCULATED (MS-60) — Has no trace of wear but may show a number of contact marks, and surface may be spotted or lack some luster.

CHOICE ABOUT UNCIRCULATED (AU-55) — Barest evidence of light wear on only the highest points of the design. Most of the mint luster remains.

ABOUT UNCIRCULATED (AU-50) — Has traces of light wear on many of the high points. At least half of the mint luster is still present.

CHOICE EXTREMELY FINE (EF-45) — Light overall wear shows on highest points. All design details are very sharp. Some of the mint luster is evident.

EXTREMELY FINE (EF-40) — Design is lightly worn throughout, but all features are sharp and well defined. Traces of luster may show.

CHOICE VERY FINE (VF-30) — Light even wear on the surface and highest parts of the design. All lettering and major features are sharp.

VERY FINE (VF-20) — Shows moderate wear on high points of design. All major details are clear.

FINE (F-12) — Moderate to considerable even wear. Entire design is bold with overall pleasing appearance.

VERY GOOD (VG-8) — Well worn with main features clear and bold although rather flat.

GOOD (G-4) — Heavily worn with design visible but faint in areas. Many details are flat.

ABOUT GOOD (AG-3) — Very heavily worn with portions of lettering, date and legends worn smooth. The date may be barely readable.

IMPORTANT: Damaged coins, such as those which are bent, corroded, scratched, holed, nicked, stained, or mutilated, are worth less than those without defects. *Flawless uncirculated coins are generally worth more than values quoted in this book.* Slightly worn coins ("sliders") which have been cleaned and conditioned ("whizzed") to simulate uncirculated luster are worth considerably less than perfect pieces.

Unlike damage inflicted after striking, manufacturing defects do not always lessen values. Examples are: Colonial coins with planchet flaws and weakly struck designs; early silver and gold with weight adjustment "file marks" (parallel cuts made prior to striking); and proofs with "lint marks" (dust or other foreign matter which may mar the surface during striking).

Brief guides to grading are placed before each major coin type in this book. For those readers who desire more detailed descriptions of all coin grades, we recommend OFFICIAL A.N.A. GRADING STANDARDS FOR UNITED STATES COINS, by the American Numismatic Association.

Preserving and Cleaning Coins

Most numismatists will tell you to "never clean a coin" and it is good advice! Cleaning coins will almost always reduce their value.

Some effort should be made to keep uncirculated and proof coins bright so they won't need cleaning. Tarnish on a coin is purely a chemical process caused by oxygen in the air acting on the metal or by chemicals with which the coin comes in contact. One of the commonest chemicals causing tarnish is sulphur; most paper, with the exception of specially manufactured "sulphur-free" kinds, contains sulphur due to the sulphuric acid that is used in paper manufacture. Therefore do not wrap coins in ordinary paper; also keep uncirculated and proof coins away from rubber bands (a rubber band placed on a silver coin for a few days will produce a black stripe on the coin where the band touched). The utmost in protection is obtained by storing the coin in an airtight box.

Many coins become marred by careless handling. Always hold the coin by the edge. The accompanying illustration shows the right and wrong way to handle numismatic specimens. It is a breach of numismatic etiquette to handle another collector's coin except by the edge, even if it is not an uncirculated or proof piece.

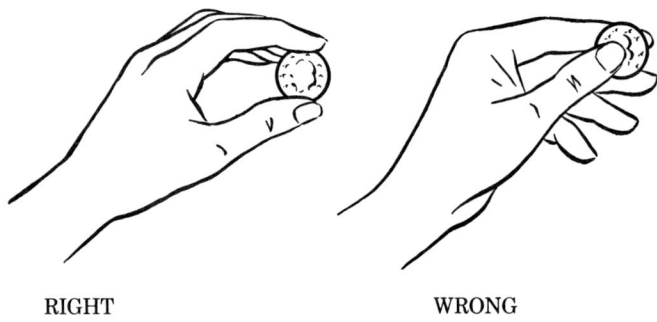

RIGHT   WRONG

Starting a Collection

One may start a collection of United States coins with very little expense by systematically assembling the various dates and mint marks of all the types and denominations that are now in general circulation. Whitman's coin folders make this possible.

With the exception of the price paid for the coin folder, collecting coins received in everyday business transactions entails no expense whatever; a Jefferson nickel taken out of circulation, for example, can always be spent for 5 cents if the occasion arrives. Filling an album or two out of circulation is probably the best method of determining whether coin collecting appeals to you. Not everyone can be a successful coin collector. It requires patience, intelligence of a high order, and a certain desire to know the meaning behind a lot of things that at first glance and to the ordinary mortal appear meaningless. You may not be cut out to be a collector but you'll never know until you look further into the subject, and if by the time an album or two of coins are collected you have no burning desire to acquire many more different coins, you will probably never be a collector. However, the chances are that you will be, because if you have read this far in this book it shows that you are interested in the subject.

Perfection is the goal of every endeavor and coin collecting is no exception. After an album has been filled with circulated specimens, the next step will be to replace them with coins in uncirculated condition, or perhaps to start collecting an obsolete series; in either case, it will be necessary to purchase some coins from dealers or other collectors. The most logical way to keep abreast with the market, or obtain the addresses of the country's leading dealers, is to subscribe to one or more of the trade publications (see page 3 for list of the coin publications). These magazines carry advertisements of various dealers listing coins for sale. Moreover, through this source the beginner may obtain price lists and catalogs from the dealers.

There are several good reference books available at reasonable prices which will be helpful to the collector who wishes to know more about U. S. coins and paper money. R. S. Yeoman's A GUIDE BOOK OF UNITED STATES COINS (Red Book) is an expanded version of THE HANDBOOK. It lists retail values of all regular U. S. coins and also lists all coins of the U. S. Colonial period and private and territorial gold coins.

Most coin, book and hobby dealers can supply the following titles:

> *Guide Book of U.S. Coins* — Yeoman
> *Let's Collect Coins* — Bressett
> *Prices for Buying and Selling U.S. Coins* — Bressett
> *Official Grading Standards for U.S. Coins* — A.N.A.
> *Common Sense Coin Investment* — Bowers
> *Basics of Coin Grading* — Bressett

Join a Coin Club

A beginner should join a "coin club" if he is fortunate enough to live in a city which has one. The association with more experienced collectors will be of great benefit. Practically all the larger cities have one or more clubs and they are being rapidly organized in the smaller towns. The publications mentioned on page 3 carry lists of coin clubs and special events such as coin shows and conventions.

UNITED STATES PAPER MONEY

Paper money issued by the United States government is collected widely in this country. The first issue of "greenbacks" was made in 1861; paper money was not issued by our government for circulation prior to that date. Collectors of U.S. notes prefer them in crisp, new condition; but the old style large-sized notes even in worn condition are usually worth more than face value.

Before the issuance of the first U.S. government paper money, many banks throughout the country issued their own currency. These issues are commonly referred to as "broken bank notes" although that is somewhat of a misnomer as many of the banks did not "go broke" (a few are still in existence) and redeemed their paper money issues. There are thousands of varieties of these notes in existence, most of which are very common and worth from $1.00 to $3.00 each. Before and during the American Revolution the various individual states and the Continental Congress issued paper money. The common varieties of these Colonial notes are worth from $3.00 to $10.00; a few are quite rare.

"Broken Bank" note of 1863

I. THE BRITISH COLONIES IN AMERICA
SOMMER ISLANDS (Bermuda)

This coinage, the first struck for the English colonies in America, was issued about 1616. The coins were known as "Hogge Money" or "Hoggies."

The pieces were made of copper lightly silvered, in four denominations: shilling, sixpence, threepence and twopence, indicated by Roman numerals. The hog is the main device and appears on the obverse side of each. SOMMER ISLANDS is inscribed within beaded circles. The reverse shows a full-rigged galleon with the flag of St. George on each of four masts.

Shilling

	Good	V. Good	Fine	V. Fine
Twopence	$900.00	$1,750	$3,750	$5,000
Threepence (V. Rare)	—	—	—	—
Sixpence	700.00	1,500	3,000	4,000
Shilling	800.00	1,750	3,750	5,000

MASSACHUSETTS
"NEW ENGLAND" COINAGE (1652)

In 1652 the General Court of Massachusetts ordered the first metallic currency to be struck in the English Americas, the New England silver threepence, sixpence, and shilling. These coins were made from silver bullion procured principally from the West Indies. Joseph Jenks made the punches for the first coins at his Iron Works in Saugus, Massachusetts, close to Boston where the mint was located. John Hull was appointed mintmaster; his assistant was Robert Sanderson.

Note: Early American coins are rare in conditions better than listed and valued much higher.

 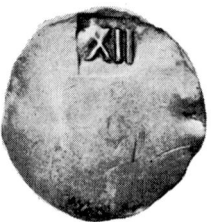

NE Shilling (1652)

	V. Good	Fine	V. Fine
NE Threepence *(2 known)*	—	—	—
NE Sixpence *(7 known)*	—	—	$25,000
NE Shilling	$2,500	$6,000	10,000

MASSACHUSETTS
WILLOW TREE COINAGE (1653-1660)

The simplicity of the design on the N.E. coins invited counterfeiting and clipping of the edges. Therefore, they were soon replaced by the Willow, Oak and Pine Tree series. The Willow Tree coins were struck from 1653 to 1660, the Oak Trees 1660 to 1667, and the Pine Trees 1667 to 1682. All of them (with the exception of the Oak Tree twopence) bore the date 1652.

Many varieties of all of these coins exist. Values shown are for the most common types.

Sixpence

	Fair	Good	Fine
Willow Tree Threepence 1652 *(3 known)*.			
Willow Tree Sixpence 1652			
Willow Tree Shilling 1652	$1,700	$3,250	$6,000

OAK TREE COINAGE (1660-1667)

Twopence   Threepence

	Good	V. Good	Fine	V. Fine
Oak Tree Twopence 1662.	$150.00	$250.00	$450.00	$900.00
Oak Tree Threepence 1652	175.00	285.00	550.00	1,300
Oak Tree Sixpence 1652.	175.00	285.00	550.00	1,400
Oak Tree Shilling 1652.	175.00	275.00	500.00	1,300

PINE TREE COINAGE (1667-1682)

The first pine tree coins were minted on the same size planchets as the Oak Tree pieces. Subsequent issues of the shilling were narrower and thicker to conform to the size of English coins.

Shilling,
Large Planchet
(1667-1674)

MASSACHUSETTS
PINE TREE COINAGE (1667-1682)

Shilling,
Small Planchet
(1675-1682)

	Good	V. Good	Fine	V. Fine
Pine Tree Threepence 1652	$100.00	$200.00	$300.00	$550.00
Pine Tree Sixpence 1652	125.00	225.00	350.00	650.00
Pine Tree Shilling, large planchet 1652	150.00	250.00	400.00	750.00
Pine Tree Shilling, small planchet 1652	125.00	225.00	350.00	650.00

MARYLAND

In 1658 Cecil Calvert, the "Lord Proprietor of Maryland," had coinage struck in England for use in Maryland.

There were four denominations: shillings, sixpence, and fourpence (groat) in silver, and a copper penny (denarium). The silver coins have the bust of Lord Baltimore on the obverse, and the Baltimore family Arms with the denomination in Roman numerals on the reverse.

Fourpence (groat)

Lord Baltimore Shilling

	Good	V. Good	Fine	V. Fine
Penny (Copper) (Ex. Rare)	—	—	—	—
Fourpence	$200.00	$500.00	$1,800	$3,500
Sixpence	200.00	475.00	1,000	2,000
Shilling	250.00	600.00	2,000	4,000

NEW JERSEY
ST. PATRICK OR MARK NEWBY COINAGE

Mark Newby, who came to America from Dublin, Ireland, in November 1681, brought copper pieces believed by numismatists to have been struck in England c. 1650. These are called St. Patrick Halfpence.

The coin received wide currency in the New Jersey Province, having been authorized to pass as legal tender by the General Assembly in May 1682.

The smaller piece, known as a farthing, was never authorized for circulation in the Colonies.

NEW JERSEY

St. Patrick Farthing

	V. Good	Fine	V. Fine
St. Patrick "Farthing"	$35.00	$75.00	$250.00
St. Patrick "Halfpenny"	50.00	100.00	250.00

II. COINAGE AUTHORIZED BY ROYAL PATENT
AMERICAN PLANTATIONS TOKEN

These tokens struck in nearly pure tin were the first authorized coinage for the British colonies in America. They were made under a franchise granted in 1688 to John Holt. Restrikes were made c. 1828 from original dies. These are valued at about half as much as the originals.

	Fine	E. Fine	Unc.
(1688) James II Plantation Token farthing, 1/24 PART REAL — Tin	$100.00	$200.00	$800.00

COINAGE OF WILLIAM WOOD
ROSA AMERICANA COINS

William Wood, an Englishman, obtained a patent from George I to make tokens for Ireland and the American Colonies.

The Rosa Americana pieces were issued in three denominations, halfpenny, penny and twopence, and were intended for use in America.

Penny

ROSA AMERICANA

	V. Good	Fine	V. Fine	E. Fine
Twopence (no date)	$25.00	$80.00	$175.00	$275.00
1722 Halfpenny DEI GRATIS REX UTILE DULCI	20.00	60.00	90.00	175.00
1722 Penny	18.00	50.00	85.00	150.00
1722 Twopence	50.00	90.00	125.00	200.00

Halfpenny

	V. Good	Fine	V. Fine	E. Fine
1723 Halfpenny	20.00	70.00	100.00	185.00

Twopence

	V. Good	Fine	V. Fine	E. Fine
1723 Penny	20.00	60.00	90.00	150.00
1723 Twopence (illustrated)	50.00	90.00	125.00	250.00

WOOD'S HIBERNIA COINAGE

The type intended for Ireland had a seated figure with a harp on the reverse side and the word HIBERNIA. Denominations struck were halfpenny and farthing with dates 1722, 1723 and 1724. Hibernia coins were unpopular in Ireland, so many of them were sent to the American colonies.

1722 Hibernia Halfpenny   First Type   Second Type

	V. Good	V. Fine	E. Fine
1722 Farthing (2nd type)		$125.00	$250.00
1722 Halfpenny (1st or 2nd type)	$10.00	35.00	95.00

WOOD'S HIBERNIA COINAGE

1723 Hibernia Farthing   1724 Hibernia Halfpenny

	V. Good	V. Fine	E. Fine
1723 Farthing	$7.00	$20.00	$80.00
1723 Halfpenny	7.00	18.00	75.00
1724 Farthing	18.00	35.00	100.00
1724 Halfpenny	15.00	22.00	90.00

VIRGINIA HALFPENNY

In 1773 coinage of a copper halfpenny was authorized for Virginia by the English Crown. The style is similar to the regular English coinage. These pieces were never popular, but did circulate by necessity.

	V. Good	V. Fine	Unc.
1773 Halfpenny	$10.00	$25.00	$250.00

III. EARLY AMERICAN TOKENS

Struck in America or England for use by American Merchants

LONDON ELEPHANT TOKENS

Struck c. 1664-1666 during the reign of Charles II, the London Token, an early historian states, was produced during the great plague raging in London. The legend on this piece relates directly to that crisis. It has also been stated that the London

LONDON ELEPHANT TOKENS

Token was to have been current in Tangier, Africa, but was never used in that locality. No date appears on this token.

It is unlikely that many ever circulated in America. They are associated with the 1694 pieces through use of a common obverse die.

	V. Good	Fine	V. Fine	E. Fine
(1664) Halfpenny GOD PRESERVE LONDON (Thick or thin planchet)	$30.00	$50.00	$100.00	$300.00

CAROLINA AND NEW ENGLAND ELEPHANT TOKENS

Although no law is known authorizing coinage for Carolina, very interesting pieces known as Elephant Tokens were made with the date 1694. These copper tokens were of halfpenny denomination. The reverse reads GOD PRESERVE CAROLINA AND THE LORDS PROPRIETERS. 1694.

The Carolina pieces were probably struck in England and perhaps intended only as tokens, or possibly as advertising to heighten interest in the Carolina Plantation.

Like the Carolina Tokens, the New England Elephant Tokens were believed to have been struck in England as a promotional piece to increase interest in the American Colonies.

	V. Good	Fine
1694 PROPRIETORS	$500.00	$2,200

NEW ENGLAND ELEPHANT TOKEN

1694 NEW ENGLAND	5,000	—

THE NEW YORKE TOKEN

Little is known about the origin of this token. The style of design and execution seem to be Dutch, and it is probable that the dies were prepared in Holland. There is no date on the piece which evidently belongs to the period between 1664, when the name New Yorke was first adopted, and 1710 after which it was rarely spelled that way.

UNDATED

	V. Good	Fine
Brass	$1,000	$2,200

GLOUCESTER TOKEN

This token appears to have been a private coinage by a merchant of Gloucester (county), Virginia. The only specimens known are struck in brass. The exact origin and use of these pieces is unknown.

1714 Shilling Brass .... —

HIGLEY OR GRANBY COPPERS

The Higley coppers were never officially authorized. All the tokens were made of pure copper. There were seven obverse and four reverse dies. The first issue, in 1737, bore the legend THE VALUE OF THREEPENCE. After a time the quantity exceeded the local demand, and a protest arose against the value of the piece. The inscription was changed to VALUE ME AS YOU PLEASE.

	Good	V. Good
1737 THE • VALVE • OF • THREE • PENCE. — 3 Hammers — CONNECTICVT	$2,750	$4,000
1737 THE • VALVE • OF • THREE • PENCE. — 3 Hammers — I • AM • GOOD • COPPER	3,000	4,200
1737 VALUE • ME • AS • YOU • PLEASE — 3 Hammers — I • AM • GOOD • COPPER	2,500	3,750
(1737) VALUE • ME • AS • YOU • PLEASE — Broad Axe — J • CUT • MY • WAY • THROUGH	3,000	4,200
1739 VALUE • ME • AS • YOU • PLEASE — Broad Axe — J • CUT • MY • WAY • THROUGH	3,500	5,000

HIBERNIA-VOCE POPULI

These coins, struck in the year 1760, were made in Dublin. Like other Irish tokens, some of these pieces found their way to Colonial America.

Farthing 1760   Halfpenny 1760

	Good	V. Fine	E. Fine
1760 Farthing	$80.00	$200.00	$500.00
1760 Halfpenny	10.00	45.00	100.00

PITT TOKENS

William Pitt is the subject of these pieces, probably intended as commemorative medalets. The halfpenny served as currency during a shortage of regular coinage.

E. Fine
1766 Farthing $1,000

1766 Halfpenny .... (illustrated)
V. Good	Fine	E. Fine
$75.00	$150.00	$400.00

RHODE ISLAND SHIP MEDAL

Although this medal has a Dutch inscription, the spelling and design indicate an English or Anglo-American origin. The satirical theme depicts the retreat from Rhode Island by Continental troops. Specimens are known in brass, copper, tin and pewter. Modern copies exist.

1778-1779
Rhode Island
Ship Medal

V. Fine	E. Fine
$200.00	$400.00

J. CHALMERS — Annapolis, Maryland

John Chalmers, a goldsmith, struck a series of silver tokens at Annapolis in 1783. The shortage of change and the refusal of the people to use underweight coins prompted the issuance of these pieces.

	V. Good	V. Fine
1783 Threepence	$200.00	$700.00
1783 Sixpence	250.00	900.00
1783 Shilling (Rev. illustrated)	200.00	800.00

IV. THE FRENCH COLONIES

None of the coins of the French regime is strictly American. They were all general issues for the French colonies of the New World. The copper of 1717 to 1722 was authorized by edicts of 1716 and 1721 for use in New France, Louisiana, and the French West Indies.

COPPER SOU OR NINE DENIERS

	V. Good	Fine
1721-B (Rouen)	$30.00	$70.00
1721-H (La Rochelle)	20.00	35.00
1722-H	15.00	30.00

FRENCH COLONIES IN GENERAL

Coined for use in the French colonies and only unofficially circulated in Louisiana along with other foreign coins and tokens. Most were counterstamped RF (République Française) for use in the West Indies.

	V. Good	V. Fine	E. Fine
1767 French Colonies, Sou	$15.00	$40.00	$125.00
1767 French Colonies, Sou. Counterstamped RF	10.00	35.00	100.00

V. SPECULATIVE ISSUES, TOKENS & PATTERNS
THE CONTINENTAL DOLLAR

The Continental Dollars were probably a pattern issue only and never reached general circulation. It was the first silver dollar size coin ever proposed for the United States. The coins were probably struck in Philadelphia. Many modern copies and replicas exist.

	Good	Fine	E. Fine	Unc.
1776 CURENCY — Pewter	$500.00	$1,750	$2,500	$5,500
1776 CURENCY — Silver				25,000
1776 CURRENCY — Pewter	600.00	2,000	3,000	7,000
1776 CURRENCY — Pewter, EG FECIT above date	500.00	1,800	2,750	6,000

NOVA CONSTELLATIO COPPERS

The Nova Constellatio pieces were struck supposedly by order of Gouverneur Morris. Evidence indicates that they were all struck in Birmingham and imported for American circulation as a private business venture.

1783 "CONSTELLATIO" Pointed Rays

V. Good	$10.00
Fine	25.00
V. Fine	50.00
Ex. Fine	200.00

1783 "CONSTELATIO" Blunt Rays

V. Good	$10.00
Fine	25.00
V. Fine	60.00
Ex. Fine	215.00

NOVA CONSTELLATIO COPPERS

1785
"CONSTELATIO"
Blunt Rays

V. Good	$12.00
Fine	35.00
V. Fine	75.00
Ex. Fine	225.00

1785
"CONSTELLATIO"
Pointed Rays

V. Good	$10.00
Fine	25.00
V. Fine	50.00
Ex. Fine	200.00

IMMUNE COLUMBIA PIECES

These are considered experimental or pattern pieces. No laws describing them are known.

1785 Copper, Star reverse.... $10,000

1785
George III Obverse

Good	$800.00
Fine	2,500

1785
Vermon Auctori Obverse

Good	$750.00
Fine	2,000

1787
IMMUNIS COLUMBIA
Eagle Reverse

V. Good	$100.00
Fine	200.00
V. Fine	500.00
Ex. Fine	1,500

CONFEDERATIO COPPERS

The Confederatio Coppers are experimental or pattern pieces. This will explain why the die with the CONFEDERATIO legend was combined with other designs such as bust of George Washington, Libertas et Justitia of 1785, Immunis Columbia of 1786, the New York "Excelsiors," Inimica Tyrannis Americana and others. There were in all thirteen dies struck in fourteen combinations.

There are two types of the Confederatio reverse. In one instance the stars are contained in a small circle; in the other larger stars are in a larger circle.

Typical Obverse　　　　　　Small Circle Reverse　　　　　Large Circle Reverse

Fine

1785 Stars in small circle — various obverses.................................... $5,000
1785 Stars in large circle — various obverses..................................... 5,000

SPECULATIVE PATTERNS

1786 IMMUNIS COLUMBIA　　　　Eagle Reverse　　　　　　　Shield Reverse

1786 IMMUNIS COLUMBIA, eagle rev... $9,000
1786 IMMUNIS COLUMBIA, shield rev... 6,000
1786 (No date) Washington obv. 20,000
1786 Eagle obverse 12,000
1786 Washington obverse, eagle reverse (Unique) .... —

VI. COINAGE OF THE STATES
NEW HAMPSHIRE

New Hampshire was the first of the states to consider the subject of coinage following the Declaration of Independence.

NEW HAMPSHIRE

William Moulton was empowered to make a limited quantity of coins of pure copper authorized by the State House of Representatives in 1776.

V. Good

1776 New Hampshire copper $6,000

MASSACHUSETTS

The coinage of Massachusetts copper cents and half cents in 1787 and 1788 was under the direction of Joshua Witherle. These were the first coins bearing the denomination Cent as established by Congress. Many varieties exist, the most valuable being that with arrows in the eagle's right talon.

	1787 Half Cent	
Good		$15.00
Fine...................		30.00
V. Fine...............		60.00
Ex. Fine..............		175.00

	Good	Fine	V. Fine	E. Fine
1787 Cent, arrows in left talon (illustrated)	$12.00	$25.00	$60.00	$175.00
1787 Cent, arrows in right talon	——	2,200	——	——

1788 Half Cent	
Good	$15.00
Fine............	30.00
Very Fine.......	65.00
Ex. Fine	200.00

MASSACHUSETTS

1788 Cent
Good	$12.00
Fine	25.00
V. Fine	60.00
Ex. Fine	175.00

CONNECTICUT

Authority for establishing a mint near New Haven was granted by the State to Samuel Bishop, Joseph Hopkins, James Hillhouse and John Goodrich in 1785.

1785 Copper
Bust Facing Right
Good	$15.00
V. Good	20.00
Fine	40.00
V. Fine	100.00

1785 Copper
Bust Facing Left
Good	$50.00
V. Good	65.00
Fine	125.00
V. Fine	200.00

	Good	V. Good	Fine	V. Fine
1786 Bust facing right	$20.00	$30.00	$55.00	$125.00
1787 Mailed bust facing right	30.00	50.00	100.00	300.00

CONNECTICUT

	Good	V. Good	Fine	V. Fine
1786 Mailed bust facing left	$12.00	$18.00	$35.00	$85.00
1787 Mailed bust facing left	8.00	15.00	25.00	70.00

1787 Draped bust facing left...................	7.00	12.00	18.00	50.00

1788 Mailed bust facing right.................	10.00	18.00	40.00	100.00

1788 Mailed bust facing left	10.00	15.00	35.00	85.00

CONNECTICUT

	Good	V. Good	Fine	V. Fine
1788 Draped bust facing left..................	$10.00	$15.00	$35.00	$85.00

NEW YORK
THE BRASHER DOUBLOON

Perhaps the most famous pieces coined before the establishment of the U.S. Mint at Philadelphia were produced by a well-known goldsmith and jeweler, Ephraim Brasher.

    Brasher produced a gold piece weighing about 408 grains, approximately equal in value to a Spanish doubloon (about $16.00).

    The punch-mark EB appears in either of two positions as illustrated. This mark is found on some foreign gold coins as well, and probably was so used by Brasher as evidence of his testing of their value.

1787 Doubloon, punch on breast. Gold (Unique) .... —
1787 Doubloon, punch on wing. Gold .... —

COPPER COINAGE

No coinage was authorized for New York following the Revolutionary War although several propositions were considered. The only coinage laws passed were those regulating coins already in use.

1786
NON VI VIRTUTE VICI
Good $1,000
Fine 2,000
V. Fine 4,000

NEW YORK

	Good	Fine	V. Fine
1787 EXCELSIOR copper, eagle on globe facing right	$300.00	$600.00	$3,000
1787 EXCELSIOR copper, eagle on globe facing left	250.00	600.00	3,000

1787 George Clinton
Good............ $1,500
Fine............ 3,500
V. Fine......... 10,000

1787
Indian and N.Y. Arms
Good $1,250
Fine.......... 2,750
V. Fine 5,000

1787
Indian and Eagle
on Globe
Good............ $1,500
Fine............ 3,500
V. Fine......... 6,000

[31]

NEW YORK
THE NOVA EBORACS

1787
NOVA EBORAC
Reverse Seated
Figure Facing Right

Fair	$10.00
Good	25.00
Fine	75.00
V. Fine	250.00

1787
NOVA EBORAC
Reverse Seated
Figure Facing Left

Fair	$8.00
Good	15.00
Fine	60.00
V. Fine	175.00

NEW JERSEY

On June 1, 1786, the New Jersey Colonial legislature granted to Thomas Goadsby, Albion Cox and Walter Mould authority to coin some three million coppers, not later than June 1788, on condition that they delivered to the Treasurer of the State, "one-tenth part of the full sum they shall strike and coin," in quarterly installments. These coppers were to pass current at 15 to the shilling.

Narrow Shield   Wide Shield

	Good	Fine	V. Fine
1786 Narrow shield	$10.00	$25.00	$55.00
1786 Wide shield	12.00	30.00	75.00

NEW JERSEY

Small Planchet

	Good	Fine	V. Fine
1787 Small planchet	$10.00	$25.00	$55.00
1787 Large planchet	10.00	25.00	55.00

	Good	Fine	V. Fine
1788 Horse's head facing right	10.00	22.00	50.00
1788 Horse's head facing left	40.00	150.00	225.00

VERMONT

Reuben Harmon, Jr., of Rupert, Vermont, was granted permission to coin copper pieces for a period of two years beginning July 1, 1785. The well-known Vermont plow coppers were first produced in that year. The franchise was extended for eight years in 1786.

	Good	Fine
1785 IMMUNE COLUMBIA	$750.00	$2,000

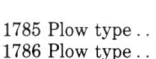

	Good	Fine
1785 Plow type	$60.00	$175.00
1786 Plow type	40.00	150.00

	Good	Fine
1786 Baby head	$70.00	$300.00

VERMONT

	Good	Fine
1786 Bust left ...	$30.00	$200.00
1787 Bust left ...	350.00	700.00

	Good	Fine
1787 BRITANNIA..	$22.00	$75.00

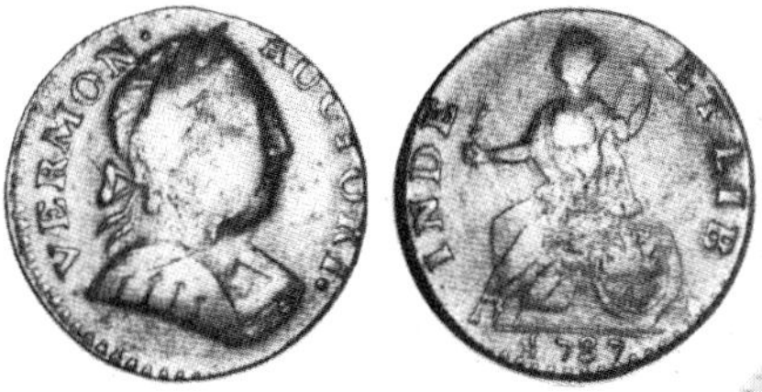

1787 Bust right..	$25.00	$85.00

1788 Bust right..	$25.00	$85.00

1788 GEORGIVS III REX*	$60.00	$200.00

*This piece should not be confused with the common English halfpence with similar design and reverse legend BRITANNIA.

VII. PRIVATE TOKENS AFTER CONFEDERATION
NORTH AMERICAN TOKEN

This piece was struck in Dublin, Ireland. The obverse shows the seated figure of Hibernia facing left.

Copper or Brass

	V. Good	Fine	V. Fine
1781 ...	$7.00	$15.00	$30.00

THE BAR "COPPER"

The Bar "Copper" is undated and of uncertain origin. It has thirteen parallel and unconnected bars on one side. On the other side is the large roman letter USA monogram. The design was supposedly copied from a Continental button.

	V. Good	Fine	V. Fine	E. Fine
Undated (about 1785) Bar "Copper"	$75.00	$100.00	$200.00	$500.00

AUCTORI PLEBIS TOKEN

This token is sometimes included with the coins of Connecticut as it greatly resembles issues of that state. It was struck in England by an unknown maker, possibly for use in America.

1787 AUCTORI PLEBIS
Good	$15.00
V. Good	25.00
Fine	50.00
V. Fine	90.00

THE MOTT TOKEN

This was one of the first tradesman's tokens issued in America. Manufactured in England, they were issued by Messrs. Mott of New York in 1789.

	V. Good	Fine	V. Fine	E. Fine
1789 Mott Token	$30.00	$50.00	$100.00	$200.00

STANDISH BARRY, BALTIMORE, MARYLAND

Standish Barry, a Baltimore silversmith, circulated a silver threepence in 1790. The tokens were believed to have been an advertising venture at a time when small change was scarce.

	Fine	V. Fine
1790 Threepence	$1,000	$3,500

KENTUCKY TOKEN

These tokens were struck in England about 1792-94. Each star in the triangle represents a state, identified by its initial letter. These pieces are usually called Kentucky Cents because the letter K (for Kentucky) happens to be at the top.

	V. Good	V. Fine	E. Fine	Unc.
Cent (1792-94)	$20.00	$50.00	$75.00	$450.00

FRANKLIN PRESS

This piece is an English tradesmans' token but, being associated with Benjamin Franklin, has accordingly been included in American collections.

	V. Good	V. Fine	E. Fine	Unc.
1794 Franklin Press Token	$18.00	$50.00	$75.00	$350.00

TALBOT, ALLUM & LEE CENTS

Talbot, Allum & Lee, engaged in the India trade and located in New York, placed a large quantity of English-made coppers in circulation during 1794 and 1795. ONE CENT appears on the 1794 issue.

1794 Cent with NEW YORK	
V. Good..............	$15.00
V. Fine	35.00
Unc..................	350.00

1794 Cent Without NEW YORK	
V. Good..............	50.00
V. Fine	200.00
Unc..................	700.00

1795 Cent	
V. Good	$14.00
V. Fine	35.00
E. Fine	75.00
Unc..............	300.00

VIII. WASHINGTON PIECES

An interesting series of coins and tokens dated from 1783 to 1795 bear the portrait of George Washington. The likenesses in most instances were faithfully reproduced and were designed to honor Washington. Many of these pieces were of English origin and made later than the dates indicate.

	Fine	V. Fine	E. Fine
1783 Large military bust	$15.00	$30.00	$85.00

1783 Draped bust..................................	15.00	30.00	85.00

WASHINGTON PIECES

UNITY STATES
V. Good	$15.00
V. Fine	45.00
Ex. Fine	100.00

Undated Double Head Cent
Fine	$20.00
V. Fine	40.00
Ex. Fine	100.00

Large Eagle

	Fine	Small Eagle E. Fine	Unc.
1791 Cent, large eagle	$55.00	$150.00	$450.00
1791 Cent, small eagle	55.00	150.00	450.00

1791 Liverpool Halfpenny Lettered Edge
Fine	$225.00
Ex. Fine	500.00
Unc.	1,000

1792 Eagle with Stars
Copper	—
Silver	—
Gold	—

WASHINGTON PIECES

(1792) Undated Cent
"WASHINGTON BORN VIRGINIA"

1792 Cent
"WASHINGTON PRESIDENT"

	Fine		Fine
Copper	$1,000	Plain edge	$2,500

	V. Good	Fine
1792 Small eagle. Copper	$1,000	$2,000

1793 Ship Halfpenny
Fine $50.00
V. Fine 75.00
Ex. Fine 150.00

1795 Halfpenny
Grate Token

	V. Fine	E. Fine	Unc.
1795 reeded edge	$30.00	$65.00	$200.00
1795 lettered edge	125.00	250.00	550.00

WASHINGTON PIECES

Liberty and Security Halfpenny

	Fine	V. Fine	E. Fine
1795 Halfpenny, plain edge	$30.00	$50.00	$125.00
1795 Halfpenny, lettered edge	20.00	40.00	100.00

Liberty and
Security Penny
Fine $60.00
V. Fine........... 100.00
Ex. Fine.......... 170.00
Unc. 900.00

SUCCESS MEDALS

	Fine	V. Fine	E. Fine
Medal, large. Plain or reeded edge	$50.00	$100.00	$150.00
Medal, small. Plain or reeded edge	50.00	100.00	175.00

NORTH WALES HALFPENNY

	Good	Fine
1795 Halfpenny..	$30.00	$75.00

IX. THE FUGIO CENTS

The first coins issued by authority of the United States were the "Fugio" cents.

The legends have been credited to Benjamin Franklin by many, and the coin, as a consequence, has been referred to as the Franklin Cent.

1787 WITH CLUB RAYS

	V. Good	Fine	V. Fine
Club Rays. Rounded ends	$50.00	$75.00	$200.00

1787 WITH POINTED RAYS

	V. Good	Fine	V. Fine	E. Fine	Unc.
STATES UNITED at sides of circle (illustrated)	$30.00	$50.00	$90.00	$150.00	$500.00
UNITED STATES at sides of circle	30.00	50.00	90.00	150.00	500.00

MODERN PROOF COINS

Proof coins can usually be distinguished by their sharpness of detail, high wire edge, and extremely brilliant, mirrorlike surface. All proofs are originally sold by the mint at a premium.

Proof coins were not struck during 1943-1949 or 1965-67. Sets from 1936 through 1972 include the cent, nickel, dime, quarter and half; from 1973 through 1981 the dollar was also included. *Values shown are for original unblemished sets.*

Figures in parentheses represent the total number of full sets minted.

1936 (3,837)	$4,000	1962 (3,218,019)	$12.50
1937 (5,542)	2,500	1963 (3,075,645)	12.50
1938 (8,045)	1,100	1964 (3,950,762)	12.00
1939 (8,795)	1,000	1968S (3,041,506)	4.00
1940 (11,246)	900.00	1969S (2,934,631)	4.00
1941 (15,287)	750.00	1970S (2,632,810)	8.00
1942 both nickels (21,120)	900.00	1971S (3,220,733)	3.00
1942 one nickel	750.00	1972S (3,260,996)	3.00
1950 (51,386)	400.00	1973S (2,760,339)	6.00
1951 (57,500)	250.00	1974S (2,612,568)	6.00
1952 (81,980)	135.00	1975S (2,909,369)	9.00
1953 (128,800)	90.00	1976S (4,149,730)	5.00
1954 (233,300)	50.00	1976S 3-pc. set (3,295,714)†	10.00
1955 (378,200)	45.00	1977S (3,251,152)	5.00
1956 (669,384)	20.00	1978S (3,127,781)	7.00
1957 (1,247,952)	15.00	1979S filled S (3,677,175)	12.00
1958 (875,652)	18.00	1979S clear S	100.00
1959 (1,149,291)	15.00	1980S (3,554,806)	6.00
1960 (1,691,602 both kinds)		1981S (4,063,083)	6.50
with lg. date 1c	14.00	1982S (3,857,479)	12.00
1960 with sm. date 1c	25.00	1983S	11.00
1961 (3,028,244)	12.50		

UNCIRCULATED MINT SETS

Official Mint Sets are specially packaged by the government for sale to collectors. They contain uncirculated specimens of each year's coins for every denomination issued from each mint. Unlike the proof sets, these are normal coins intended for circulation and are not minted with any special consideration for quality.

1947 P-D-S	$500.00	1965 *(2,360,000)	$3.25
1948 P-D-S	200.00	1966 *(2,261,583)	3.50
1949 P-D-S	750.00	1967 *(1,863,344)	8.50
1951 P-D-S (8,654)	375.00	1968 P-D-S (2,105,128)	2.25
1952 P-D-S (11,499)	200.00	1969 P-D-S (1,817,392)	2.50
1953 P-D-S (15,538)	160.00	1970 P-D-S (2,038,134)	22.50
1954 P-D-S (25,599)	80.00	1971 P-D-S (2,193,396)	2.00
1955 P-D-S (49,656)	40.00	1972 P-D-S (2,750,000)	2.00
1956 P-D (45,475)	30.00	1973 P-D-S (1,767,691)	14.00
1957 P-D (34,324)	50.00	1974 P-D-S (1,975,981)	4.00
1958 P-D (50,314)	40.00	1975 P-D-S (1,921,488)	4.25
1959 P-D (187,000)	20.00	1976 3 pieces (3,400,000)†	8.00
1960 P-D Lg. Date (260,485)	20.00	1976 P-D (1,892,513)	4.00
1960 P-D Sm. Date	21.00	1977 P-D (2,006,869)	4.25
1961 P-D (223,704)	15.00	1978 P-D (2,162,609)	4.50
1962 P-D (385,285)	15.00	1979 P-D (2,526,000)	3.50
1963 P-D (606,612)	15.00	1980 P-D-S (2,813,118)	5.00
1964 P-D (1,008,108)	14.00	1981 P-D-S (2,902,823)	13.00

*Special Mint Sets †Estimated

UNITED STATES REGULAR ISSUES
HALF CENTS — 1793-1857

The half cent was authorized to be coined April 2, 1792. Originally the weight was to have been 132 grains, but this was changed to 104 grains by the Act of January 14, 1793, before coinage commenced. The weight was again changed to 84 grains January 26, 1796 by presidential proclamation in conformity with the Act of March 3, 1795. Coinage was discontinued by the Act of February 21, 1857. All were coined at the Philadelphia Mint.

LIBERTY CAP TYPE 1793-1797

AG-3 ABOUT GOOD—*Clear enough to identify.*
G-4 GOOD—*Outline of bust clear, no details. Date readable. Reverse lettering incomplete.*
VG-8 VERY GOOD—*Some hair details. Reverse lettering complete.*
F-12 FINE—*Most of hair detail shows. Leaves worn but all visible.*
VF-20 VERY FINE—*Hair near ear and forehead worn, other areas distinct. Some details in leaves show.*
EF-40 EXTREMELY FINE—*Light wear on highest parts of head and wreath.*

Head Facing Left 1793

	Quan. Minted	AG-3	G-4	VG-8	F-12	VF-20	EF-40
1793	35,334	$350.00	$900.00	$1,400	$1,650	$2,500	$5,000

Head Facing Right 1794-1797

1794	81,600	50.00	125.00	225.00	450.00	750.00	1,200

Pole to Cap	Punctuated Date	No Pole to Cap

	Quan. Minted	AG-3	G-4	VG-8	F-12	VF-20	EF-40
1795 Lettered edge, with pole	25,600	$40.00	$90.00	$130.00	$275.00	$500.00	$1,000
1795 Lettered edge, punctuated date		40.00	90.00	130.00	275.00	500.00	1,000

HALF CENTS

	Quan. Minted	AG-3	G-4	VG-8	F-12	VF-20	EF-40
1795 Plain edge, punctuated date	109,000	$40.00	$90.00	$130.00	$275.00	$500.00	$1,000
1795 Pl. edge, no pole		40.00	90.00	130.00	275.00	500.00	1,000
1796 With pole	5,090	650.00	1,400	2,000	4,000	6,000	—
1796 No pole	1,390	1,100	2,400	4,000	6,000	12,000	

1797 Plain Edge   1797, 1 above 1, Plain Edge

1797 All kinds 119,215						
1797 Lettered edge..................	90.00	200.00	300.00	650.00	1,300	2,400
1797 Plain edge.....................	30.00	75.00	125.00	275.00	500.00	900.00
1797, 1 above 1, plain edge	30.00	75.00	125.00	275.00	500.00	900.00

DRAPED BUST TYPE 1800-1808

AG-3 ABOUT GOOD—*Clear enough to identify.*
G-4 GOOD—*Bust outline clear, few details, date readable. Reverse lettering worn and incomplete.*
VG-8 VERY GOOD—*Some drapery shows. Date and legends complete.*
F-12 FINE—*Shoulder drapery and hair over brow worn smooth.*
VF-20 VERY FINE—*Only slight wear in above areas. Slight wear on reverse.*
EF-40 EXTREMELY FINE—*Light wear on highest parts of head and wreath.*

	Quan. Minted	AG-3	G-4	VG-8	F-12	VF-20	EF-40
1800	211,530	$6.50	$13.00	$20.00	$27.50	$45.00	$115.00
1802, 2 over 0	14,366	40.00	100.00	175.00	375.00	800.00	1,900
1803	97,900	7.00	15.00	21.00	30.00	47.50	130.00

Plain 4   Crosslet 4   Stemless Wreath   Stems to Wreath

1804 Plain 4, stems	}		6.50	13.00	20.00	27.50	47.50	135.00
1804 Pl. 4, stemless	} 1,055,312	6.00	12.00	19.00	22.00	42.00	90.00
1804 Cr. 4, stems		6.00	12.00	19.00	22.00	42.00	90.00
1804 Cr. 4, stemless		6.00	12.00	19.00	22.00	42.00	90.00

HALF CENTS

1804 "Spiked Chin" Variety   Small 5   Large 5

	Quan. Minted	AG-3	G-4	VG-8	F-12	VF-20	EF-40
1804 "Spiked chin"	Inc. above	$8.00	$15.00	$20.00	$30.00	$50.00	$150.00
1805 Sm. 5, stemless	}	6.00	12.00	19.00	22.00	42.00	80.00
1805 Small 5, stems	} 814,464	20.00	50.00	80.00	200.00	400.00	850.00
1805 Large 5, stems	}	6.00	12.00	19.00	22.00	42.00	80.00

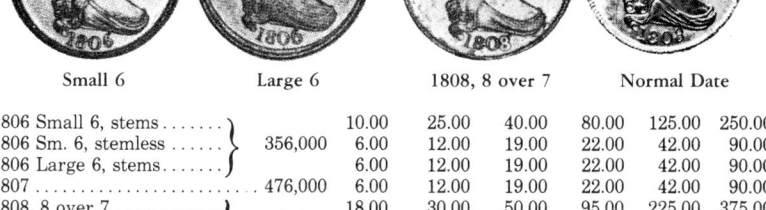

Small 6   Large 6   1808, 8 over 7   Normal Date

1806 Small 6, stems	}		10.00	25.00	40.00	80.00	125.00	250.00
1806 Sm. 6, stemless	}	356,000	6.00	12.00	19.00	22.00	42.00	90.00
1806 Large 6, stems	}		6.00	12.00	19.00	22.00	42.00	90.00
1807		476,000	6.00	12.00	19.00	22.00	42.00	90.00
1808, 8 over 7	}		18.00	30.00	50.00	95.00	225.00	375.00
1808 Normal date	}	400,000	6.50	13.00	20.00	27.50	47.50	115.00

CLASSIC HEAD TYPE 1809-1836

G-4 GOOD—*LIBERTY only partly visible on hair band. Lettering, date, stars, worn but visible.*
VG-8 VERY GOOD—*LIBERTY entirely visible on hair band. Lower curls worn.*
F-12 FINE—*Only part wear on LIBERTY and hair at top worn in spots.*
VF-20 VERY FINE—*Lettering clear-cut. Hair only slightly worn.*
EF-40 EXTREMELY FINE—*Light wear on highest points of hair and leaves.*
MS-60 UNCIRCULATED—*Typical brown to red surface. No trace of wear.*

Brilliant or red uncirculated coins are worth more than prices shown. Spotted, cleaned or discolored pieces are worth less.

	Quan. Minted	G-4	VG-8	F-12	VF-20	EF-40	MS-60
1809	1,154,572	$11.00	$13.00	$18.00	$32.50	$50.00	$300.00
1810	215,000	13.00	18.00	27.00	50.00	90.00	600.00
1811	63,140	40.00	60.00	120.00	350.00	650.00	1,500
1825	63,000	12.00	16.00	22.00	32.50	50.00	200.00
1826	234,000	10.00	12.00	17.00	28.00	40.00	200.00

HALF CENTS

13 Stars    12 Stars

	Quan. Minted	G-4	VG-8	F-12	VF-20	EF-40	MS-60	Proof-63
1828, 13 Stars	} 606,000	$10.00	$12.00	$16.00	$25.00	$35.00	$175.00	
1828, 12 Stars		11.00	14.00	20.00	35.00	50.00	300.00	
1829	487,000	10.00	12.00	16.00	25.00	35.00	175.00	
1831 (Beware of altered date)	2,200						2,400	$4,200
1832	154,000	10.00	13.00	17.00	26.00	40.00	165.00	1,800
1833	120,000	10.00	13.00	17.00	26.00	40.00	165.00	1,800
1834	141,000	10.00	13.00	17.00	26.00	40.00	165.00	1,800
1835	398,000	10.00	13.00	17.00	26.00	40.00	165.00	1,800
1836								3,300

BRAIDED HAIR TYPE 1840-1857

	Proof-63		Proof-63
1840 Original	$1,900	1845 Original	$2,800
1840 Restrike	1,800	1845 Restrike	2,400
1841 Original	1,900	1846 Original	2,400
1841 Restrike	2,000	1846 Restrike	2,000
1842 Original	2,100	1847 Original	2,000
1842 Restrike	1,900	1847 Restrike	2,000
1843 Original	2,000	1848 Original	2,000
1843 Restrike	2,000	1848 Restrike	2,000
1844 Original	2,800	1849 Original. Small date	2,300
1844 Restrike	2,000	1849 Restrike. Small date	2,300

Brilliant or red uncirculated coins are worth more than prices shown. Spotted, cleaned or discolored pieces are worth less.

G-4 GOOD—*Hair and bun show few details, parts of LIBERTY show.*
VG-8 VERY GOOD—*Beads uniformly distinct. Hairlines show in spots.*
F-12 FINE—*Hairlines above ear worn. Beads sharp.*
VF-20 VERY FINE—*Lowest curl shows wear, hair otherwise distinct.*
EF-40 EXTREMELY FINE—*Light wear on highest points of hair and leaves.*
MS-60 UNCIRCULATED—*No trace of wear, light blemishes.*

Small Date   Large Date

	Quan. Minted	G-4	VG-8	F-12	VF-20	EF-40	MS-60	Proof-63
1849 Large date	39,864	$14.00	$17.00	$20.00	$30.00	$45.00	$200.00	—
1850	39,812	14.00	17.00	20.00	30.00	45.00	200.00	—
1851	147,672	11.00	15.00	17.00	25.00	38.00	175.00	—
1852								$2,400
1853	129,694	11.00	15.00	17.00	25.00	38.00	175.00	
1854	55,358	11.00	15.00	17.00	25.00	38.00	175.00	2,400
1855	56,500	11.00	15.00	17.00	25.00	38.00	175.00	2,400
1856	40,430	13.00	16.00	19.00	30.00	45.00	200.00	2,400
1857	35,180	14.00	17.00	20.00	32.50	50.00	235.00	2,400

LARGE CENTS — 1793-1857

Cents and half cents were the first coins struck under the authority of the United States Government. Coinage began in 1793 with laws specifying that the cent should weigh exactly twice as much as the half cent. Large cents were coined every year from 1793 to 1857 with the exception of 1815, when a lack of copper prevented production. All were coined at the Philadelphia Mint. Varieties listed are those most significant to collectors. Numerous other die varieties may be found because each of the early dies was individually made.

FLOWING HAIR, CHAIN TYPE REVERSE 1793

AG-3 ABOUT GOOD—*Date and devices clear enough to identify.*
G-4 GOOD—*Lettering worn but readable. Bust has no detail.*
VG-8 VERY GOOD—*Date and lettering distinct, some details of head visible.*
F-12 FINE—*About half of hair, etc. details show.*
VF-20 VERY FINE—*Ear visible. Most of details can be seen.*
EF-40 EXTREMELY FINE—*Highest points of hair and back of temple show wear.*

Obverse AMERI. Reverse AMERICA Reverse

	Quan. Minted	AG-3	G-4	VG-8	F-12	VF-20	EF-40
1793 Chain	36,103						
1793 AMERI. in legend		$350.00	$1,000	$1,500	$2,250	$4,750	$9,000
1793 AMERICA		325.00	900.00	1,350	2,000	4,500	8,000

FLOWING HAIR, WREATH TYPE REVERSE 1793

Wreath Type Strawberry Leaf Var.

	Quan. Minted	AG-3	G-4	VG-8	F-12	VF-20	EF-40
1793 Wreath	63,353						
1793 Vine/bars edge		$150.00	$400.00	$700.00	$1,250	$2,000	$4,500
1793 Lettered Edge		175.00	450.00	750.00	1,400	2,250	5,000
1793 Strawberry leaf				(4 known)			

LARGE CENTS
LIBERTY CAP TYPE 1793-1796

1793 Vine and Bar edge
Chain and Wreath Type Only

Lettered edge 1793-1795
ONE HUNDRED FOR A DOLLAR

Beaded Border, 1793 Only

1793-1794   **1794 Only**   **1794-1796**

"Head of 1793"
Head is in high
rounded relief

"Head of 1794"
Well defined hair,
hook on lowest curl

"Head of 1795"
Head in low relief,
no hook on lowest curl

	Quan. Minted	AG-3	G-4	VG-8	F-12	VF-20	EF-40
1793 Lib. Cap.	11,056	$300.00	$650.00	$1,100	$1,750	$3,600	$10,000
1794 All kinds	918,521						
1794 "Head of 1793"		75.00	150.00	250.00	650.00	1,500	3,500
1794 "Head of 1794"		20.00	60.00	85.00	150.00	400.00	1,000
1794 "Head of 1795"		20.00	60.00	85.00	150.00	400.00	1,000
1795 Ltd. ed.	37,000	20.00	60.00	110.00	200.00	450.00	1,200
1795 Plain ed.	501,500	18.00	50.00	75.00	130.00	350.00	650.00
1796 Lib. Cap.	109,825	20.00	60.00	90.00	150.00	350.00	800.00

DRAPED BUST TYPE 1796-1807

AG-3 ABOUT GOOD—*Clear enough to identify.*
G-4 GOOD—*Lettering worn, but clear; date clear. Bust lacks details.*
VG-8 VERY GOOD—*Drapery partly visible. Less wear in date and lettering.*
F-12 FINE—*Hair over brow is smooth, some details showing in other parts of hair.*
VF-20 VERY FINE—*Hairlines slightly worn. Hair over brow better defined.*
EF-40 EXTREMELY FINE—*Hair above forehead and left of eye outlined and detailed. Only slight wear on olive leaves.*

LARGE CENTS

 LIHERTY error

 Stems

 Stemless

 Gripped or Milled Edge

	Quan. Minted	AG-3	G-4	VG-8	F-12	VF-20	EF-40
1796 Draped Bust....	363,375	$20.00	$40.00	$70.00	$110.00	$275.00	$725.00
1796 LIHERTY error..........		25.00	50.00	90.00	185.00	450.00	1,200
1797 All kinds.......	897,510						
1797 Gr. edge, '96 rev.......		10.00	17.00	40.00	75.00	175.00	375.00
1797 Pl. edge, '96 rev		10.00	19.00	42.00	85.00	190.00	450.00
1797, '97 rev., Stems........		8.00	16.00	24.00	55.00	150.00	325.00
1797, '97 rev., Stemless......		15.00	28.00	60.00	115.00	250.00	625.00

1798, 8 over 7

1799, 9 over 8

1800 over 1798

1800, 80 over 79

1798 All kinds......	1,841,745						
1798, 8 over 7..............		10.00	21.00	52.50	125.00	300.00	750.00
1798......................		7.00	13.00	22.00	50.00	110.00	300.00
1799, 9 over 8.............	*	175.00	400.00	800.00	1,400	3,200	—
1799 Nor. date........	42,540	150.00	375.00	750.00	1,300	3,000	—
1800 All kds.	2,822,175						
1800 over 1798		6.00	11.00	19.00	40.00	110.00	375.00
1800, 80 over 79		4.50	10.00	18.00	35.00	100.00	250.00
1800 Normal date...........		4.50	10.00	18.00	35.00	100.00	250.00

*Mintage for 1799, 9 over 8 variety is included with the 1798 figure.

Fraction 1/000

Corrected Fraction

1801 Reverse, 3 Errors

1801 All kds.	1,362,837						
1801 Normal rev............		4.50	10.00	18.00	35.00	100.00	250.00
1801, 3 errors: 1/000, one stem & IINITED		10.00	20.00	40.00	100.00	225.00	725.00
1801 Fraction 1/000.........		6.00	12.00	25.00	60.00	120.00	375.00
1801, 1/100 over 1/000		6.00	13.00	27.00	65.00	150.00	400.00
1802 All kds.	3,435,100						
1802 Normal rev............		4.25	9.00	16.00	30.00	80.00	200.00
1802 Fraction 1/000.........		6.00	12.00	21.00	40.00	110.00	275.00
1802 Stemless wreath		4.50	10.00	18.00	35.00	90.00	250.00

LARGE CENTS

1803 Sm. Date, Blunt 1	1803 Large Date, Pointed 1	Small Fraction		Large Fraction	
	Quan. Minted	AG-3	G-4	VG-8	F-12	VF-20	EF-40

	Quan. Minted	AG-3	G-4	VG-8	F-12	VF-20	EF-40
1803 All kds.	3,131,691						
1803 Sm. dt., sm. fract.		$4.25	$9.00	$16.00	$30.00	$80.00	$200.00
1803 Sm. dt., lg. fract.		4.25	9.00	16.00	30.00	80.00	200.00
1803 Lg. dt., sm. fract.		100.00	200.00	350.00	800.00	2,000	
1803 Lg. dt., lg. fract.		14.00	25.00	60.00	125.00	200.00	600.00
1803, 1/100 over 1/000		6.00	13.00	27.50	50.00	125.00	350.00
1803 Stemless wreath		5.00	10.00	22.00	40.00	110.00	325.00

1804 With Broken Dies (see arrows)

All genuine 1804 Cents have a crosslet 4 in the date and a large fraction. The 0 in the date is in line with the O in OF on the reverse of the coin.

1804	96,500	100.00	175.00	400.00	675.00	1,200	2,500
1805	941,116	4.25	9.00	16.00	30.00	80.00	200.00
1806	348,000	6.00	12.00	27.50	60.00	125.00	375.00

Sm. 1807, 7 over 6, blunt 1   Lg. 1807, 7 over 6, pointed 1

1807 All kinds	829,221						
1807 Small 7 over 6		75.00	175.00	325.00	600.00	1,300	—
1807 Large 7 over 6		4.25	9.00	16.00	30.00	80.00	250.00
1807 Small fraction		5.00	11.00	22.00	40.00	100.00	350.00
1807 Large fraction		4.25	9.00	16.00	30.00	80.00	250.00

CLASSIC HEAD TYPE 1808-1814

AG-3 ABOUT GOOD—*Details clear enough to identify.*

G-4 GOOD—*Legends, stars, date worn, but plain.*

VG-8 VERY GOOD—*LIBERTY all readable. Ear shows. Details worn but plain.*

F-12 FINE—*Hair on forehead and before ear nearly smooth. Ear and hair under ear sharp.*

VF-20 VERY FINE—*All hairlines show some detail. Leaves on rev. show slight wear.*

EF-40 EXTREMELY FINE—*All hairlines sharp. Very slight wear on high points.*

LARGE CENTS

	Quan. Minted	AG-3	G-4	VG-8	F-12	VF-20	EF-40
1808	1,007,000	$6.25	$15.00	$27.00	$50.00	$140.00	$450.00
1809	222,867	17.00	35.00	60.00	125.00	325.00	750.00

1810, 10 over 09   1810 Normal Date   1811, last 1 over 0   1811 Normal Date

	G-4	VG-8	F-12	VF-20	EF-40
1810 All kds. 1,458,500					
1810, 10 over 09	6.00	13.00	25.00	45.00	135.00	375.00
1810 Normal date	6.00	13.00	25.00	45.00	135.00	375.00
1811 All kds. 218,025					
1811 Last 1 over 0	12.00	23.00	45.00	110.00	250.00	625.00
1811 Normal date	10.00	20.00	42.00	100.00	235.00	600.00
1812 ... 1,075,500	6.00	13.00	25.00	45.00	135.00	375.00
1813 ... 418,000	8.00	18.00	40.00	65.00	175.00	400.00
1814 ... 357,830	6.00	13.00	25.00	45.00	135.00	375.00

CORONET TYPE 1816-1857

G-4 GOOD—*Head details partly visible. Even wear in date and legends.*
VG-8 VERY GOOD—*LIBERTY, date, stars, legends clear. Part of hair cord visible.*
F-12 FINE—*All hairlines show. Hair cords show uniformly.*
VF-20 VERY FINE—*Hair cords only slightly worn. Hairlines only partly worn, all well defined.*
EF-40 EXTREMELY FINE—*Both hair cords stand out sharply. All hairlines sharp.*
MS-60 UNCIRCULATED—*Typical brown to red surface. No trace of wear.*

13 Stars   15 Stars

Brilliant or red uncirculated coins are worth more than prices shown. Spotted, cleaned or discolored pieces are worth less.

	Quan. Minted	G-4	VG-8	F-12	VF-20	EF-40	MS-60
1816	2,820,982	$3.75	$4.50	$7.00	$12.00	$32.00	$185.00
1817, 13 stars	} 3,948,400	3.75	4.50	6.00	10.00	32.00	185.00
1817, 15 stars		4.00	5.00	9.00	18.00	45.00	275.00
1818	3,167,000	3.75	4.50	6.00	10.00	32.00	185.00

LARGE CENTS

1819, 9 over 8   1820, 20 over 19

	Quan. Minted	G-4	VG-8	F-12	VF-20	EF-40	MS-60
1819, 9 over 8	} 2,671,000	$4.00	$5.00	$8.00	$11.00	$35.00	$200.00
1819		3.75	4.50	6.00	10.00	32.00	185.00
1820, 20 over 19		4.00	5.00	8.00	14.00	35.00	200.00
1820	4,407,550	3.75	4.50	6.00	10.00	30.00	185.00
1821	389,000	7.00	12.00	20.00	45.00	125.00	750.00
1822	2,072,339	3.75	4.50	6.00	10.00	35.00	200.00

1823, 3 over 2   1824, 4 over 2   1826, 6 over 5

1823, 3 over 2	} Included with 1824	12.00	16.00	30.00	75.00	200.00	—
1823 Normal date		13.00	20.00	35.00	80.00	325.00	—
1824, 4 over 2	} 1,262,000	4.50	6.00	13.00	35.00	100.00	—
1824 Normal date		4.00	5.00	8.00	17.00	45.00	300.00
1825	1,461,100	3.75	4.50	7.00	15.00	35.00	200.00
1826, 6 over 5	} 1,517,425	5.00	9.00	14.00	30.00	75.00	275.00
1826 Normal date		3.75	4.50	6.00	10.00	30.00	185.00
1827	2,357,732	3.75	4.50	6.00	10.00	30.00	185.00

This date size appears on cents before 1828.

This date size appears on cents after 1828.

1828 Lg. nar. date	} 2,260,624	3.75	4.50	6.00	10.00	30.00	200.00
1828 Sm. wide date		4.00	5.00	8.00	15.00	35.00	225.00
1829	1,414,500	3.75	4.50	6.00	10.00	30.00	185.00
1830	1,711,500	3.75	4.50	6.00	10.00	30.00	185.00
1831	3,359,260	3.50	4.25	5.50	8.00	27.00	185.00
1832	2,362,000	3.50	4.25	5.50	8.00	27.00	185.00
1833	2,739,000	3.50	4.25	5.50	8.00	27.00	185.00
1834	1,855,100	3.50	4.25	5.50	10.00	30.00	225.00
1835	3,878,400	4.00	5.00	7.00	12.00	30.00	200.00
1836	2,111,000	3.50	4.25	5.50	9.00	27.00	185.00

LARGE CENTS

G-4 GOOD—*Considerably worn. LIBERTY readable.*
VG-8 VERY GOOD—*Hairlines smooth but visible, outline of ear clearly defined.*
F-12 FINE—*Hairlines at top of head and behind ear worn but visible. Braid over brow plain, ear clear.*
VF-20 VERY FINE—*All details more sharp. Hair over brow shows only slight wear.*
EF-40 EXTREMELY FINE—*Hair above ear detailed, but slightly worn.*
MS-60 UNCIRCULATED—*Typical brown to red surface. No trace of wear.*

1839 over 1836

Brilliant or red uncirculated coins are worth more than prices shown. Spotted, cleaned or discolored pieces are worth less.

	Quan. Minted	G-4	VG-8	F-12	VF-20	EF-40	MS-60
1837	5,558,300	$3.75	$4.50	$6.00	$10.00	$30.00	$200.00
1838	6,370,200	3.50	4.25	5.50	8.00	27.00	185.00
1839	} 3,128,661	3.50	5.00	6.00	10.00	30.00	200.00
1839, 9 over 6		35.00	70.00	140.00	250.00	725.00	——
1840	2,462,700	3.00	4.00	5.00	8.00	25.00	185.00
1841	1,597,367	3.00	4.00	5.00	8.00	25.00	185.00
1842	2,383,390	3.00	4.00	5.00	8.00	25.00	175.00

Small Letters

Large Letters

"Head of 1840"
Petite Head
1839-1843

"Head of 1844"
Mature Head
1843-1857

1843 Petite, sm. let.	} 2,425,342	3.00	4.00	5.00	8.00	25.00	175.00
1843 Petite, lg. let.		5.00	8.00	12.00	25.00	45.00	300.00
1843 Mature, lg. let.		3.50	5.00	8.00	14.00	30.00	175.00
1844 Normal date	} 2,398,752	3.00	4.00	5.00	8.00	25.00	175.00
1844 over 81 (error-photo page 54)		4.00	5.00	9.00	17.00	60.00	325.00
1845	3,894,804	2.75	3.75	4.75	7.00	22.00	165.00
1846	4,120,800	3.00	4.00	5.00	8.00	25.00	175.00
1847	} 6,183,669	2.75	3.75	4.75	7.00	22.00	165.00
1847, 7 over "sm." 7		4.00	5.00	9.00	15.00	35.00	200.00

LARGE CENTS

	Quan. Minted	G-4	VG-8	F-12	VF-20	EF-40	MS-60
1848	6,415,799	$2.75	$3.75	$4.75	$7.00	$22.00	$165.00
1849	4,178,500	2.75	3.75	4.75	7.00	22.00	165.00
1850	4,426,844	2.75	2.75	4.75	7.00	22.00	165.00

1844, 44 over 81   1851, 51 over 81   1847, 7 over "Small" 7

Brilliant or red uncirculated coins are worth more than prices shown. Spotted, cleaned or discolored pieces are worth less.

1851 Normal date	} 9,889,707	2.75	3.75	4.75	7.00	22.00	165.00
1851 over 81 (error)		4.00	5.00	8.00	17.00	30.00	200.00
1852	5,063,094	2.75	3.75	4.75	7.00	22.00	165.00
1853	6,641,131	2.75	3.75	4.75	7.00	22.00	165.00
1854	4,236,156	2.75	3.75	4.75	7.00	22.00	165.00

1855 Upright 5's   1855 Slanting 5's   1855 Knob on ear

1855 All kinds	1,574,829						
1855 Upright 5's		2.75	3.75	4.75	7.00	22.00	165.00
1855 Slanting 5's		2.75	3.75	4.75	7.00	22.00	165.00
1855 Slanting 5's, knob on ear		3.00	4.00	5.50	12.00	27.00	185.00
1856 Upright 5	} 2,690,463	2.75	3.75	4.75	7.00	22.00	165.00
1856 Slanting 5		2.75	3.75	4.75	7.00	22.00	165.00

1857 Large Date   1857 Small Date

1857 Large date	} 333,456	9.00	13.00	19.00	24.00	26.00	200.00
1857 Small date		10.00	15.00	22.00	26.00	30.00	225.00

SMALL CENTS — 1856 to Date
FLYING EAGLE TYPE 1856-1858

The Act of February 21, 1857 provided for the coinage of the small cent. The 1856 Eagle cent was not an authorized mint issue, as the law governing the new size coin was enacted after the date of issue. It is believed that about 1,000 of these pieces were struck. They are properly referred to as patterns.

G-4 GOOD—*All details worn, but readable.*
VG-8 VERY GOOD—*Feather details and eye of eagle are evident but worn.*
F-12 FINE—*Eagle head details and feather tips sharp.*
VF-20 VERY FINE—*Feathers in right wing and tail show considerable detail.*
EF-40 EXTREMELY FINE—*Slight wear, all details sharp.*
MS-60 UNCIRCULATED—*No trace of wear. Light blemishes.*

1858, 8 over 7

1856-1858 Large Letters

1858 Small Letters

Brilliant uncirculated and proof coins are worth more than prices shown. Spotted, cleaned or discolored pieces are worth less.

	Quan. Minted			Quan. Minted
1856	est. *1,000*	1858 Lg. letters	*(80)*	24,600,000
1857	17,450,000	1858 Sm. letters	*(200)*	

	G-4	VG-8	F-12	VF-20	EF-40	MS-60	Proof-60
1856	$600.00	$850.00	$1,000	$1,300	$1,600	$2,000	$2,200
1857	4.50	6.00	9.00	16.00	40.00	185.00	1,000
1858 Lg. let.	4.50	6.00	9.00	16.00	40.00	185.00	1,000
1858, 8 over 7			60.00	125.00	250.00	500.00	
1858 Sm let.	4.50	6.00	9.00	16.00	40.00	185.00	1,000

SMALL CENTS
INDIAN HEAD TYPE 1859-1909

The small cent was redesigned in 1859, and a representation of an Indian princess was adopted as the obverse device. The 1859 reverse was also changed to represent a laurel wreath. In 1860 the reverse was modified to display an oak wreath with a small shield at the top. From 1859 to 1863 cents were struck in copper-nickel. In 1864 the composition was changed to bronze, although copper-nickel cents were also struck during that year.

SMALL CENTS

G-4 GOOD—*No LIBERTY visible.*
VG-8 VERY GOOD—*At least three letters of LIBERTY readable on head band.*
F-12 FINE—*LIBERTY completely visible.*
VF-20 VERY FINE—*Slight but even wear on LIBERTY.*
EF-40 EXTREMELY FINE—*LIBERTY sharp. All other details sharp. Only slight wear on ribbon end.*
MS-60 UNCIRCULATED—*No trace of wear. Light blemishes.*

Without Shield at Top of Wreath
1859 Only

With Shield on Reverse
1860 to 1909

Brilliant uncirculated and proof coins are worth more than prices shown. Spotted, cleaned or discolored pieces are worth less.

Copper-nickel, Laurel Wreath Reverse 1859

	Quan. Minted	G-4	VG-8	F-12	VF-20	EF-40	MS-60	Proof-63
1859 .... (800)	36,400,000	$2.50	$3.00	$5.00	$12.00	$35.00	$185.00	$650.00

Copper-nickel, Oak Wreath with Shield Reverse 1860-1864

	Quan. Minted	G-4	VG-8	F-12	VF-20	EF-40	MS-60	Proof-63
1860 .... (1,000)	20,566,000	2.50	3.00	4.00	7.00	15.00	80.00	575.00
1861 .... (1,000)	10,100,000	5.00	7.00	10.00	17.00	25.00	120.00	600.00
1862 .... (550)	28,075,000	1.75	2.00	3.00	5.00	10.00	70.00	500.00
1863 .... (460)	49,840,000	1.75	2.00	3.00	5.00	10.00	70.00	500.00
1864 .... (370)	13,740,000	4.00	5.00	7.00	10.00	15.00	80.00	575.00

Bronze 1864-1909

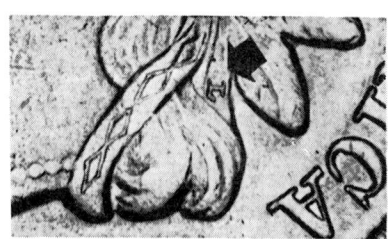

1864 Indian Head Cent with "L"

1869, "9 over 8"

	Quan. Minted	G-4	VG-8	F-12	VF-20	EF-40	MS-60	Proof-63
1864 All kinds	39,233,714							
1864 No L .... (150)		$2.00	$3.00	$5.00	$10.00	$15.00	$40.00	$600.00
1864 L must show .... (20)		17.00	22.00	35.00	60.00	85.00	215.00	——
1865 .... (500)	35,429,286	2.00	2.50	4.50	9.00	15.00	35.00	300.00
1866 .... (725)	9,826,500	13.00	15.00	22.00	35.00	50.00	100.00	300.00
1867 .... (625)	9,821,000	13.00	15.00	22.00	35.00	50.00	100.00	300.00
1868 .... (600)	10,266,500	13.00	15.00	22.00	35.00	50.00	100.00	275.00
1869 over 8. } (600)	6,420,000	45.00	65.00	100.00	175.00	250.00	550.00	——
1869 .... }		18.00	25.00	45.00	65.00	90.00	215.00	400.00

SMALL CENTS

Brilliant or red uncirculated coins are worth more than prices shown. Spotted, cleaned or discolored pieces are worth less.

	Quan. Minted	G-4	VG-8	F-12	VF-20	EF-40	MS-60	Proof-63
1870 .... (1,000)	5,275,000	$16.00	$20.00	$35.00	$45.00	$65.00	$150.00	$300.00
1871 .... (960)	3,929,500	20.00	25.00	45.00	60.00	80.00	165.00	350.00
1872 .... (950)	4,042,000	28.00	32.00	50.00	75.00	100.00	230.00	375.00
1873 .... (1,100)	11,676,500	5.50	6.50	11.00	17.00	30.00	70.00	250.00
1874 .... (700)	14,187,500	5.50	6.50	11.00	17.00	30.00	65.00	225.00
1875 .... (700)	13,528,000	5.50	6.50	11.00	17.00	30.00	65.00	225.00
1876 .... (1,150)	7,944,000	10.00	12.00	16.00	25.00	38.00	85.00	225.00
1877 .... (510)	852,500	150.00	175.00	225.00	350.00	500.00	1,000	1,700
1878 .... (2,350)	5,799,850	10.00	12.00	16.00	25.00	40.00	80.00	200.00
1879 .... (3,200)	16,231,200	2.00	2.25	3.50	7.00	12.00	40.00	200.00
1880 .... (3,955)	38,964,955	.60	1.00	1.75	2.75	7.00	25.00	190.00
1881 .... (3,575)	39,211,575	.60	1.00	1.75	2.75	7.00	25.00	190.00
1882 .... (3,100)	38,581,100	.60	1.00	1.75	2.75	7.00	25.00	190.00
1883 .... (6,609)	45,598,109	.60	1.00	1.75	2.75	7.00	25.00	190.00
1884 .... (3,942)	23,261,742	.75	1.25	2.25	4.00	8.00	30.00	200.00
1885 .... (3,790)	11,765,384	2.00	2.75	5.00	9.00	15.00	40.00	210.00
1886 .... (4,290)	17,654,290	.60	1.25	3.25	5.00	9.00	35.00	190.00
1887 .... (2,960)	45,226,483	.50	.60	.90	1.75	5.50	22.00	190.00
1888 .... (4,582)	37,494,414	.50	.60	.90	1.75	5.50	22.00	190.00
1889 .... (3,336)	48,869,361	.50	.60	.90	1.75	5.50	22.00	180.00
1890 .... (2,740)	57,182,854	.50	.60	.90	1.75	5.50	22.00	180.00
1891 .... (2,350)	47,072,350	.50	.60	.90	1.75	5.50	22.00	180.00
1892 .... (2,745)	37,649,832	.50	.60	.90	1.75	5.50	22.00	180.00
1893 .... (2,195)	46,642,195	.50	.60	.90	1.75	5.50	22.00	180.00
1894 .... (2,632)	16,752,132	.75	1.25	2.75	4.50	8.00	27.00	185.00
1895 .... (2,062)	38,343,636	.35	.50	.75	1.25	4.50	20.00	175.00
1896 .... (1,862)	39,057,293	.35	.50	.75	1.25	4.50	20.00	175.00
1897 .... (1,938)	50,466,330	.35	.50	.75	1.25	4.50	20.00	175.00
1898 .... (1,795)	49,823,079	.35	.50	.75	1.25	4.50	20.00	175.00
1899 .... (2,031)	53,600,031	.35	.50	.75	1.25	4.50	20.00	175.00
1900 .... (2,262)	66,833,764	.30	.40	.60	.85	3.50	18.00	175.00
1901 .... (1,985)	79,611,143	.30	.40	.60	.85	3.50	18.00	175.00
1902 .... (2,018)	87,376,722	.30	.40	.60	.85	3.50	18.00	175.00
1903 .... (1,790)	85,094,493	.30	.40	.60	.85	3.50	18.00	175.00
1904 .... (1,817)	61,328,015	.30	.40	.60	.85	3.50	18.00	175.00
1905 .... (2,152)	80,719,163	.30	.40	.60	.85	3.50	18.00	175.00
1906 .... (1,725)	96,022,255	.30	.40	.60	.85	3.50	18.00	175.00
1907 .... (1,475)	108,138,618	.30	.40	.60	.85	3.50	18.00	175.00

Location of mint mark S on reverse of Indian cent (1908 and 1909 only).

1908 .... (1,620)	32,327,987	.30	.40	.60	.85	3.50	18.00	185.00
1908S	1,115,000	13.00	14.00	15.00	18.00	30.00	85.00	
1909 .... (2,175)	14,370,645	.50	.65	.80	1.50	5.00	20.00	200.00
1909S	309,000	60.00	75.00	90.00	110.00	145.00	250.00	

[57]

SMALL CENTS
LINCOLN TYPE, WHEAT EARS REVERSE 1909-1958

Victor D. Brenner designed this cent which was issued to commemorate the hundredth anniversary of Lincoln's birth. The designer's initials VDB appear on the reverse of a limited quantity of cents of 1909. Later in the year they were removed from the dies but restored in 1918 as very small incuse letters beneath the shoulder. The Lincoln type was the first cent to have the motto IN GOD WE TRUST.

G-4 GOOD—*Date worn but apparent. Lines in wheat ears missing. Full rims.*
VG-8 VERY GOOD—*Half of lines show in upper wheat ears.*
F-12 FINE—*Wheat lines worn but visible.*
VF-20 VERY FINE—*Cheek and jaw bones worn but separated. No worn spots on wheat ears.*
EF-40 EXTREMELY FINE—*Slight wear. All details sharp.*
MS-60 UNCIRCULATED—*No trace of wear. Light blemishes or discoloration.*
MS-63 SELECT UNCIRCULATED—*No trace of wear. Slight blemishes.*
MS-65 CHOICE UNCIRCULATED—*No trace of wear. Barely noticeable blemishes.*

Location of mint mark S or D on obverse of Lincoln cent.

Bronze 1909-1942

Location of designer's initials V.D.B. on 1909 only.

No V.D.B. on reverse 1909-1958.

Brilliant uncirculated coins are worth more than prices shown. Spotted, cleaned, or discolored pieces are worth less.

	Quan. Minted	G-4	VG-8	F-12	VF-20	EF-40	MS-60
1909 V.D.B.	27,995,000	$1.25	$1.50	$1.75	$2.00	$2.50	$7.00
1909 V.D.B. Matte proof-63	(420)						500.00
1909S, V.D.B.	484,000	175.00	190.00	210.00	225.00	265.00	375.00
1909	72,702,618	.15	.20	.25	.40	.75	6.00
1909 Matte proof-63	(2,198)						100.00
1909S	1,825,000	25.00	30.00	35.00	40.00	60.00	125.00
1910	146,801,218	.05	.08	.10	.20	.50	7.00
1910 Matte proof-63	(2,405)						100.00
1910S	6,045,000	4.00	4.50	5.00	6.00	10.00	55.00
1911	101,177,787	.05	.08	.15	.40	.75	8.00
1911 Matte proof-63	(1,733)						100.00
1911D	12,672,000	2.50	2.75	3.25	6.00	12.00	60.00
1911S	4,026,000	8.00	8.50	9.00	12.00	18.00	65.00
1912	68,153,060	.05	.10	.40	1.00	1.75	11.00
1912 Matte proof-63	(2,145)						100.00
1912D	10,411,000	2.50	2.75	3.50	6.00	15.00	63.00
1912S	4,431,000	6.00	7.00	8.00	9.00	15.00	63.00
1913	76,532,352	.05	.10	.30	.75	1.25	11.00
1913 Matte proof-63	(2,848)						100.00
1913D	15,804,000	1.00	1.25	1.75	3.00	8.00	45.00

SMALL CENTS

Brilliant uncirculated coins before 1934 are worth more than prices shown. Spotted, cleaned or discolored pieces are worth less

	Quan. Minted	G-4	VG-8	F-12	VF-20	EF-40	MS-60
1913S	6,101,000	$4.00	$5.00	$5.50	$6.00	$10.00	$60.00
1914	75,238,432	.05	.10	.30	.75	3.00	35.00
1914 Matte proof-63	(1,365)						160.00
1914D*	1,193,000	45.00	50.00	70.00	100.00	235.00	550.00
1914S	4,137,000	5.50	6.00	6.50	8.00	16.00	90.00
1915	29,092,120	.30	.50	1.25	3.00	14.00	60.00
1915 Matte proof-63	(1,150)						160.00
1915D	22,050,000	.20	.40	.65	1.50	4.00	20.00
1915S	4,833,000	5.00	5.50	6.00	7.00	12.00	55.00
1916	131,833,677	.03	.05	.10	.20	.80	5.00
1916 Matte proof-63	(1,050)						185.00
1916D	35,956,000	.08	.13	.40	1.00	2.50	25.00
1916S	22,510,000	.30	.40	.75	1.25	3.50	32.50
1917	196,429,785	.03	.05	.10	.20	.50	6.00
1917D	55,120,000	.08	.13	.35	.80	2.50	30.00
1917S	32,620,000	.08	.13	.35	.80	2.50	36.00

Designer's initials restored starting 1918.

	Quan. Minted	G-4	VG-8	F-12	VF-20	EF-40	MS-60
1918	288,104,634	.03	.05	.10	.20	.75	5.50
1918D	47,830,000	.08	.13	.35	.80	2.50	30.00
1918S	34,680,000	.08	.13	.35	.80	2.50	35.00
1919	392,021,000	.02	.03	.05	.15	.50	4.00
1919D	57,154,000	.04	.06	.10	.30	1.00	26.00
1919S	139,760,000	.04	.06	.10	.25	.50	17.50
1920	310,165,000	.02	.03	.05	.15	.50	4.50
1920D	49,280,000	.04	.06	.10	.30	1.00	28.00
1920S	46,220,000	.04	.06	.10	.30	1.25	35.00
1921	39,157,000	.05	.08	.15	.35	1.50	21.00
1921S	15,274,000	.35	.45	.70	1.25	6.00	78.00
1922D	} 7,160,000	3.00	3.75	4.50	6.00	10.00	45.00
1922 Plain†		120.00	150.00	200.00	335.00	550.00	1,950
1923	74,723,000	.02	.03	.05	.15	.50	4.00
1923S	8,700,000	.75	.85	1.25	2.00	6.00	100.00
1924	75,178,000	.02	.03	.05	.15	.75	11.00
1924D	2,520,000	6.50	7.00	8.00	11.00	21.00	135.00
1924S	11,696,000	.35	.45	.70	1.00	2.00	65.00
1925	139,949,000	.02	.03	.05	.15	.45	4.00
1925D	22,580,000	.04	.06	.10	.30	1.50	25.00
1925S	26,380,000	.04	.06	.10	.25	1.25	35.00
1926	157,088,000	.02	.03	.05	.15	.45	3.50
1926D	28,020,000	.04	.06	.10	.25	1.50	24.00
1926S	4,550,000	1.50	1.75	2.25	2.75	5.00	55.00
1927	144,440,000	.02	.03	.05	.15	.45	3.25
1927D	27,170,000	.04	.06	.10	.25	.85	15.00
1927S	14,276,000	.25	.30	.50	.75	1.25	35.00
1928	134,116,000	.02	.03	.05	.15	.45	3.25
1928D	31,170,000	.04	.06	.10	.25	.75	12.00
1928S	17,266,000	.06	.10	.25	.50	1.00	27.50
1929	185,262,000	.02	.03	.05	.15	.25	2.50
1929D	41,730,000	.04	.06	.10	.25	.60	8.00
1929S	50,148,000	.03	.05	.10	.15	.40	4.00

*Beware of altered date or mint mark. No VDB on shoulder of genuine 1914D cent.
†The 1922 without D caused by defective die. Beware removed mint mark.

SMALL CENTS

	Quan. Minted	G-4	VG-8	F-12	VF-20	EF-40	MS-60	MS-65
1930	157,415,000	$.02	$.03	$.05	$.15	$.25	$2.50	$25.00
1930D	40,100,000	.04	.06	.10	.25	.60	6.00	65.00
1930S	24,286,000	.03	.05	.10	.15	.40	3.00	40.00
1931	19,396,000	.15	.20	.30	.40	.60	7.50	55.00
1931D	4,480,000	1.50	1.75	2.00	2.50	4.00	25.00	175.00
1931S	866,000	21.00	23.00	25.00	26.00	30.00	45.00	150.00
1932	9,062,000	.70	.80	1.00	1.15	1.75	9.00	50.00
1932D	10,500,000	.25	.35	.40	.50	.75	7.00	45.00
1933	14,360,000	.25	.35	.45	.60	1.00	9.00	70.00
1933D	6,200,000	.80	1.00	1.20	1.50	1.75	11.00	60.00
1934	219,080,000	.02	.02	.02	.03	.10	1.50	5.00
1934D	28,446,000	.04	.06	.08	.10	.25	9.00	25.00
1935	245,388,000	.02	.02	.02	.03	.06	.75	2.00
1935D	47,000,000	.02	.02	.02	.03	.10	1.25	4.00
1935S	38,702,000	.02	.03	.03	.04	.08	5.00	18.00
1936	309,637,569	.02	.02	.02	.03	.06	.50	1.15
1936 Proof-65	(5,569)							225.00
1936D	40,620,000	.02	.02	.02	.03	.08	.75	2.00
1936S	29,130,000	.03	.03	.03	.04	.10	1.00	3.00
1937	309,179,320	.02	.02	.02	.03	.05	.60	1.50
1937 Proof-65	(9,320)							90.00
1937D	50,430,000	.02	.02	.02	.03	.06	.50	2.25
1937S	34,500,000	.03	.03	.03	.04	.06	.50	2.25
1938	156,696,734	.02	.02	.02	.03	.05	.60	1.25
1938 Proof-65	(14,784)							60.00
1938D	20,010,000	.02	.03	.04	.06	.15	1.00	2.00
1938S	15,180,000	.06	.08	.10	.12	.15	1.00	2.50
1939	316,479,520	.02	.02	.02	.03	.05	.25	.75
1939 Proof-65	(13,520)							55.00
1939D	15,160,000	.06	.08	.10	.12	.15	.95	3.25
1939S	52,070,000	.03	.03	.03	.04	.10	.50	1.50
1940	586,825,872	.02	.02	.02	.02	.03	.20	.40
1940 Proof-65	(15,872)							50.00
1940D	81,390,000	.02	.02	.02	.02	.03	.40	1.25
1940S	112,940,000	.04	.02	.02	.03	.04	.60	2.25
1941	887,039,100	.02	.02	.02	.02	.03	.25	.60
1941 Proof-65	(21,100)							45.00
1941D	128,700,000	.02	.02	.02	.02	.03	.60	2.25
1941S	92,360,000	.02	.02	.02	.03	.04	.75	2.75
1942	657,828,600	.02	.02	.02	.02	.03	.10	.30
1942 Proof-65	(32,600)							45.00
1942D	206,698,000	.02	.02	.02	.02	.03	.10	.45
1942S	85,590,000	.02	.02	.02	.03	.05	1.00	3.50

Zinc-coated Steel 1943 Only

1943	684,628,670				.03	.03	.08	.25	.90
1943D	217,660,000				.03	.04	.10	.30	1.50
1943S	191,550,000				.04	.05	.15	.30	3.00

Bronze Resumed 1944-1958

	Quan. Minted	VF-20	EF-40	MS-65
1944	1,435,400,000	$.02	$.02	$.25
1944D	} 430,578,000	.02	.02	.45
1944D, D over S (varieties)		35.00	45.00	*125.00
1944S	282,760,000	.02	.03	.25
1945	1,040,515,000	.02	.02	.10
1945D	266,268,000	.02	.02	.35
1945S	181,770,000	.02	.03	.25

*Value is for MS-60 uncirculated.

SMALL CENTS

1944D, D over S

	Quan. Minted	VF-20	EF-40	MS-65	Proof-65
1946	991,655,000	$.02	$.02	$.15	
1946D	315,690,000	.02	.02	.15	
1946S	198,100,000	.02	.03	.25	
1947	190,555,000	.02	.02	.45	
1947D	194,750,000	.02	.02	.25	
1947S	99,000,000	.02	.03	.45	
1948	317,570,000	.02	.02	.30	
1948D	172,637,500	.02	.02	.50	
1948S	81,735,000	.02	.03	.50	
1949	217,775,000	.02	.02	.75	
1949D	153,132,500	.02	.02	.55	
1949S	64,290,000	.03	.05	1.25	
1950 (51,386)	272,686,386	.02	.02	.80	$45.00
1950D	334,950,000	.02	.02	.15	
1950S	118,505,000	.02	.03	.45	
1951 (57,500)	284,633,500	.02	.02	.55	30.00
1951D	625,355,000	.02	.02	.20	
1951S	136,010,000	.02	.03	.85	
1952 (81,980)	186,856,980	.02	.02	.30	20.00
1952D	746,130,000	.02	.02	.35	
1952S	137,800,004	.02	.03	.50	
1953 (128,800)	256,883,800	.02	.03	.15	12.00
1953D	700,515,000	.02	.02	.20	
1953S	181,835,000	.02	.03	.25	
1954 (233,300)	71,873,350	.03	.05	.25	6.00
1954D	251,552,500	.02	.02	.10	
1954S	96,190,000	.02	.03	.10	
1955 Doubled die obv	} 330,958,200	235.00	275.00	*1,800	
1955 (378,200)		.02	.02	.08	4.50
1955D	563,257,500	.02	.02	.08	
1955S	44,610,000	.10	.15	.25	
1956 (669,384)	421,414,384	.02	.02	.08	1.50
1956D	1,098,201,100	.02	.02	.05	
1957 (1,247,952)	283,787,952	.02	.02	.05	1.00
1957D	1,051,342,000	.02	.02	.03	
1958 (875,652)	253,400,652	.02	.02	.03	1.10
1958D	800,953,300	.02	.02	.03	

*Value for MS-60 Uncirculated is $450.00; MS-63 is $775.00

1955 Doubled Die Error

Enlarged Detail of 1972
Doubled Die Error

1969S Doubled Die Error

SMALL CENTS
LINCOLN TYPE, MEMORIAL REVERSE 1959 TO DATE

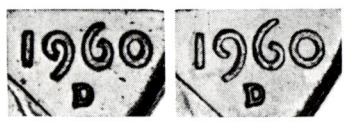

| Small Date | Large Date | Small Date
Numbers aligned at top | Large Date
Low 7 in date |

	Quan. Minted	MS-65	Proof-65
1959 .... (1,149,291)	610,864,291	$.01	$.65
1959D	1,279,760,000	.01	
1960 Large date .... } (1,691,602)	588,096,602	.01	.45
1960 Sm. date		1.50	8.00
1960D Large date .... }	1,580,884,000	.01	
1960D Small date		.02	
1961 .... (3,028,244)	756,373,244	.01	.35
1961D	1,753,266,700	.01	

	Quan. Minted	MS-65	Proof-65
1962 (3,218,019)			
....	609,263,019	$.01	$.35
1962D	1,793,148,400	.01	
1963 (3,075,645)			
....	757,185,645	.01	.35
1963D	1,774,020,400	.01	
1964 (3,950,762)			
....	2,652,525,762	.01	.35
1964D	3,799,071,500	.01	
1965	1,497,224,900	.03	
1966	2,188,147,783	.15	
1967	3,048,667,100	.13	
1968	1,707,880,970	.06	
1968D	2,886,269,600	.02	
1968S (3,041,506)			
....	261,311,510	.02	.35
1969	1,136,910,000	.25	
1969D	4,002,832,200	.04	
1969S (2,934,631)			
....	547,309,631	.03	.35
1969S Doubled die obv		—	
1970	1,898,315,000	.18	
1970D	2,891,438,900	.05	
1970S (2,632,810)			
....	693,192,814		
1970S Sm. date		6.00	65.00
1970S Lg. date (low 7)		.04	.35
1971	1,919,490,000	.10	
1971D	2,911,045,600	.09	
1971S (3,220,733)			
....	528,354,192	.13	.35

	Quan. Minted	MS-65	Proof-65
1972 Doubled die obv	$225.00		
1972	2,933,255,000	.02	
1972D	2,665,071,400	.05	
1972S (3,260,996)			
....	380,200,104	.02	$.35
1973	3,728,245,000	.01	
1973D	3,549,576,588	.01	
1973S (2,760,339)			
....	319,937,634	.02	.35
1974	4,232,140,523	.01	
1974D	4,235,098,000	.01	
1974S (2,612,568)			
....	412,039,228	.05	.35
1975	5,451,476,142	.01	
1975D	4,505,275,300	.02	
1975S Proof	(2,845,450)		5.00
1976	4,674,292,426	.01	
1976D	4,221,592,455	.03	
1976S Proof	(4,149,730)		1.75
1977	4,469,930,000	.02	
1977D	4,194,062,300	.01	
1977S Proof	(3,251,152)		1.50
1978	5,558,605,000	.04	
1978D	4,280,233,400	.03	
1978S Proof	(3,127,781)		2.10
1979	6,018,515,000	.01	
1979D	4,139,357,254	.01	
1979S Proof	(3,677,175)		
Filled S			2.10
Clear S			3.85

 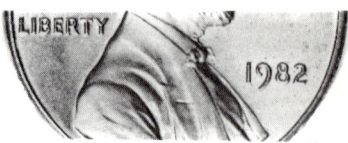

| Large Date | Small Date |

SMALL CENTS

	Quan. Minted	MS-65	Proof-65
1980	7,414,705,000	$.01	
1980D	5,140,098,660	.01	
1980S Proof	(3,554,806)		$1.35
1981	7,491,750,000	.01	
1981D	5,373,235,677	.01	
1981S Proof	(4,063,083)		1.50
1982	10,712,525,000		
Lg. Date		.01	
Sm. Date		.04	
1982D	6,012,979,368		
Lg. Date		.01	
1982S Proof	(3,857,479)		2.50

	Quan. Minted	MS-65	Proof-65
Copper Plated Zinc			
1982 Lg. Date	inc. above	$.01	
1982 Sm. Date	inc. above	.01	
1982D Lg. Date	inc. above	.06	
1982D Sm. Date	inc. above	.01	
1983		.01	
1983D		.01	
1983S Proof			$1.50

TWO-CENT PIECES — 1864-1873

The Act of April 22, 1864, which changed the weight and composition of the cent, included a provision for the bronze two-cent piece. The weight was specified as 96 grains, the alloy being the same as for the cent.

There are two varieties for the first year of issue, 1864: the small motto and the large motto. The differences are explained in the illustrations below.

1864 Small Motto

1864 Large Motto

On the obverse the D in GOD is narrow on the large motto. The stem to the leaf shows plainly on the small motto variety.

G-4 GOOD—At least IN GOD visible.
F-12 FINE—Complete motto visible. WE weak.
EF-40 EXTREMELY FINE—WE is bold.
MS-60 UNCIRCULATED—No trace of wear. Light blemishes.
MS-63 SELECT UNCIRCULATED—No trace of wear. Nice color, few blemishes.

Brilliant red choice uncirculated and proof coins are worth more than prices shown. Cleaned or discolored pieces are worth less.

	Quan. Minted	G-4	F-12	EF-40	MS-60	MS-63	Proof-63
1864 Sm. motto	} 19,847,500	$25.00	$55.00	$125.00	$325.00	$725.00	—
1864 Lg. motto		2.75	4.00	18.00	120.00	310.00	$600.00
1865	13,640,000	2.75	4.00	18.00	120.00	310.00	575.00
1866	3,177,000	2.75	4.00	18.00	120.00	310.00	575.00
1867	2,938,750	2.75	4.00	18.00	120.00	310.00	575.00
1868	2,803,750	2.75	4.00	18.00	120.00	310.00	575.00
1869, 9 over 8	} 1,546,500	50.00	100.00	300.00			
1869		3.00	5.50	19.00	150.00	325.00	600.00
1870	861,250	4.00	7.50	20.00	175.00	350.00	650.00
1871	721,250	4.25	7.75	25.00	200.00	400.00	800.00
1872	65,000	30.00	65.00	175.00	475.00	850.00	1,000
1873 Proofs only (Est. 1,100)							1,400

SILVER THREE-CENT PIECES 1851-1873

This smallest of United States silver coins was authorized by Congress March 3, 1851. The first three-cent silver pieces had no lines bordering the six-pointed star. From 1854 through 1858 there were three lines, while issues of the last fifteen years show only two lines. Issues from 1854 through 1873 have an olive sprig over the III and a bundle of three arrows beneath.

Mint Mark
O
←

G-4 GOOD—*Star worn smooth. Legend and date readable.*
VG-8 VERY GOOD—*Outline of shield defined. Legend and date clear.*
F-12 FINE—*Only star points worn smooth.*
VF-20 VERY FINE—*Only partial wear on star ridges.*
EF-40 EXTREMELY FINE—*Ridges on star points show.*
MS-60 UNCIRCULATED—*No trace of wear. Light blemishes.*

No outline around star.

Well struck specimens command higher prices.

	Quan. Minted	G-4	VG-8	F-12	VF-20	EF-40	MS-60	Proof-63
1851	5,447,440	$4.50	$6.00	$8.00	$13.00	$25.00	$180.00	—
1851O	720,000	6.00	9.00	14.00	24.00	40.00	275.00	
1852	18,663,500	4.00	5.00	7.00	12.00	25.00	180.00	—
1853	11,400,000	4.00	5.00	7.00	12.00	25.00	180.00	

Three outlines to star, large date.

1854	671,000	7.00	8.00	11.00	20.00	42.00	275.00	—
1855	139,000	9.00	12.00	20.00	35.00	85.00	325.00	$1,900
1856	1,458,000	6.00	7.50	10.00	18.00	40.00	275.00	1,800
1857	1,042,000	6.00	7.50	10.00	18.00	40.00	275.00	1,800
1858	1,604,000	6.00	7.50	10.00	18.00	40.00	275.00	1,400

Two outlines to star, small date.   1862 2 over 1

1859 .... (800)	365,000	6.00	7.00	10.00	17.00	30.00	170.00	650.00
1860 .... (1,000)	287,000	6.00	7.00	10.00	17.00	30.00	170.00	650.00
1861 .... (1,000)	498,000	6.00	7.00	10.00	17.00	30.00	170.00	650.00
1862, 2 over 1	343,550	7.00	8.00	12.00	20.00	40.00	190.00	
1862 .... (550)		6.00	7.00	10.00	17.00	30.00	170.00	650.00
1863 .... (460)	21,460						325.00	700.00
1864 .... (470)	12,470						325.00	700.00
1865 .... (500)	8,500						350.00	700.00
1866 .... (725)	22,725						350.00	700.00
1867 .... (625)	4,625						350.00	700.00
1868 .... (600)	4,100						350.00	700.00
1869 .... (600)	5,100						350.00	700.00
1870 .... (1,000)	4,000						350.00	700.00
1871 .... (960)	4,360						350.00	700.00
1872 .... (950)	1,950						350.00	700.00
1873 .... (600)	600							800.00

THREE-CENT PIECES (NICKEL)
ISSUED 1865-1889

The three-cent pieces struck in nickel composition were designed to replace the silver three cent coins. Composition is 75% copper and 25% nickel. All were coined at Philadelphia and have plain edges.

G-4 GOOD—*Date and legends complete though worn. III smooth.*
VG-8 VERY GOOD—*III is half worn. Rims complete.*
F-12 FINE—*Hair curls well defined.*
EF-40 EXTREMELY FINE—*Slight, even wear.*
MS-60 UNCIRCULATED—*No trace of wear. Light blemishes.*

Brilliant choice uncirculated and proof coins are worth more than prices shown. Spotted, cleaned or discolored pieces are worth less.

	Quan. Minted	G-4	VG-8	F-12	EF-40	MS-60	Proof-63
1865	11,382,000	$2.50	$3.00	$4.00	$8.00	$70.00	$500.00
1866	4,801,000	2.50	3.00	4.00	8.00	70.00	350.00
1867	3,915,000	2.50	3.00	4.00	8.00	70.00	300.00
1868	3,252,000	2.50	3.00	4.00	8.00	70.00	300.00
1869	1,604,000	2.50	3.00	4.00	8.00	70.00	300.00
1870	1,335,000	3.00	4.00	5.00	9.00	70.00	300.00
1871	604,000	3.00	4.00	5.00	9.00	75.00	300.00
1872	862,000	3.00	4.00	5.00	9.00	75.00	300.00
1873 (1,100)	1,173,000	3.00	4.00	5.00	9.00	70.00	300.00
1874	790,000	3.50	4.50	5.50	10.00	75.00	300.00
1875	228,000	5.00	6.00	7.00	14.00	100.00	300.00
1876	162,000	5.00	6.00	7.00	14.00	110.00	300.00
1877 (Proofs only)							750.00
1878 (2,350)	2,350						550.00
1879 (3,200)	41,200	22.00	27.50	35.00	45.00	175.00	300.00
1880 (3,955)	24,955	35.00	40.00	50.00	70.00	185.00	300.00
1881 (3,575)	1,080,575	2.50	3.00	4.00	8.00	70.00	300.00
1882 (3,100)	25,300	30.00	35.00	40.00	50.00	185.00	350.00
1883 (6,609)	10,609	60.00	70.00	85.00	110.00	245.00	475.00
1884 (3,942)	5,642	100.00	135.00	160.00	200.00	375.00	450.00
1885 (3,790)	4,790	150.00	175.00	200.00	250.00	400.00	600.00
1886 (4,290)	4,290						675.00
1887, 7 over 6							675.00
1887 All kinds (2,960)	7,961	100.00	135.00	160.00	200.00	375.00	625.00
1888 (4,582)	41,083	20.00	25.00	30.00	40.00	175.00	300.00
1889 (3,436)	21,561	25.00	30.00	35.00	55.00	185.00	300.00

NICKEL FIVE-CENT PIECES — 1866 to Date
SHIELD TYPE 1866-1883

The shield type nickel was made possible by the Act of May 16, 1866. Its weight was set at 77-16/100 grains with the same composition as the nickel three-cent piece which was authorized in 1865.

G-4 GOOD—*All letters in motto readable.*
VG-8 VERY GOOD—*Motto stands out clearly. Rims worn slightly but even. Part of shield lines visible.*
F-12 FINE—*Half of each olive leaf is smooth.*
EF-40 EXTREMELY FINE—*Leaf tips show slight wear. Cross over shield slightly worn.*
MS-60 UNCIRCULATED—*No trace of wear. Light blemishes.*

Rays Between Stars 1866-1867

NICKEL FIVE-CENT PIECES

Brilliant choice uncirculated and proof coins are worth more than prices shown. Spotted, cleaned or discolored pieces are worth less.

	Quan. Minted	G-4	VG-8	F-12	EF-40	MS-60	Proof-63
1866 Rays	14,742,500	$6.00	$7.50	$12.00	$40.00	$225.00	$1,225
1867 Rays	2,019,000	7.00	9.00	15.00	45.00	250.00	4,500

Without Rays 1867-1883

Typical example of 1883, 3 over 2. Other varieties exist.

Year	Quan. Minted	G-4	VG-8	F-12	EF-40	MS-60	Proof-63
1867 No rays	28,890,500	4.00	5.00	6.00	15.00	90.00	400.00
1868	28,817,000	4.00	5.00	6.00	15.00	90.00	400.00
1869	16,395,000	4.00	5.00	6.00	15.00	90.00	400.00
1870	4,806,000	4.00	5.00	6.00	16.00	100.00	400.00
1871	561,000	15.00	20.00	27.00	50.00	170.00	500.00
1872	6,036,000	4.00	5.00	6.00	16.00	90.00	400.00
1873 Closed 3 (1,100)	436,050	4.00	5.00	6.00	16.00	100.00	400.00
1873 Open 3	4,113,950	4.00	5.00	6.00	16.00	100.00	
1874	3,538,000	5.00	6.00	7.00	16.00	100.00	400.00
1875	2,097,000	6.00	7.00	10.00	20.00	110.00	400.00
1876	2,530,000	6.00	7.00	10.00	20.00	100.00	400.00
1877 Est. Issued (500)	500						1,200
1878 (2,350)	2,350						725.00
1879 (3,200)	29,100	100.00	125.00	150.00	200.00	400.00	600.00
1880 (3,955)	19,955	110.00	135.00	185.00	235.00	375.00	600.00
1881 (3,575)	72,375	75.00	100.00	125.00	175.00	350.00	600.00
1882 (3,100)	11,476,000	4.00	5.00	6.00	15.00	90.00	400.00
1883 (5,419)	1,456,919	4.00	5.00	6.00	15.00	90.00	400.00
1883, 3 over 2			15.00	25.00	65.00	200.00	

LIBERTY HEAD TYPE 1883-1913

In 1883 the design was changed to the familiar "Liberty head." This type first appeared without the word CENTS on the coin, merely a large letter "V." These "centless" coins were goldplated and passed for five dollars. Later in that year the word CENTS was added.

Without CENTS 1883 Only

G-4 GOOD—*No details in head. LIBERTY obliterated.*
VG-8 VERY GOOD—*At least 3 letters in LIBERTY readable.*
F-12 FINE—*All letters in LIBERTY show.*
VF-20 VERY FINE—*LIBERTY bold, including letter I.*
EF-40 EXTREMELY FINE—*LIBERTY sharp. Corn grains at bottom of wreath show, on reverse.*
MS-60 UNCIRCULATED—*No trace of wear. Light blemishes.*

	Quan. Minted	G-4	VG-8	F-12	VF-20	EF-40	MS-60	Proof-63
1883 without CENTS (5,219)	5,479,519	$1.00	$1.50	$2.00	$3.00	$4.00	$25.00	$425.00

NICKEL FIVE-CENT PIECES
With CENTS 1883-1913

Location of mint mark

Brilliant choice uncirculated and proof coins are worth more than prices shown. Spotted, cleaned or discolored pieces are worth less.

	Quan. Minted	G-4	VG-8	F-12	VF-20	EF-40	MS-60	Proof-63
1883 with CENTS								
.... (6,783)	16,032,983	$2.00	$3.00	$5.00	$10.00	$15.00	$90.00	$300.00
1884 .... (3,942)	11,273,942	2.50	3.50	5.50	11.00	16.00	100.00	300.00
1885 .... (3,790)	1,476,490	175.00	200.00	300.00	400.00	500.00	800.00	1,000
1886 .... (4,290)	3,330,290	25.00	30.00	40.00	60.00	125.00	275.00	635.00
1887 .... (2,960)	15,263,652	1.50	2.00	5.00	8.00	15.00	90.00	285.00
1888 .... (4,582)	10,720,483	2.50	4.00	6.00	12.00	18.00	100.00	285.00
1889 .... (3,336)	15,881,361	1.50	2.00	4.00	8.00	15.00	90.00	285.00
1890 .... (2,740)	16,259,272	1.50	2.00	4.00	8.00	15.00	100.00	285.00
1891 .... (2,350)	16,834,350	1.50	2.00	4.00	8.00	15.00	90.00	285.00
1892 .... (2,745)	11,699,642	1.50	2.00	4.00	8.00	15.00	90.00	285.00
1893 .... (2,195)	13,370,195	1.50	2.00	4.00	8.00	15.00	90.00	285.00
1894 .... (2,632)	5,413,132	2.00	3.00	6.00	12.00	19.00	110.00	285.00
1895 .... (2,062)	9,979,884	1.25	2.00	4.00	7.00	13.00	80.00	285.00
1896 .... (1,862)	8,842,920	1.50	2.00	5.00	8.00	15.00	80.00	285.00
1897 .... (1,938)	20,428,735	.40	.50	1.50	3.00	10.00	75.00	285.00
1898 .... (1,795)	12,532,087	.40	.50	1.50	3.00	10.00	75.00	285.00
1899 .... (2,031)	26,029,031	.40	.50	1.50	3.00	10.00	75.00	285.00
1900 .... (2,262)	27,255,995	.25	.40	.80	2.50	9.00	70.00	275.00
1901 .... (1,985)	26,480,213	.25	.40	.80	2.50	9.00	70.00	275.00
1902 .... (2,018)	31,489,579	.25	.40	.80	2.50	9.00	70.00	275.00
1903 .... (1,790)	28,006,725	.25	.40	.80	2.50	9.00	70.00	275.00
1904 .... (1,817)	21,404,984	.25	.40	.80	2.50	9.00	70.00	275.00
1905 .... (2,152)	29,827,276	.25	.40	.80	2.50	9.00	70.00	275.00
1906 .... (1,725)	38,613,725	.25	.40	.80	2.50	9.00	70.00	275.00
1907 .... (1,475)	39,214,800	.25	.40	.80	2.50	9.00	70.00	275.00
1908 .... (1,620)	22,686,177	.25	.40	.80	2.50	9.00	70.00	275.00
1909 .... (4,763)	11,590,526	.25	.40	.80	3.00	10.00	70.00	275.00
1910 .... (2,405)	30,169,353	.25	.40	.80	2.50	9.00	70.00	275.00
1911 .... (1,733)	39,559,372	.25	.40	.80	2.50	9.00	70.00	275.00
1912 .... (2,145)	26,236,714	.25	.40	.80	2.50	9.00	70.00	275.00
1912D	8,474,000	.40	.50	1.50	5.00	22.00	160.00	
1912S	238,000	22.00	27.00	35.00	80.00	165.00	400.00	
1913 Liberty Head (5 known)								—

INDIAN HEAD or BUFFALO TYPE 1913-1938

The Buffalo nickel was designed by James E. Fraser, whose initial F is below the date. He modeled the bison after Black Diamond in the New York Zoological Gardens. The three Indians used in the portrait were Irontail, Two Moons, and John Big Tree.

NICKEL FIVE-CENT PIECES
Variety 1 — FIVE CENTS on Raised Ground

G-4 GOOD—*Legends and date readable. Horn worn off.*
VG-8 VERY GOOD—*Half horn shows.*
F-12 FINE—*Three-quarters of horn shows. Obv. rim intact.*
VF-20 VERY FINE—*Full horn shows. Indian's cheekbone worn.*
EF-40 EXTREMELY FINE—*Full horn. Slight wear on Indian's hair ribbon.*
MS-63 SELECT UNCIRCULATED—*No trace of wear. Light blemishes. Attractive mint luster.*

Brilliant choice uncirculated coins are worth more than prices shown. Spotted, cleaned, weakly struck or discolored pieces are worth less.

	Quan. Minted	G-4	VG-8	F-12	VF-20	EF-40	MS-63	Matte Proof-63
1913 Var. 1. (1,520)	30,993,520	$1.25	$2.00	$2.50	$3.00	$7.50	$25.00	$1,200
1913D Var. 1	5,337,000	2.50	3.00	3.50	6.00	12.00	60.00	
1913S Var. 1	2,105,000	5.50	6.50	9.00	11.00	25.00	100.00	

Variety 2 — FIVE CENTS Recessed

Mint mark below FIVE CENTS   1916 Doubled Die Obverse   1918D, 8 over 7

	Quan. Minted	G-4	VG-8	F-12	VF-20	EF-40	MS-63	Matte Proof-63
1913 Var. 2. (1,514)	29,858,700	1.50	2.25	3.00	3.75	6.00	35.00	625.00
1913D Var. 2	4,156,000	25.00	28.00	33.00	40.00	50.00	175.00	
1913S Var. 2	1,209,000	40.00	50.00	65.00	80.00	110.00	225.00	
1914 (1,275)	20,665,738	2.00	2.50	3.00	4.00	9.00	50.00	625.00
1914D	3,912,000	17.00	20.00	25.00	40.00	70.00	225.00	
1914S	3,470,000	2.00	3.00	5.00	8.00	22.00	100.00	
1915 (1,050)	20,987,270	1.00	1.25	2.00	3.00	7.00	50.00	625.00
1915D	7,569,000	3.00	4.00	6.50	15.00	30.00	140.00	
1915S	1,505,000	6.00	7.50	10.00	30.00	55.00	250.00	
1916 (600)	63,498,066	.35	.50	.90	1.40	2.80	30.00	1,400
1916 Doubled die obv		25.00	60.00	125.00	175.00	350.00	—	
1916D	13,333,000	2.00	3.00	4.50	12.00	25.00	140.00	
1916S	11,860,000	1.50	2.00	3.00	12.00	30.00	120.00	
1917	51,424,019	.30	.40	.75	1.00	5.00	35.00	—
1917D	9,910,000	2.50	3.00	6.00	15.00	50.00	200.00	
1917S	4,193,000	2.00	2.50	5.00	20.00	40.00	210.00	
1918	32,086,314	.25	.50	1.00	3.00	8.00	65.00	
1918D, 8 over 7	} 8,362,000	275.00	325.00	500.00	825.00	1,750	6,500	
1918D		2.50	3.50	6.50	35.00	50.00	275.00	
1918S	4,882,000	2.00	3.00	6.00	22.00	45.00	220.00	
1919	60,868,000	.20	.30	.55	1.00	4.00	35.00	
1919D†	8,006,000	2.00	3.00	7.50	45.00	65.00	300.00	
1919S†	7,521,000	1.50	2.00	4.00	30.00	50.00	225.00	

†Uncirculated pieces with full sharp details are worth considerably more.

NICKEL FIVE-CENT PIECES

Brilliant choice uncirculated coins are worth more than prices shown. Spotted, cleaned, weakly struck or discolored pieces are worth less.

	Quan. Minted	G-4	VG-8	F-12	VF-20	EF-40	MS-63
1920	63,093,000	$.20	$.30	$.55	$1.00	$4.00	$35.00
1920D†	9,418,000	2.00	2.50	5.00	35.00	60.00	300.00
1920S	9,689,000	.90	1.25	2.50	15.00	50.00	200.00
1921	10,663,000	.25	.50	1.00	3.00	10.00	80.00
1921S†	1,557,000	7.50	10.00	20.00	50.00	140.00	450.00
1923	35,715,000	.15	.20	.30	.90	3.00	35.00
1923S†	6,142,000	1.00	1.50	2.50	12.00	35.00	165.00
1924	21,620,000	.15	.20	.30	1.00	4.50	60.00
1924D	5,258,000	1.25	1.75	3.00	25.00	43.00	195.00
1924S	1,437,000	2.00	3.00	7.50	65.00	150.00	550.00
1925	35,565,100	.15	.20	.30	1.00	3.00	30.00
1925D†	4,450,000	2.00	3.00	5.00	32.00	50.00	275.00
1925S	6,256,000	1.00	1.50	3.00	12.00	30.00	200.00
1926	44,693,000	.12	.15	.20	.50	1.50	30.00
1926D†	5,638,000	1.00	1.50	4.00	25.00	50.00	125.00
1926S	970,000	2.00	3.00	7.00	35.00	125.00	450.00
1927	37,981,000	.12	.15	.20	.50	1.50	30.00
1927D	5,730,000	.40	.85	1.00	6.00	22.00	100.00
1927S	3,430,000	.25	.35	.75	8.00	30.00	175.00
1928	23,411,000	.12	.15	.20	.50	1.50	30.00
1928D	6,436,000	.25	.35	.65	2.00	6.00	40.00
1928S	6,936,000	.20	.30	.50	1.00	4.50	60.00
1929	36,446,000	.12	.15	.20	.40	1.50	25.00
1929D	8,370,000	.25	.40	.60	1.75	6.00	40.00
1929S	7,754,000	.12	.15	.20	.75	3.50	30.00
1930	22,849,000	.12	.15	.20	.50	1.75	27.50
1930S	5,435,000	.15	.20	.25	.50	3.50	45.00
1931S	1,200,000	1.50	1.75	2.00	2.50	5.00	45.00
1934	20,213,003	.11	.14	.18	.25	1.10	20.00
1934D	7,480,000	.11	.14	.18	.25	2.00	30.00
1935	58,264,000	.11	.14	.18	.20	.60	12.00
1935D	12,092,000	.11	.14	.18	.30	1.10	30.00
1935S	10,300,000	.11	.14	.18	.25	.90	20.00
1936	119,001,420	.11	.14	.18	.20	.50	11.00
1936 Proof-65	(4,420)						750.00
1936D	24,814,000	.11	.14	.18	.25	.60	12.00
1936S	14,930,000	.11	.14	.18	.25	.60	15.00
1937	79,485,769	.11	.14	.18	.20	.50	9.00
1937 Proof-65	(5,769)						800.00
1937D	} 17,826,000	.11	.14	.18	.25	.60	11.00
1937D 3-Legged*		45.00	60.00	70.00	100.00	135.00	425.00
1937S	5,635,000	.11	.14	.18	.25	.60	12.00
1938D	} 7,020,000	.11	.14	.18	.25	.60	9.00
1938D, D over S				2.00	3.00	4.00	15.00

*Beware of removed leg.
†Uncirculated pieces with full sharp details are worth considerably more.

1937D "3-Legged" Variety

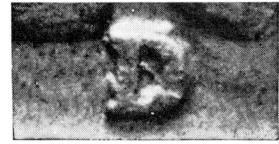

1938D, D over S

NICKEL FIVE-CENT PIECES
JEFFERSON TYPE 1938 to Date

This nickel was designed by Felix Schlag. He won an award of $1,000 in a competition with some 390 artists. It established the definite public approval of portrait and pictorial rather than symbolic devices on our coinage. On October 8, 1942, the wartime five-cent piece composed of copper (56%), silver (35%) and manganese (9%) was introduced to eliminate nickel, a critical war material. A larger mint mark was placed above the dome. Letter P (Philadelphia) was used for the first time, indicating the change of alloy. The designer's initials FS were added below the bust starting in 1966. Mint mark position was moved to the obverse starting in 1968.

VG-8 VERY GOOD—*Second porch pillar from right nearly gone, other three still visible but weak.*

F-12 FINE—*Cheekbone worn flat. Hairlines and eyebrow faint. Second pillar weak, especially at bottom.*

VF-20 VERY FINE—*Second pillar plain and complete on both sides.*

EF-40 EXTREMELY FINE—*Cheekbone, hairlines, eyebrow slightly worn but well defined. Base of triangle above pillars visible but weak.*

MS-65 CHOICE UNCIRCULATED—*No trace of wear. Barely noticeable blemishes.*

Mint mark located at right of building   Wartime Silver   Mint mark location starting 1968

Uncirculated pieces with fully struck steps are valued higher.

	Quan. Minted	VG-8	F-12	VF-20	EF-40	MS-65	Proof-65
1938	(19,365) 19,515,365	$.06	$.08	$.10	$.20	$1.00	$47.50
1938D	5,376,000	.30	.40	.50	.75	4.00	
1938S	4,105,000	.50	.75	1.00	1.25	5.00	
1939	(12,535) 120,627,535	.06	.08	.10	.20	1.00	50.00
1939D	3,514,000	1.00	1.50	2.00	4.00	38.00	
1939S	6,630,000	.20	.25	.30	1.00	25.00	
1940	(14,158) 176,499,158			.05	.08	.50	40.00
1940D	43,540,000			.05	.08	1.25	
1940S	39,690,000			.05	.10	1.25	
1941	(18,720) 203,283,720			.05	.08	.40	32.00
1941D	53,432,000			.05	.08	2.25	
1941S	43,445,000			.05	.09	3.00	
1942	(29,600) 49,818,600			.05	.08	.90	30.00
1942D	13,938,000	.06	.08	.20	.40	14.00	

Wartime Silver Five-Cent Pieces 1942-1945

	Quan. Minted	VG-8	F-12	VF-20	EF-40	MS-65	Proof-65
1942P	(27,600) 579,900,600	*.40*	*.40*	*.40*	*.50*	8.00	165.00
1942S	32,900,000	*.40*	*.40*	*.40*	*.50*	6.00	
1943P, 3 over 2	} 271,165,000		20.00	30.00	60.00	400.00	
1943P		*.40*	*.40*	*.40*	*.50*	2.25	
1943D	15,294,000	*.40*	*.40*	*.40*	*.50*	2.35	
1943S	104,060,000	*.40*	*.40*	*.40*	*.50*	2.60	
1944P	119,150,000	*.40*	*.40*	*.40*	*.50*	2.75	
1944D	32,309,000	*.40*	*.40*	*.40*	*.50*	7.00	
1944S	21,640,000	*.40*	*.40*	*.40*	*.50*	6.00	
1945P	119,408,100	*.40*	*.40*	*.40*	*.50*	5.00	
1945D	37,158,000	*.40*	*.40*	*.40*	*.50*	3.50	
1945S	58,939,000	*.40*	*.40*	*.40*	*.50*	2.00	

Italic prices indicate unsettled values due to fluctuating bullion market. See Bullion Chart.

NICKEL FIVE-CENT PIECES
Prewar composition and mint mark style resumed

	Quan. Minted	VF-20	EF-40	MS-65	Proof-65
1946	161,116,000	$.05	$.05	$.25	
1946D	45,292,200	.05	.05	.30	
1946S	13,560,000	.05	.06	.30	
1947	95,000,000	.05	.05	.20	
1947D	37,822,000	.05	.05	.30	
1947S	24,720,000	.05	.06	.30	
1948	89,348,000	.05	.05	.25	
1948D	44,734,000	.05	.06	.50	
1948S	11,300,000	.05	.06	.40	
1949	60,652,000	.05	.05	.60	
1949D	36,498,000	.05	.05	.45	
1949D, D over S		15.00	25.00	150.00	
1949S	9,716,000	.05	.10	.85	
1950 (51,386)	9,847,386	.05	.10	.75	$32.50
1950D	2,630,030	4.00	4.50	5.50	
1951 (57,500)	28,609,500	.05	.05	.50	25.00
1951D	20,460,000	.05	.05	.50	
1951S	7,776,000	.05	.10	1.20	
1952 (81,980)	64,069,980	.05	.05	.30	15.00
1952D	30,638,000	.05	.05	.90	
1952S	20,572,000	.05	.05	.50	
1953 (128,800)	46,772,800	.05	.05	.10	9.50
1953D	59,878,600	.05	.05	.10	
1953S	19,210,900	.05	.05	.20	
1954 (233,300)	47,917,350	.05	.05	.10	6.25
1954D	117,183,060	.05	.05	.10	
1954S	29,384,000	.05	.05	.12	
1954S, S over D		2.50	5.00	15.00	
1955 (378,200)	8,266,200	.06	.08	.25	4.00
1955D	74,464,100	.05	.05	.07	
1955D, D over S*		3.00	5.00	25.00	

1943, 3 over 2   1954S, S over D   1955D, D over S*

	Quan. Minted	VF-20	EF-40	MS-65	Proof-65
1956 (669,384)	35,885,384		.05	.06	1.25
1956D	67,222,940		.05	.06	
1957 (1,247,952)	39,655,952		.05	.07	1.00
1957D	136,828,900		.05	.07	
1958 (875,652)	17,963,652		.05	.08	1.25
1958D	168,249,120		.05	.06	
1959 (1,149,291)	28,397,291		.05	.06	.65
1959D	160,738,240		.05	.05	
1960 (1,691,602)	57,107,602		.05	.05	.40
1960D	192,582,180		.05	.05	
1961 (3,028,144)	76,668,244		.05	.05	.40
1961D	229,342,760		.05	.05	
1962 (3,218,019)	100,602,019		.05	.05	.40
1962D	280,195,720		.05	.07	
1963 (3,075,645)	178,851,645		.05	.05	.40

*Varieties exist.

NICKEL FIVE-CENT PIECES

	Quan. Minted	MS-65	Proof-65
1963D	276,829,460	$.05	
1964	1,028,622,762	.05	
1964 Proof	(3,950,762)		$.40
1964D	1,787,297,160	.05	
1965	136,131,380	.05	
1966	156,208,283	.05	
1967	107,325,800	.05	
1968D	91,227,880	.05	
1968S	103,437,510	.05	
1968S Proof	(3,041,506)		.25
1969D	202,807,500	.05	
1969S	123,009,631	.05	
1969S Proof	(2,934,631)		.25
1970D	515,485,380	.05	
1970S	241,464,814	.05	
1970S Proof	(2,632,810)		.35
1971	106,884,000	.30	
1971D	316,144,800	.05	
1971S Proof	(3,220,733)		.75
1972	202,036,000	.05	
1972D	351,694,600	.05	
1972S Proof	(3,260,996)		.75
1973	384,396,000	.05	
1973D	261,405,000	.05	
1973S Proof	(2,760,339)		1.00
1974	601,752,000	.05	
1974D	277,373,000	.07	
1974S Proof	(2,612,568)		1.25
1975	181,772,000	.06	
1975D	401,875,300	$.07	
1975S Proof	(2,845,450)		$.75
1976	367,124,000	.05	
1976D	563,964,147	.05	
1976S Proof	(4,149,730)		.35
1977	585,376,000	.05	
1977D	297,313,422	.07	
1977S Proof	(3,251,152)		.35
1978	391,308,000	.05	
1978D	313,092,780	.05	
1978S Proof	(3,127,781)		.50
1979	463,188,000	.05	
1979D	325,867,672	.05	
1979S Proof	(3,677,175)		
Filled S			.65
Clear S			1.90
1980P	593,004,000	.05	
1980D	502,323,448	.05	
1980S Proof	(3,554,806)		.35
1981P	657,504,000	.05	
1981D	364,801,843	.05	
1981S Proof	(4,063,083)		.35
1982P	292,355,000	.05	
1982D	373,726,544	.05	
1982S Proof	(3,857,479)		1.00
1983P		.05	
1983D		.05	
1983S Proof			.35

HALF DIMES 1794-1873

The half dime types present the same general characteristics as larger United States silver coins. Authorized by the Act of April 2, 1792, they were not coined until February, 1795, although dated 1794. At first the weight was 20.8 grains, and fineness 892.4. By the Act of January 18, 1837, the weight was slightly reduced to 20 5/8 grains and the fineness changed to .900. Finally the weight was reduced to 19.2 grains by the Act of February 21, 1853.

FLOWING HAIR TYPE 1794-1795

AG-3 ABOUT GOOD—*Details clear enough to identify.*
G-5 GOOD—*Eagle, wreath, bust outlined but lack details.*
VG-8 VERY GOOD—*Some details remain on face. All lettering readable.*
F-12 FINE—*Hair ends show. Hair at top smooth.*
VF-20 VERY FINE—*Hairlines at top show. Hair about ear defined.*
EF-40 EXTREMELY FINE—*Hair above forehead and at neck well defined but shows some wear.*
MS-60 UNCIRCULATED—*No trace of wear. Light blemishes.*

Weakly struck uncirculated coins are worth less than values shown.

	Quan. Minted	AG-3	G-4	VG-8	F-12	VF-20	EF-40	MS-60
1794	} 86,416	$200.00	$475.00	$600.00	$950.00	$1,500	$2,100	$6,300
1795		200.00	475.00	600.00	900.00	1,400	2,000	5,300

HALF DIMES

DRAPED BUST TYPE, SMALL EAGLE REVERSE 1796-1797

AG-3 ABOUT GOOD—*Details clear enough to identify.*
G-4 GOOD—*Date, stars, LIBERTY readable. Bust outlined but no details.*
VG-8 VERY GOOD—*Some details show.*
F-12 FINE—*Hair and drapery lines worn, but visible.*
VF-20 VERY FINE—*Only left of drapery indistinct.*
EF-40 EXTREMELY FINE—*All hairlines show details.*
MS-60 UNCIRCULATED—*No trace of wear. Light blemishes.*

	Quan. Minted	AG-3	G-4	VG-8	F-12	VF-20	EF-40	MS-60
1796, 6 over 5	} 10,230	$225.00	$475.00	$675.00	$950.00	$1,400	$2,350	$6,500
1796 Nor. dt.		200.00	450.00	650.00	900.00	1,300	2,200	5,500
1796 LIKERTY		200.00	450.00	650.00	900.00	1,300	2,200	6,500
1797, 15 Stars	} 44,527	175.00	425.00	550.00	800.00	1,200	1,950	5,000
1797, 16 stars		175.00	425.00	550.00	800.00	1,200	1,950	5,000
1797, 13 stars		175.00	425.00	550.00	800.00	1,200	1,950	6,250

DRAPED BUST TYPE, HERALDIC EAGLE REVERSE 1800-1805

1800 LIBEKTY

	AG-3	G-4	VG-8	F-12	VF-20	EF-40	MS-60
1800 24,000	110.00	350.00	450.00	600.00	875.00	1,500	4,500
1800 LIBERTY ... 16,000	110.00	350.00	450.00	600.00	875.00	1,500	5,000
1801 27,760	110.00	350.00	450.00	600.00	875.00	1,650	5,600
1802 3,060	1,250	2,500	3,250	6,000	9,000	17,000	———
1803 37,850	110.00	350.00	450.00	600.00	875.00	1,500	4,500
1805 15,600	130.00	375.00	475.00	650.00	1,000	2,000	———

CAPPED BUST TYPE 1829-1837

G-4 GOOD—*Bust outlined, no detail. Date and legend readable.*
VG-8 VERY GOOD—*Complete legend and date plain. At least 3 letters of LIBERTY show clearly.*
F-12 FINE—*All letters in LIBERTY show.*
VF-20 VERY FINE—*Full rims. Ear and shoulder clasp show plainly.*
EF-40 EXTREMELY FINE—*Ear very distinct, eyebrow and hair well defined.*
MS-60 UNCIRCULATED—*No trace of wear. Light blemishes.*

	Quan. Minted	G-4	VG-8	F-12	VF-20	EF-40	MS-60
1829	1,230,000	$9.00	$12.00	$14.00	$25.00	$65.00	$350.00
1830	1,240,000	9.00	12.00	14.00	25.00	65.00	325.00
1831	1,242,700	9.00	12.00	14.00	25.00	65.00	325.00
1832	965,000	9.00	12.00	14.00	25.00	65.00	325.00
1833	1,370,000	9.00	12.00	14.00	25.00	65.00	325.00
1834	1,480,000	9.00	12.00	14.00	25.00	65.00	325.00
1835	2,760,000	9.00	12.00	14.00	25.00	65.00	325.00
1836	1,900,000	9.00	12.00	14.00	25.00	65.00	325.00
1837 Small 5c.	} 871,000	10.00	17.00	25.00	40.00	85.00	575.00
1837 Large 5c		9.00	12.00	14.00	25.00	65.00	325.00

HALF DIMES
LIBERTY SEATED TYPE 1837-1873
No Stars on Obverse 1837-1838

G-4 GOOD—*LIBERTY On shield smooth. Date and letters readable.*
VG-8 VERY GOOD—*At least 3 letters in LIBERTY are visible.*
F-12 FINE—*Entire LIBERTY visible, weak spots.*
VF-20 VERY FINE—*Entire LIBERTY strong and even.*
EF-40 EXTREMELY FINE—*LIBERTY and scroll edges distinct.*
MS-60 UNCIRCULATED—*No trace of wear. Light blemishes.*

	Quan. Minted	G-4	VG-8	F-12	VF-20	EF-40	MS-60
1837	1,405,000	$15.00	$20.00	$27.50	$47.50	$125.00	$375.00
1838O No stars	70,000	27.50	40.00	55.00	110.00	275.00	2,500

Stars on Obverse 1838-1853

From 1838 through 1859 mint mark is located above bow on reverse. Large, medium or small mint mark varieties occur for several dates.

	Quan. Minted	G-4	VG-8	F-12	VF-20	EF-40	MS-60
1838	2,255,000	3.00	4.00	6.00	13.00	23.00	300.00
1839	1,069,150	3.00	4.00	6.00	13.00	23.00	280.00
1839O	1,034,039	4.00	6.00	9.00	15.00	27.50	350.00
1840	1,344,085	3.00	4.00	6.00	12.00	22.00	300.00
1840O	935,000	3.50	5.00	9.00	17.00	30.00	280.00
1841	1,150,000	3.00	4.00	6.00	11.00	22.00	200.00
1841O	815,000	5.00	8.00	12.00	20.00	30.00	350.00
1842	815,000	3.00	4.00	6.00	11.00	22.00	200.00
1842O	350,000	6.00	10.00	17.00	40.00	90.00	———
1843	1,165,000	3.00	4.00	6.00	11.00	22.00	200.00
1844	430,000	3.00	4.00	6.00	11.00	22.00	200.00
1844O	220,000	15.00	21.00	45.00	125.00	315.00	———
1845	1,564,000	3.00	4.00	6.00	11.00	22.00	200.00
1846	27,000	55.00	70.00	110.00	200.00	425.00	———
1847	1,274,000	3.00	4.00	6.00	11.00	22.00	200.00
1848	668,000	3.00	4.00	6.00	11.00	22.00	200.00
1848O	600,000	5.00	10.00	13.00	25.00	35.00	325.00
1849, 9 over 6	}	3.50	6.00	9.00	12.00	25.00	280.00
1849, 9 over 8	1,309,000	4.00	7.00	10.00	15.00	35.00	300.00
1849 Nor. date		3.00	4.00	6.00	11.00	22.00	200.00
1849O	140,000	12.00	20.00	35.00	90.00	200.00	———
1850	955,000	3.00	4.00	6.00	11.00	22.00	200.00
1850O	690,000	5.00	10.00	13.00	20.00	35.00	375.00
1851	781,000	3.00	4.00	6.00	11.00	22.00	200.00
1851O	860,000	5.00	8.00	12.00	20.00	35.00	325.00
1852	1,000,500	3.00	4.00	6.00	11.00	22.00	200.00
1852O	260,000	11.00	16.00	25.00	60.00	110.00	———
1853 No arrows	135,000	6.00	12.00	18.00	25.00	50.00	325.00
1853O No arrows	160,000	50.00	75.00	100.00	170.00	350.00	———

Arrows at Date 1853-1855

As on the dimes, quarters and halves, arrows were placed at the sides of the date for a short period starting in 1853 to denote reduction of weight.

HALF DIMES

	Quan. Minted	G-4	VG-8	F-12	VF-20	EF-40	MS-60	Proof-60
1853	13,210,020	$3.00	$4.00	$5.00	$10.00	$20.00	$210.00	
1853O	2,200,000	4.00	5.00	7.00	12.00	30.00	225.00	
1854	5,740,000	3.00	4.00	5.00	9.00	18.00	210.00	
1854O	1,560,000	3.00	4.00	6.00	11.00	22.00	350.00	
1855	1,750,000	3.00	4.00	5.00	10.00	20.00	210.00	$1,800
1855O	600,000	4.00	7.00	10.00	17.00	40.00	400.00	

No Arrows at Date 1856-1859

1856	4,880,000	3.00	4.00	5.00	10.00	17.00	200.00	800.00
1856O	1,100,000	3.00	4.00	6.00	11.00	20.00	250.00	
1857	7,280,000	3.00	4.00	5.00	10.00	17.00	200.00	750.00
1857O	1,380,000	3.00	4.00	6.00	11.00	20.00	250.00	

1858 over Inverted Date

1858	} 3,500,000	3.00	4.00	5.00	10.00	17.00	200.00	650.00
1858 over inv. date		9.00	15.00	30.00	60.00	115.00	300.00	
1858O	1,660,000	3.00	4.00	6.00	11.00	20.00	250.00	
1859O	560,000	5.00	8.00	12.00	20.00	30.00	275.00	
1859	340,000	5.00	8.00	12.00	20.00	30.00	225.00	600.00

Legend on Obverse 1860-1873

	Quan. Minted	G-4	VG-8	F-12	VF-20	EF-40	MS-60	Proof-60
1860 .... (1,000)	799,000	3.00	4.00	5.00	8.00	15.00	185.00	275.00
1860O	1,060,000	3.00	4.00	5.00	9.00	18.00	200.00	
1861 .... (1,000)	3,361,000	3.00	4.00	5.00	7.00	14.00	175.00	235.00
1862 ..... (550)	1,492,550	3.00	4.00	5.00	7.00	14.00	175.00	235.00
1863 ..... (460)	18,460	30.00	40.00	50.00	75.00	125.00	325.00	300.00
1863S	100,000	7.00	9.00	12.00	21.00	45.00	425.00	
1864 ..... (470)	48,470	75.00	100.00	125.00	175.00	250.00	900.00	500.00
1864S	90,000	10.00	15.00	25.00	40.00	100.00	450.00	
1865 ..... (500)	13,500	30.00	40.00	60.00	90.00	125.00	300.00	275.00
1865S	120,000	6.00	9.00	13.00	22.00	40.00	350.00	
1866 ..... (725)	10,725	50.00	75.00	100.00	125.00	200.00	375.00	275.00
1866S	120,000	6.00	9.00	12.00	21.00	40.00	350.00	
1867 ..... (625)	8,625	60.00	75.00	100.00	125.00	200.00	450.00	275.00
1867S	120,000	6.00	9.00	12.00	21.00	30.00	350.00	
1868 ..... (600)	89,200	9.00	15.00	25.00	50.00	100.00	300.00	235.00
1868S	280,000	4.00	6.00	7.00	10.00	19.00	210.00	
1869 ..... (600)	208,600	4.00	5.00	6.00	9.00	15.00	175.00	235.00
1869S	230,000	4.00	6.00	7.00	10.00	19.00	225.00	
1870 .... (1,000)	536,000	3.00	4.00	5.00	8.00	15.00	175.00	235.00
1870S	Unique						—	
1871 ..... (960)	1,873,960	3.00	4.00	5.00	8.00	15.00	175.00	235.00
1871S	161,000	7.00	9.00	15.00	35.00	45.00	275.00	
1872 ..... (950)	2,947,950	3.00	4.00	5.00	8.00	15.00	175.00	235.00
1872S	837,000	3.00	4.00	5.00	8.00	15.00	175.00	
1873 ..... (600)	712,600	3.00	4.00	5.00	8.00	15.00	175.00	235.00
1873S	324,000	3.00	4.00	5.00	8.00	15.00	175.00	

DIMES — 1796 to Date

The designs of the dimes, first coined in 1796, follow closely those of the half dimes up through the Liberty seated type. The dimes in each instance weigh twice as much as the half dimes.

DRAPED BUST TYPE, SMALL EAGLE REVERSE 1796-1797

AG-3 ABOUT GOOD—*Details clear enough to identify.*
G-4 GOOD—*Date readable. Bust outlined, but no detail.*
VG-8 VERY GOOD—*All but deepest drapery folds worn smooth. Hairlines nearly gone and curls lack detail.*
F-12 FINE—*All drapery lines visible. Hair partly worn.*
VF-20 VERY FINE—*Only left side of drapery is indistinct.*
EF-40 EXTREMELY FINE—*Hair well outlined and shows details.*
MS-60 UNCIRCULATED—*No trace of wear. Light blemishes.*

1797, 16 Stars   1797, 13 Stars

	Quan. Minted	AG-3	G-4	VG-8	F-12	VF-20	EF-40	MS-60
1796	22,135	$300.00	$550.00	$800.00	$1,100	$1,750	$2,750	$6,000
1797 16 stars	} 25,261	250.00	500.00	700.00	1,000	1,600	2,500	5,500
1797 13 stars		250.00	500.00	700.00	1,000	1,600	2,500	7,000

DRAPED BUST TYPE, HERALDIC EAGLE REVERSE 1798-1807

1798 All kinds 27,550							
1798 over 97, 16 stars on rev.	100.00	250.00	400.00	750.00	950.00	1,250	3,800
1798 over 97, 13 stars			600.00	1,000	1,800	—	
1798	100.00	250.00	400.00	750.00	950.00	1,250	3,800
1800 21,760	100.00	250.00	400.00	700.00	900.00	1,200	3,500
1801 34,640	100.00	250.00	400.00	700.00	900.00	1,200	3,500
1802 10,975	100.00	250.00	400.00	700.00	900.00	1,200	3,500
1803 33,040	100.00	250.00	400.00	700.00	900.00	1,200	3,500
1804 8,265	225.00	450.00	850.00	1,200	1,850	3,250	4,500
1805 120,780	100.00	250.00	400.00	700.00	900.00	1,200	3,000
1807 165,000	100.00	250.00	400.00	700.00	900.00	1,200	3,000

CAPPED BUST TYPE 1809-1837

G-4 GOOD—*Date, letters and stars discernible. Bust outlined, no details.*
VG-8 VERY GOOD—*Legends and date plain. Minimum of 3 letters in LIBERTY.*
F-12 FINE—*Full LIBERTY. Ear and shoulder clasp visible. Part of rim shows both sides.*
VF-20 VERY FINE—*LIBERTY distinct. Full rim. Ear and clasp plain and distinct.*
EF-40 EXTREMELY FINE—*LIBERTY sharp. Ear distinct. Hair above eye well defined.*
MS-60 UNCIRCULATED—*No trace of wear. Light blemishes.*

DIMES

Large Size 1809-1828

	Quan. Minted	G-4	VG-8	F-12	VF-20	EF-40	MS-60
1809	51,065	$35.00	$55.00	$80.00	$135.00	$250.00	$2,200
1811 over 9	65,180	25.00	37.00	50.00	90.00	185.00	1,900
1814	421,500	12.00	14.00	20.00	60.00	150.00	1,000
1820	942,587	9.00	12.00	18.00	50.00	150.00	800.00
1821	1,186,512	9.00	12.00	18.00	50.00	150.00	800.00
1822	100,000	32.00	45.00	100.00	200.00	400.00	2,100
1823, 3 over 2, all kinds	440,000						
1823, 3 over 2, sm. E's		9.00	12.00	18.00	50.00	150.00	1,000
1823, 3 over 2, lg. E's		9.00	12.00	18.00	50.00	150.00	1,000

1823, 3 over 2   1824, 4 over 2   1828 Large Date   1828 Small Date

	Quan. Minted	G-4	VG-8	F-12	VF-20	EF-40	MS-60
1824, 4 over 2	} 510,000	13.00	16.00	22.50	60.00	175.00	1,100
1825		9.00	12.00	18.00	50.00	150.00	800.00
1827	1,215,000	9.00	12.00	18.00	50.00	150.00	800.00
1828 Both vars	125,000						
1828 Lg. date, curl base 2		15.00	20.00	40.00	70.00	185.00	1,000

Reduced Size 1828-1837

1829 Small 10c   Large 10c   1830, 30 over 29

	Quan. Minted	G-4	F-12	VF-20	EF-40	MS-60
1828 Small date, sq. base 2		$14.00	$23.00	$45.00	$125.00	$700.00
1829 Small 10c		7.00	13.00	22.00	100.00	550.00
1829 Medium 10c	} 770,000	7.00	13.00	20.00	100.00	500.00
1829 Large 10c		10.00	18.00	30.00	110.00	550.00
1830, 30 over 29		25.00	50.00	100.00	200.00	650.00
1830 Large 10c	} 510,000	7.00	13.00	20.00	100.00	500.00
1830 Small 10c		7.00	13.00	20.00	100.00	500.00

DIMES

	Quan. Minted	G-4	F-12	VF-20	EF-40	MS-60
1831	771,350	$7.00	$13.00	$20.00	$100.00	$500.00
1832	522,500	7.00	13.00	20.00	100.00	500.00
1833	485,000	7.00	13.00	20.00	100.00	500.00
1834	635,000	7.00	13.00	20.00	100.00	600.00
1835	1,410,000	7.00	13.00	20.00	100.00	500.00
1836	1,190,000	7.00	13.00	20.00	100.00	500.00
1837	359,500	7.00	13.00	20.00	100.00	500.00

LIBERTY SEATED TYPE 1837-1891

No Stars on Obverse 1837-1838

G-4 GOOD—*LIBERTY on shield smooth. Date and letters readable.*
F-12 FINE—*Entire LIBERTY visible, weak spots.*
VF-20 VERY FINE—*Entire LIBERTY strong and even.*
EF-40 EXTREMELY FINE—*LIBERTY and scroll edges distinct.*
MS-60 UNCIRCULATED—*No trace of wear. Light blemishes.*

No Drapery from Elbow
No Stars on Obverse

Mint marks on Liberty seated dimes are placed on the reverse, within or below the wreath.

1837	682,500	14.00	27.00	65.00	125.00	550.00
1838O	406,034	20.00	45.00	100.00	200.00	1,500

Stars on Obverse 1838-1853

No Drapery from Elbow
Tilted Shield

1838 Small Stars   1838 Large Stars

1838 Small stars	⎫	7.00	16.00	27.00	50.00	700.00
1838 Large stars	⎬ 1,992,500	4.00	6.00	10.00	25.00	200.00
1838 Partial drapery	⎭	7.00	15.00	25.00	50.00	600.00
1839	1,053,115	3.00	5.00	9.00	25.00	200.00
1839O	1,323,000	3.50	7.00	14.00	27.00	225.00
1840	981,500	3.00	5.00	9.00	20.00	200.00
1840O	1,175,000	3.50	7.00	15.00	27.00	600.00

DIMES

 Drapery from Elbow
Upright Shield

	Quan. Minted	G-4	F-12	VF-20	EF-40	MS-60	Proof-60
1840	377,500	$10.00	$25.00	$50.00	$200.00	—	
1841	1,622,500	2.50	4.00	9.00	18.00	$200.00	
1841O	2,007,500	3.50	7.00	12.00	25.00	600.00	
1842	1,887,500	2.50	4.00	9.00	18.00	200.00	
1842O	2,020,000	2.50	4.00	10.00	30.00	—	
1843	1,370,000	2.50	4.00	9.00	18.00	200.00	
1843O	150,000	13.00	45.00	120.00	310.00	—	
1844	72,500	13.00	45.00	90.00	185.00	1,200	
1845	1,755,000	2.50	4.00	9.00	18.00	200.00	
1845O	230,000	7.00	20.00	60.00	350.00	—	
1846	31,300	25.00	50.00	135.00	375.00	—	
1847	245,000	5.00	14.00	25.00	75.00	500.00	
1848	451,500	3.00	5.00	10.00	21.00	225.00	
1849	839,000	2.50	4.00	9.00	18.00	210.00	
1849O	300,000	5.00	10.00	40.00	140.00	—	
1850	1,931,500	2.50	4.00	9.00	18.00	200.00	
1850O	510,000	4.00	7.00	30.00	65.00	550.00	
1851	1,026,500	2.50	4.00	9.00	18.00	200.00	
1851O	400,000	5.00	10.00	25.00	75.00	750.00	
1852	1,535,500	2.50	4.00	9.00	18.00	210.00	
1852O	430,000	5.00	12.00	35.00	90.00	850.00	
1853 No arrows	95,000	13.00	22.00	50.00	135.00	675.00	

Arrows at Date 1853-1855

Arrows at Date   Small Date, Arrows Removed

1853 With arrows	12,078,010	3.00	4.50	9.00	25.00	210.00	
1853O	1,100,000	3.50	5.00	12.00	45.00	350.00	
1854	4,470,000	3.00	4.50	9.00	25.00	210.00	
1854O	1,770,000	3.50	5.00	11.00	40.00	350.00	
1855	2,075,000	3.00	4.50	9.00	25.00	210.00	$1,250

No Arrows at Date 1856-1860

1856 Lg. date	} 5,780,000	2.35	3.75	7.00	16.00	210.00	800.00
1856 Sm. date		2.35	3.75	7.00	16.00	200.00	
1856O	1,180,000	2.35	3.75	9.00	20.00	210.00	
1856S	70,000	18.00	40.00	80.00	200.00	—	
1857	5,580,000	2.25	3.50	7.00	15.00	200.00	750.00
1857O	1,540,000	2.25	3.50	7.00	15.00	210.00	

DIMES

	Quan. Minted	G-4	F-12	VF-20	EF-40	MS-60	Proof-60
1858	1,540,000	$2.25	$3.50	$7.00	$15.00	$200.00	$700.00
1858O	290,000	5.00	12.00	30.00	75.00	450.00	
1858S	60,000	15.00	40.00	90.00	200.00	—	
1859 (800)	430,000	2.50	4.00	10.00	25.00	200.00	675.00
1859O	480,000	2.50	5.00	17.00	35.00	210.00	
1859S	60,000	18.00	40.00	100.00	225.00	1,200	
1860S	140,000	5.00	15.00	40.00	100.00	—	

Legend on Obverse 1860-1873

	Quan. Minted	G-4	F-12	VF-20	EF-40	MS-60	Proof-60
1860 (1,000)	607,000	2.00	3.50	6.50	13.00	145.00	200.00
1860O	40,000	150.00	350.00	550.00	1,100	—	
1861 (1,000)	1,884,000	2.00	3.50	6.50	13.00	145.00	200.00
1861S	172,500	7.00	18.00	40.00	90.00	425.00	
1862 (550)	847,550	2.00	3.50	6.50	13.00	145.00	200.00
1862S	180,750	7.00	15.00	35.00	80.00	475.00	
1863 (460)	14,460	30.00	60.00	100.00	150.00	500.00	225.00
1863S	157,500	9.00	20.00	40.00	90.00	525.00	
1864 (470)	11,470	30.00	55.00	80.00	140.00	350.00	225.00
1864S	230,000	6.00	15.00	30.00	75.00	525.00	
1865 (500)	10,500	35.00	75.00	125.00	185.00	475.00	225.00
1865S	175,000	6.00	15.00	30.00	75.00	525.00	
1866 (725)	8,725	50.00	100.00	150.00	200.00	525.00	225.00
1866S	135,000	7.00	15.00	30.00	70.00	525.00	
1867 (625)	6,625	80.00	150.00	200.00	250.00	650.00	225.00
1867S	140,000	6.00	14.00	30.00	65.00	650.00	
1868 (600)	464,600	2.50	5.00	14.00	35.00	225.00	200.00
1868S	260,000	5.00	10.00	30.00	70.00	185.00	
1869 (600)	256,000	2.50	5.00	14.00	35.00	185.00	200.00
1869S	450,000	4.00	7.00	15.00	40.00	200.00	
1870 (1,000)	471,500	2.00	3.50	8.00	17.00	145.00	200.00
1870S	50,000	20.00	50.00	100.00	200.00	1,700	
1871 (960)	907,710	2.00	3.50	6.50	13.00	145.00	200.00
1871CC	20,100	160.00	425.00	600.00	1,200	—	
1871S	320,000	5.00	14.00	25.00	60.00	300.00	
1872 (950)	2,396,450	2.00	3.50	6.50	13.00	145.00	200.00
1872CC	35,480	75.00	200.00	325.00	650.00	2,000	
1872S	190,000	8.00	20.00	35.00	80.00	375.00	
1873 Closed 3 (1,100)	1,508,000	2.00	3.50	6.50	13.00	175.00	200.00
1873 Open 3	60,000	7.00	15.00	30.00	70.00	250.00	
1873CC (Unique)	12,400					—	

Arrows at Date 1873-1874

In 1873 the dime was increased in weight to 2.50 grams. Arrows at date in 1873 and 1874 indicate this change.

DIMES

	Quan. Minted	G-4	F-12	VF-20	EF-40	MS-60	Proof-60
1873	(800) 2,378,500	$4.00	$9.00	$20.00	$50.00	$500.00	$450.00
1873CC	18,791	200.00	425.00	650.00	1,200	—	
1873S	455,000	8.00	16.00	30.00	55.00	550.00	
1874	(700) 2,940,000	4.00	9.00	20.00	50.00	500.00	450.00
1874CC	10,817	325.00	750.00	1,200	1,800	—	
1874S	240,000	9.00	20.00	45.00	75.00	575.00	

No Arrows at Date 1875-1891

	Quan. Minted	G-4	F-12	VF-20	EF-40	MS-60	Proof-60
1875	(700) 10,350,700	2.00	3.00	6.00	11.00	140.00	200.00
1875CC	4,645,000	2.00	3.00	6.00	11.00	160.00	
1875S	9,070,000	2.00	3.00	6.00	11.00	140.00	
1876	(1,150) 11,461,150	2.00	3.00	6.00	11.00	140.00	200.00
1876CC	8,270,000	2.00	3.00	6.00	11.00	150.00	
1876S	10,420,000	2.00	3.00	6.00	11.00	140.00	
1877	(510) 7,310,510	2.00	3.00	6.00	11.00	140.00	210.00
1877CC	7,700,000	2.00	3.00	6.00	11.00	150.00	
1877S	2,340,000	2.00	3.00	6.00	11.00	150.00	
1878	(800) 1,678,000	2.00	3.00	6.00	11.00	140.00	200.00
1878CC	200,000	10.00	35.00	50.00	90.00	375.00	
1879	(1,100) 15,100	22.00	60.00	100.00	150.00	300.00	210.00
1880	(1,355) 37,355	20.00	50.00	75.00	110.00	275.00	210.00
1881	(975) 24,975	21.00	55.00	80.00	135.00	275.00	210.00
1882	(1,100) 3,911,100	2.00	3.00	6.00	11.00	140.00	200.00
1883	(1,039) 7,675,712	2.00	3.00	6.00	11.00	140.00	200.00
1884	(875) 3,366,380	2.00	3.00	6.00	11.00	140.00	200.00
1884S	564,969	5.00	10.00	20.00	30.00	250.00	
1885	(930) 2,533,427	2.00	3.00	6.00	11.00	140.00	200.00
1885S	43,690	45.00	85.00	135.00	225.00	1,000	
1886	(886) 6,377,570	2.00	3.00	6.00	11.00	140.00	175.00
1886S	206,524	5.00	10.00	18.00	25.00	250.00	
1887	(710) 11,283,939	2.00	3.00	6.00	11.00	140.00	175.00
1887S	4,454,450	2.00	3.00	6.00	11.00	140.00	
1888	(832) 5,496,487	2.00	3.00	6.00	11.00	140.00	175.00
1888S	1,720,000	2.00	3.00	6.00	11.00	150.00	
1889	(711) 7,380,711	2.00	3.00	6.00	11.00	140.00	175.00
1889S	972,678	5.00	10.00	22.00	45.00	250.00	
1890	(590) 9,911,541	2.00	3.00	6.00	11.00	140.00	200.00
1890S	1,423,076	2.00	4.00	7.00	12.00	150.00	
1891	(600) 15,310,600	2.00	3.00	6.00	11.00	140.00	200.00
1891O	4,540,000	2.00	3.00	6.00	18.00	160.00	
1891S	3,196,116	2.00	3.00	6.00	13.00	140.00	

BARBER or LIBERTY HEAD TYPE 1892-1916

This type was designed by Charles E. Barber, Chief Engraver of the Mint. His initial B is at the truncation of the neck. He also designed quarters and half dollars of the same period.

G-4 GOOD—*Date and letters plain. LIBERTY is obliterated.*
VG-8 VERY GOOD—*At least 3 letters visible in LIBERTY.*
F-12 FINE—*All letters in LIBERTY visible, though some are weak.*
VF-20 VERY FINE—*All letters of LBERTY evenly plain.*
EF-40 EXTREMELY FINE—*All letters in LIBERTY are sharp, distinct. Headband edges are distinct.*
MS-60 UNCIRCULATED—*No trace of wear. Light blemishes.*

Mint mark location is on the reverse below the wreath.

DIMES

	Quan. Minted	G-4	VG-8	F-12	VF-20	EF-40	MS-60	Proof-63
1892 ...... (1,245)	12,121,245	$1.00	$1.50	$3.00	$4.00	$9.00	$90.00	$400.00
1892O...............	3,841,700	2.25	3.00	4.00	6.00	14.00	100.00	
1892S...............	990,710	12.00	14.00	20.00	25.00	40.00	150.00	
1893, 3 over 2 ..					—	75.00	225.00	500.00
1893 .... (792)	3,340,792	2.00	2.75	3.75	5.00	13.00	90.00	400.00
1893O...............	1,760,000	7.00	8.00	62.00	20.00	25.00	135.00	
1893S...............	2,491,401	3.00	4.00	6.00	11.00	18.00	115.00	
1894 .... (972)	1,330,972	3.00	4.00	6.00	12.00	20.00	125.00	400.00
1894O...............	720,000	18.00	22.00	32.00	50.00	125.00	650.00	
1894S...............	24						—	
1895 .... (880)	690,880	30.00	35.00	45.00	65.00	100.00	350.00	400.00
1895O...............	440,000	90.00	100.00	120.00	170.00	250.00	625.00	
1895S...............	1,120,000	6.00	9.00	14.00	20.00	30.00	140.00	
1896 .... (762)	2,000,762	2.00	3.00	5.00	9.00	18.00	90.00	400.00
1896O...............	610,000	20.00	25.00	30.00	40.00	70.00	350.00	
1896S...............	575,056	20.00	24.00	27.50	37.50	65.00	235.00	
1897 .... (731)	10,869,264	.80	.90	1.35	3.50	9.00	75.00	400.00
1897O...............	666,000	20.00	22.00	32.00	42.00	100.00	385.00	
1897S...............	1,342,844	3.00	4.00	8.00	15.00	30.00	130.00	
1898 .... (735)	16,320,735	.80	.90	1.35	3.50	9.00	75.00	400.00
1898O...............	2,130,000	1.00	2.00	4.00	10.00	25.00	175.00	
1898S...............	1,702,507	1.00	2.00	4.00	8.00	17.00	100.00	
1899 .... (846)	19,580,846	.80	.90	1.35	3.50	9.00	75.00	400.00
1899O...............	2,650,000	1.00	2.00	4.00	10.00	23.00	175.00	
1899S...............	1,867,493	1.00	2.00	4.00	7.00	12.00	100.00	
1900 .... (912)	17,600,912	.80	.90	1.35	3.50	9.00	75.00	400.00
1900O...............	2,010,000	2.00	3.00	5.00	12.00	22.00	200.00	
1900S...............	5,168,270	1.00	1.50	2.50	4.00	12.00	100.00	
1901 .... (813)	18,860,478	.80	.90	1.35	3.50	9.00	75.00	400.00
1901O...............	5,620,000	1.00	1.50	2.50	6.00	20.00	175.00	
1901S...............	593,022	20.00	24.00	40.00	60.00	120.00	475.00	
1902 .... (777)	21,380,777	.80	.90	1.35	3.50	9.00	75.00	400.00
1902O...............	4,500,000	1.00	1.50	2.50	4.00	14.00	135.00	
1902S...............	2,070,000	1.50	2.50	5.00	11.00	25.00	150.00	
1903 .... (755)	19,500,755	.80	.90	1.35	3.50	9.00	75.00	400.00
1903O...............	8,180,000	1.00	1.50	2.00	4.00	13.00	135.00	
1903S...............	613,300	15.00	18.00	26.00	40.00	70.00	375.00	
1904 .... (670)	14,601,027	.80	.90	1.35	3.50	9.00	75.00	400.00
1904S...............	800,000	10.00	14.00	20.00	36.00	65.00	325.00	
1905 .... (727)	14,552,350	.80	.90	1.35	3.50	9.00	75.00	400.00
1905O...............	3,400,000	.90	1.50	3.00	6.00	12.00	110.00	
1905S...............	6,855,199	.90	1.50	2.50	4.50	12.00	110.00	
1906 .... (675)	19,958,406	.80	.90	1.35	3.50	9.00	75.00	400.00
1906D...............	4,060,000	.90	1.50	2.50	4.50	11.00	100.00	
1906O...............	2,610,000	1.00	2.00	4.00	7.00	15.00	110.00	
1906S...............	3,136,640	.90	1.50	2.50	5.00	13.00	110.00	
1907 .... (575)	22,220,575	.80	.90	1.35	3.50	9.00	75.00	400.00
1907D...............	4,080,000	.80	1.25	2.25	4.25	12.00	110.00	
1907O...............	5,058,000	.80	1.25	2.25	4.25	12.00	85.00	
1907S...............	3,178,470	1.00	1.50	2.50	5.00	14.00	125.00	
1908 .... (545)	10,600,545	.80	.90	1.35	3.50	9.00	75.00	400.00
1908D...............	7,490,000	.80	1.25	2.25	2.75	10.00	85.00	
1908O...............	1,789,000	1.00	1.75	4.00	9.00	18.00	135.00	
1908S...............	3,220,000	.80	1.25	2.25	4.00	12.00	110.00	

Italic prices indicate unsettled values due to fluctuating bullion market. See Bullion Chart.

DIMES

	Quan. Minted	G-4	VG-8	F-12	VF-20	EF-40	MS-60	Proof-63
1909 .... (650)	10,240,650	$.80	$.90	$1.35	$2.75	$9.00	$75.00	$400.00
1909D	954,000	1.25	2.75	7.00	14.00	25.00	125.00	
1909O	2,287,000	1.00	1.50	3.00	7.00	15.00	100.00	
1909S	1,000,000	1.25	2.75	6.00	10.00	20.00	135.00	
1910 .... (551)	11,520,551	.80	.90	1.35	2.75	9.00	75.00	400.00
1910D	3,490,000	.80	1.25	2.25	4.00	14.00	135.00	
1910S	1,240,000	.80	1.25	3.25	7.00	14.00	100.00	
1911 .... (543)	18,870,543	.80	.90	1.35	2.75	9.00	75.00	400.00
1911D	11,209,000	.80	.90	1.35	2.75	9.00	90.00	
1911S	3,520,000	.80	1.25	2.25	4.00	10.00	100.00	
1912 .... (700)	19,350,000	.80	.90	1.35	2.75	9.00	75.00	400.00
1912D	11,760,000	.80	.90	1.35	2.75	9.00	90.00	
1912S	3,420,000	.80	1.25	2.25	4.00	10.00	100.00	
1913 .... (622)	19,760,622	.80	.90	1.35	2.75	9.00	75.00	400.00
1913S	510,000	3.00	5.00	12.00	25.00	50.00	190.00	
1914 .... (425)	17,360,655	.80	.90	1.35	2.75	9.00	75.00	400.00
1914D	11,908,000	.80	.90	1.35	2.75	9.00	75.00	
1914S	2,100,000	.80	1.25	2.25	4.00	10.00	100.00	
1915 .... (450)	5,620,450	.80	.90	1.35	2.75	9.00	75.00	400.00
1915S	960,000	.90	1.50	2.75	4.25	14.00	110.00	
1916	18,490,000	.80	.90	1.35	2.75	9.00	75.00	
1916S	5,820,000	.80	.90	1.35	2.75	9.00	75.00	

WINGED LIBERTY HEAD or "MERCURY" TYPE 1916-1945

Although this coin is commonly called the "Mercury Dime," the main device is in fact a representation of Liberty. The wings crowning her cap are intended to symbolize liberty of thought. The designer's monogram AW is right of neck.

Mint mark location is on reverse left of fasces.

G-4 GOOD—*Letters and date clear. Lines and bands in fasces are obliterated.*
VG-8 VERY GOOD—*One-half of sticks discernible in fasces.*
F-12 FINE—*All sticks in fasces are defined. Diagonal bands worn nearly flat.*
VF-20 VERY FINE—*The two crossing diagonal bands must show.*
EF-40 EXTREMELY FINE—*Diagonal bands show only slight wear. Braids and hair before ear show clearly.*
MS-60 UNCIRCULATED—*No trace of wear. Light blemishes.*
MS-65—**CHOICE UNCIRCULATED**—*No trace of wear. Barely noticeable blemishes.*

Uncirculated values shown are for average pieces with minimum blemishes, those with sharp strikes and split bands on reverse are worth much more

	Quan. Minted	G-4	VG-8	F-12	VF-20	EF-40	MS-60	MS-65
1916	22,180,080	$.80	$.80	$.80	$1.50	$2.50	$14.00	$32.50
1916D	264,000	275.00	350.00	550.00	800.00	1,000	1,600	2,250
1916S	10,450,000	.80	.80	1.00	3.00	7.00	22.50	75.00
1917	55,230,000	.80	.80	.80	1.25	2.50	12.00	27.50
1917D	9,402,000	.80	.80	1.50	5.00	12.50	55.00	225.00
1917S	27,330,000	.80	.80	.80	1.50	3.50	20.00	95.00

Italic prices indicate unsettled values due to fluctuating bullion market. See Bullion Chart.

DIMES

	Quan. Minted	G-4	VG-8	F-12	VF-20	EF-40	MS-60	MS-65
1918	26,680,000	*$.80*	*$.80*	*$.80*	$3.00	$8.00	$30.00	$125.00
1918D	22,674,800	*.80*	*.80*	*.80*	3.00	8.00	35.00	170.00
1918S	19,300,000	*.80*	*.80*	*.80*	2.00	5.00	25.00	115.00
1919	35,740,000	*.80*	*.80*	*.80*	1.50	2.50	12.00	55.00
1919D	9,939,000	*.80*	*.80*	1.00	5.00	12.00	65.00	260.00
1919S	8,850,000	*.80*	*.80*	*.80*	4.50	10.00	75.00	325.00
1920	59,030,000	*.80*	*.80*	*.80*	2.00	3.00	11.00	40.00
1920D	19,171,000	*.80*	*.80*	*.80*	3.00	8.00	40.00	165.00
1920S	13,820,000	*.80*	*.80*	*.80*	2.50	7.00	36.00	145.00
1921	1,230,000	12.00	18.00	40.00	75.00	240.00	525.00	900.00
1921D	1,080,000	19.00	25.00	58.00	100.00	240.00	525.00	900.00
1923	50,130,000	*.80*	*.80*	*.80*	1.00	1.75	11.00	35.00
1923S	6,440,000	*.80*	*.80*	*.80*	2.50	8.00	47.00	240.00
1924	24,010,000	*.80*	*.80*	*.80*	1.25	3.00	22.50	65.00
1924D	6,810,000	*.80*	*.80*	1.00	2.50	7.00	52.00	240.00
1924S	7,120,000	*.80*	*.80*	1.00	2.25	6.00	55.00	265.00
1925	25,610,000	*.80*	*.80*	*.80*	1.25	2.25	20.00	60.00
1925D	5,117,000	1.50	2.00	4.00	12.00	35.00	140.00	435.00
1925S	5,850,000	*.80*	*.80*	1.00	2.25	8.00	65.00	325.00
1926	32,160,000	*.80*	*.80*	*.80*	1.25	2.00	10.00	30.00
1926D	6,828,000	*.80*	*.80*	*.80*	2.00	6.00	39.00	150.00
1926S	1,520,000	3.00	4.00	8.00	15.00	40.00	240.00	825.00
1927	28,080,000	*.80*	*.80*	*.80*	1.00	1.75	10.00	30.00
1927D	4,812,000	*.80*	*.80*	1.00	5.00	12.00	100.00	325.00
1927S	4,770,000	*.80*	*.80*	*.80*	1.25	5.00	47.50	200.00
1928	19,480,000	*.80*	*.80*	*.80*	1.00	1.75	10.00	30.00
1928D	4,161,000	*.80*	*.80*	1.75	5.00	11.00	75.00	235.00
1928S	7,400,000	*.80*	*.80*	*.80*	1.25	4.00	30.00	150.00
1929	25,970,000	*.80*	*.80*	*.80*	1.00	1.50	8.00	25.00
1929D	5,034,000	*.80*	*.80*	*.80*	1.75	3.00	20.00	62.50
1929S	4,730,000	*.80*	*.80*	*.80*	1.25	2.00	25.00	75.00
1930	6,770,000	*.80*	*.80*	*.80*	1.00	2.00	12.00	40.00
1930S	1,843,000	*.80*	1.00	1.25	1.50	3.00	40.00	150.00
1931	3,150,000	*.80*	*.80*	*.80*	1.50	3.50	20.00	60.00
1931D	1,260,000	3.00	4.00	5.00	8.00	18.00	65.00	145.00
1931S	1,800,000	*.80*	1.00	1.50	2.00	4.00	40.00	150.00

	Quan. Minted	VG-8	F-12	VF-20	EF-40	MS-60	MS-65	Proof-65
1934	24,080,000	*.80*	*.80*	*.80*	*.80*	9.00	37.00	
1934D	6,772,000	*.80*	*.80*	*.80*	*.80*	19.00	60.00	
1935	58,830,000	*.80*	*.80*	*.80*	*.80*	7.00	27.00	
1935D	10,477,000	*.80*	*.80*	*.80*	*.80*	25.00	85.00	
1935S	15,840,000	*.80*	*.80*	*.80*	*.80*	16.00	32.00	
1936 (4,130)	87,504,130	*.80*	*.80*	*.80*	*.80*	6.00	25.00	500.00
1936D	16,132,000	*.80*	*.80*	*.80*	*.80*	17.00	50.00	
1936S	9,210,000	*.80*	*.80*	*.80*	*.80*	11.00	30.00	
1937 (5,756)	56,865,756	*.80*	*.80*	*.80*	*.80*	6.00	25.00	375.00
1937D	14,146,000	*.80*	*.80*	*.80*	*.80*	16.00	42.00	
1937S	9,740,000	*.80*	*.80*	*.80*	*.80*	10.00	27.50	
1938 (8,728)	22,198,728	*.80*	*.80*	*.80*	*.80*	7.00	26.00	325.00
1938D	5,537,000	*.80*	*.80*	*.80*	*.80*	16.00	45.00	
1938S	8,090,000	*.80*	*.80*	*.80*	*.80*	9.00	33.00	
1939 (9,321)	67,749,321	*.80*	*.80*	*.80*	*.80*	4.00	18.00	300.00
1939D	24,394,000	*.80*	*.80*	*.80*	*.80*	4.00	18.00	
1939S	10,540,000	*.80*	*.80*	*.80*	*.80*	10.00	36.00	

Italic prices indicate unsettled values due to fluctuating bullion market. See Bullion Chart.

DIMES

	Quan. Minted	VG-8	F-12	VF-20	EF-40	MS-60	MS-65	Proof-65
1940 ..... (11,827)	65,361,827	$.80	$.80	$.80	$.80	$2.00	$13.00	$275.00
1940D.............	21,198,000	.80	.80	.80	.80	8.00	20.00	
1940S.............	21,560,000	.80	.80	.80	.80	2.50	14.00	
1941 ..... (16,557)	175,106,557	.80	.80	.80	.80	2.00	13.00	250.00
1941D.............	45,634,000	.80	.80	.80	.80	5.00	20.00	
1941S.............	43,090,000	.80	.80	.80	.80	3.00	18.00	

1942, 2 over 1   1942D, 2 over 1

	Quan. Minted	VG-8	F-12	VF-20	EF-40	MS-60	MS-65	Proof-65
1942, 2 over 1 ...	205,432,329	120.00	140.00	150.00	180.00	675.00	1,500	
1942 ..... (22,329)		.80	.80	.80	.80	2.00	12.00	250.00
1942D, 2 over 1..	60,740,000	120.00	140.00	155.00	185.00	750.00	1,750	
1942D............		.80	.80	.80	.80	2.00	18.00	
1942S.............	49,300,000	.80	.80	.80	.80	4.00	22.00	
1943	191,710,000	.80	.80	.80	.80	2.00	12.00	
1943D.............	71,949,000	.80	.80	.80	.80	2.00	15.00	
1943S.............	60,400,000	.80	.80	.80	.80	3.00	15.00	
1944	231,410,000	.80	.80	.80	.80	2.00	12.00	
1944D.............	62,224,000	.80	.80	.80	.80	2.00	14.00	
1944S.............	49,490,000	.80	.80	.80	.80	2.00	14.00	
1945	159,130,000	.80	.80	.80	.80	2.00	13.00	
1945D.............	40,245,000	.80	.80	.80	.80	2.00	14.00	
1945S Normal S .	41,920,000	.80	.80	.80	.80	2.00	14.00	
1945S Micro S....		.80	.80	.80	.80	5.00	22.50	

ROOSEVELT TYPE 1946 to Date

John R. Sinnock (whose initials JS are at the truncation of the neck) designed this dime showing a portrait of Franklin D. Roosevelt. The design has heavier lettering and a more modernistic character than preceding types.

VF-20 VERY FINE—*Hair above ear slightly worn. All vertical lines on torch plain.*
EF-40 EXTREMELY FINE—*All lines of torch, flame and hair very plain.*
MS-63 SELECT UNCIRCULATED—*No trace of wear. Slight blemishes.*
MS-65 CHOICE UNCIRCULATED—*No trace of wear. Barely noticeable blemishes.*

Mint mark on reverse 1946-1964.

	Quan. Minted	VF-20	EF-40	MS-63	Proof-65
1946	255,250,000	$.80	$.80	$1.00	
1946D.................................	61,043,500	.80	.80	2.00	
1946S.................................	27,900,000	.80	.80	2.50	

Italic prices indicate unsettled values due to fluctuating bullion market. See Bullion Chart.

DIMES

	Quan. Minted	VF-20	EF-40	MS-63	Proof-65
1947	121,520,000	*$.80*	*$.80*	$1.25	
1947D	46,835,000	*.80*	*.80*	2.50	
1947S	34,840,000	*.80*	*.80*	1.60	
1948	74,950,000	*.80*	*.80*	4.50	
1948D	52,841,000	*.80*	*.80*	3.00	
1948S	35,520,000	*.80*	*.80*	3.00	
1949	30,940,000	*.80*	*.80*	8.00	
1949D	26,034,000	*.80*	*.80*	4.00	
1949S	13,510,000	*.80*	*.80*	19.00	
1950 (51,386)	50,181,500	*.80*	*.80*	1.40	$40.00
1950D	46,803,000	*.80*	*.80*	1.45	
1950S	20,440,000	*.80*	*.80*	8.25	
1951 (57,500)	103,937,602	*.80*	*.80*	1.00	27.50
1951D	56,529,000	*.80*	*.80*	1.00	
1951S	31,630,000	*.80*	*.80*	6.00	
1952 (81,980)	99,122,073	*.80*	*.80*	1.00	16.00
1952D	122,100,000	*.80*	*.80*	1.00	
1952S	44,419,500	*.80*	*.80*	2.20	
1953 (128,800)	53,618,920	*.80*	*.80*	1.00	11.00
1953D	136,433,000	*.80*	*.80*	1.00	
1953S	39,180,000	*.80*	*.80*	1.00	
1954 (233,300)	114,243,503	*.80*	*.80*	1.00	5.00
1954D	106,397,000	*.80*	*.80*	1.00	
1954S	22,860,000	*.80*	*.80*	1.00	
1955 (378,200)	12,828,381	*.80*	*.80*	1.15	6.00
1955D	13,959,000	*.80*	*.80*	1.00	
1955S	18,510,000	*.80*	*.80*	1.00	
1956 (669,384)	109,309,384	*.80*	*.80*	1.00	1.75
1956D	108,015,100	*.80*	*.80*	1.00	
1957 (1,247,952)	161,407,952	*.80*	*.80*	*.80*	1.50
1957D	113,354,330	*.80*	*.80*	*.80*	
1958 (875,652)	32,785,652	*.80*	*.80*	1.00	1.75
1958D	136,564,600	*.80*	*.80*	*.80*	
1959 (1,149,291)	86,929,291	*.80*	*.80*	*.80*	1.25
1959D	164,919,790	*.80*	*.80*	*.80*	
1960 (1,691,602)	72,081,602	*.80*	*.80*	*.80*	1.25
1960D	200,160,400	*.80*	*.80*	*.80*	
1961 (3,028,244)	96,758,244	*.80*	*.80*	*.80*	1.00
1961D	209,146,550	*.80*	*.80*	*.80*	
1962 (3,218,019)	75,668,019	*.80*	*.80*	*.80*	1.00
1962D	334,948,380	*.80*	*.80*	*.80*	
1963 (3,075,645)	126,725,645	*.80*	*.80*	*.80*	1.00
1963D	421,476,530	*.80*	*.80*	*.80*	
1964 (3,950,762)	933,310,762	*.80*	*.80*	*.80*	1.00
1964D	1,357,517,180	*.80*	*.80*	*.80*	

Clad Coinage

Mint mark on obverse starting 1968

	Quan. Minted	MS-65	Proof-65
1965	1,652,140,570	.15	
1966	1,382,734,540	.12	

Italic prices indicate unsettled values due to fluctuating bullion market. See Bullion Chart.

DIMES

	Quan. Minted	MS-65	Proof-65
1967	2,244,007,320	$.12	
1968	424,470,400	.11	
1968D	480,748,280	.11	
1968S Proof	(3,041,506)		$.25
1969	145,790,000	.18	
1969D	563,323,870	.14	
1969S Proof	(2,934,631)		.25
1970	345,570,000	.12	
1970D	754,942,100	.12	
1970S Proof	(2,632,810)		.40
1971	162,690,000	.14	
1971D	377,914,240	.14	
1971S Proof	(3,220,733)		.40
1972	431,540,000	.11	
1972D	330,290,000	.11	
1972S Proof	(3,260,996)		.40
1973	315,670,000	.11	
1973D	455,032,426	.11	
1973S Proof	(2,760,339)		.25
1974	470,248,000	.12	
1974D	571,083,000	.12	
1974S Proof	(2,612,568)		.40
1975	585,673,900	.11	
1975D	313,705,300	.11	
1975S Proof	(2,845,450)		.40
1976	568,760,000	.10	
1976D	695,222,774	$.10	
1976S Proof	(4,149,730)		$.25
1977	796,930,000	.10	
1977D	376,607,228	.10	
1977S Proof	(3,251,152)		.20
1978	663,980,000	.10	
1978D	282,847,540	.10	
1978S Proof	(3,127,781)		.40
1979	315,440,000	.12	
1979D	390,921,184	.13	
1979S Proof	(3,677,175)		
Filled S			.55
Clear S			1.75
1980P	735,170,000	.10	
1980D	719,354,321	.10	
1980S Proof	(3,554,806)		.40
1981P	676,650,000	.10	
1981D	712,284,143	.10	
1981S Proof	(4,063,083)		.40
1982 (no mint mark)		250.00	
1982P	519,475,000	.10	
1982D	542,713,584	.10	
1982S Proof	(3,857,479)		.55
1983P		.10	
1983D		.10	
1983S Proof			.55

TWENTY-CENT PIECES — 1875-1878

This short-lived coin was authorized by the Act of March 3, 1875. The edge of the coin is plain. Most of the 1876CC coins were melted at the mint and never released. Mint mark is on the reverse below the eagle.

G-4 GOOD—*LIBERTY on shield obliterated. Letters and date legible.*
VG-8 VERY GOOD—*One or two letters in LIBERTY may show. Other details will be bold.*
F-12 FINE—*At least 3 letters of LIBERTY show.*
VF-20 VERY FINE—*LIBERTY completely readable, but partly weak.*
EF-40 EXTREMELY FINE—*LIBERTY sharp. Only slight wear on high points of coin.*
MS-60 UNCIRCULATED—*No trace of wear. Light blemishes.*

	Quan. Minted	G-4	VG-8	F-12	VF-20	EF-40	MS-60	Proof-60
1875 (2,790)	39,700	$23.00	$28.00	$35.00	$50.00	$100.00	$650.00	$700.00
1875CC	133,290	23.00	28.00	35.00	50.00	90.00	600.00	
1875S	1,155,000	18.00	23.00	30.00	45.00	80.00	550.00	—
1876 (1,260)	15,900	33.00	42.00	55.00	65.00	130.00	700.00	850.00
1876CC	10,000						—	
1877 (350)	350							1,200
1878 (600)	600							1,000

QUARTER DOLLARS — 1796 to Date

Authorized in 1792, this denomination was not issued until four years later. The first type weighed 104 grains which remained standard until modified to 103⅛ grains by the Act of January 18, 1837. As with the dime and half dime, the weight was reduced and arrows placed at the date in 1853. Rays were placed in the field of the reverse during that year only.

DRAPED BUST TYPE, SMALL EAGLE REVERSE 1796

AG-3 ABOUT GOOD—*Details clear enough to identify.*
G-4 GOOD—*Date readable. Bust outlined, but no detail.*
VG-8 VERY GOOD—*All but deepest drapery folds worn smooth. Hairlines nearly gone and curls lack detail.*
F-12 FINE—*All drapery lines visible. Hair partly worn.*
VF-20 VERY FINE—*Only left side of drapery is indistinct.*
EF-40 EXTREMELY FINE—*Hair well outlined and detailed.*
MS-60 UNCIRCULATED—*No trace of wear. Light blemishes.*

	Quan. Minted	AG-3	G-4	VG-8	F-12	VF-20	EF-40	MS-60
1796	6,146	$700.00	$1,400	$1,900	$2,600	$3,900	$5,800	$12,500

DRAPED BUST TYPE, HERALDIC EAGLE REVERSE 1804-1807

1804	6,738	175.00	325.00	400.00	1,100	2,000	4,300	—
1805	121,395	70.00	125.00	150.00	275.00	600.00	1,000	4,500
1806 6 over 5	} 206,124	70.00	125.00	150.00	275.00	600.00	1,000	4,500
1806		70.00	125.00	150.00	275.00	600.00	1,000	4,500
1807	220,643	70.00	125.00	150.00	275.00	600.00	1,000	4,500

CAPPED BUST TYPE 1815-1838
Large Size 1815-1828

AG-3 ABOUT GOOD—*Details clear enough to identify.*
G-4 GOOD—*Date, letters and stars readable. Hair under headband smooth. Cap lines worn smooth.*
VG-8 VERY GOOD—*Rim well defined. Main details visible. Full LIBERTY on cap. Hair above eye nearly smooth.*
F-12 FINE—*All hairlines show but drapery has only part details. Shoulder clasp distinct.*
VF-20 VERY FINE—*All details show, but some wear. Clasp and ear sharp.*
EF-40 EXTREMELY FINE—*All details show distinctly. Hair well outlined.*
MS-60 UNCIRCULATED—*No trace of wear. Light blemishes.*

QUARTER DOLLARS

	Quan. Minted	AG-3	G-4	VG-8	F-12	VF-20	EF-40	MS-60
1815	89,235	$13.00	$25.00	$35.00	$60.00	$150.00	$425.00	$1,300
1818 8 over 5	} 361,174	13.00	25.00	35.00	55.00	150.00	425.00	1,300
1818 Normal		13.00	25.00	35.00	55.00	135.00	375.00	1,200
1819	144,000	13.00	25.00	35.00	55.00	135.00	375.00	1,200
1820	127,444	13.00	25.00	35.00	55.00	135.00	375.00	1,200
1821	216,851	13.00	25.00	35.00	55.00	135.00	375.00	1,200
1822 All kinds	64,080	13.00	25.00	35.00	55.00	135.00	375.00	1,300
1822, 25 over 50c		70.00	100.00	150.00	250.00	475.00	800.00	2,600
1823, 3 over 2	17,800	650.00	1,200	3,000	5,000	7,000	12,000	—
1824	} 168,000	15.00	30.00	37.00	65.00	160.00	385.00	1,500
1825		12.00	23.00	30.00	50.00	125.00	350.00	1,300
1827 Original (Curled base 2 in 25c) 4,000 Minted								—
1827 Restrike (Square base 2 in 25c)								—
1828 All kds...	102,000	12.00	23.00	30.00	50.00	125.00	350.00	1,400
1828, 25 over 50c		22.00	40.00	60.00	110.00	250.00	400.00	2,400

Reduced Size, No Motto on Reverse 1831-1838

G-4 GOOD—*Bust well defined. Hair under headband smooth. Date, letters, stars readable. Scant rims.*
VG-8 VERY GOOD—*Details apparent but worn on high spots. Rims strong. Full LIBERTY.*
F-12 FINE—*All hairlines visible. Drapery partly worn. Shoulder clasp distinct.*
VF-20 VERY FINE—*Only top spots worn. Clasp sharp. Ear distinct.*
EF-40 EXTREMELY FINE—*Hair details and clasp are bold and clear.*
MS-60 UNCIRCULATED—*No trace of wear. Light blemishes.*

	Quan. Minted	G-4	VG-8	F-12	VF-20	EF-40	MS-60
1831	398,000	$20.00	$24.00	$30.00	$60.00	$150.00	$675.00
1832	320,000	20.00	24.00	30.00	60.00	150.00	675.00
1833	156,000	21.00	25.00	35.00	70.00	165.00	850.00
1834	286,000	20.00	24.00	30.00	60.00	150.00	675.00
1835	1,952,000	20.00	24.00	30.00	60.00	150.00	675.00
1836	472,000	20.00	24.00	30.00	60.00	150.00	675.00
1837	252,400	20.00	24.00	30.00	60.00	150.00	675.00
1838	366,000	20.00	24.00	30.00	60.00	150.00	675.00

QUARTER DOLLARS
LIBERTY SEATED TYPE 1838-1891
No Motto Above Eagle 1838-1853

G-4 GOOD—*Scant rim. LIBERTY on shield worn off. Date and letters readable.*
VG-8 VERY GOOD—*Rim fairly defined, at least 3 letters in LIBERTY evident.*
F-12 FINE—*LIBERTY complete, but partly weak.*
VF-20 VERY FINE—*LIBERTY strong.*
EF-40 EXTREMELY FINE—*Complete LIBERTY and edges of scroll. Clasp shows plainly.*
MS-60 UNCIRCULATED—*No trace of wear. Light blemishes.*

Mint mark location is on the reverse below the eagle.

	Quan. Minted	G-4	VG-8	F-12	VF-20	EF-40	MS-60
1838	466,000	$4.00	$6.00	$11.00	$21.00	$60.00	$1,100
1839	491,146	4.00	6.00	11.00	21.00	70.00	1,100
1840	188,127	7.00	9.00	15.00	30.00	60.00	950.00
1840O	425,200	4.00	6.00	11.00	21.00	70.00	950.00
1841	120,000	11.00	14.00	30.00	50.00	90.00	450.00
1841O	452,000	4.00	6.00	11.00	24.00	70.00	450.00

Small Date

Large Date

	Quan. Minted	G-4	VG-8	F-12	VF-20	EF-40	MS-60
1842	88,000	30.00	40.00	70.00	130.00	225.00	900.00
1842O Small date	} 769,000	60.00	125.00	185.00	300.00	850.00	—
1842O Large date		5.00	7.00	11.00	18.00	40.00	500.00
1843	645,600	4.50	6.00	9.00	18.00	40.00	500.00
1843O	968,000	7.00	12.00	20.00	35.00	100.00	600.00
1844	421,200	4.50	6.00	11.00	19.00	40.00	300.00
1844O	740,000	4.50	6.00	11.00	21.00	50.00	700.00
1845	922,000	4.50	6.00	9.00	18.00	40.00	300.00
1846	510,000	4.50	6.00	11.00	19.00	40.00	300.00
1847	734,000	4.50	6.00	11.00	18.00	40.00	300.00
1847O	368,000	9.00	14.00	24.00	40.00	90.00	500.00
1848	146,000	8.00	12.00	24.00	40.00	70.00	450.00
1849	340,000	7.00	9.00	15.00	21.00	65.00	325.00
1849O	†incl. below	125.00	200.00	350.00	600.00	1,600	—
1850	190,800	4.50	9.00	14.00	21.00	40.00	450.00
1850O	412,000	12.00	16.00	22.00	35.00	65.00	500.00
1851	160,000	4.50	9.00	14.00	21.00	60.00	400.00
1851O	88,000	60.00	85.00	150.00	225.00	600.00	1,100
1852	177,060	9.00	14.00	21.00	30.00	60.00	450.00
1852O	96,000	100.00	140.00	185.00	325.00	650.00	1,600
1853 No arrows or rays	44,200	70.00	90.00	125.00	225.00	325.00	1,800

†Coinage for 1849O included with 1850O.

Arrows at Date, Rays Around Eagle 1853 Only

1853, 3 over 4

[90]

QUARTER DOLLARS

	Quan. Minted	G-4	VG-8	F-12	VF-20	EF-40	MS-60
1853	} 15,210,000	$5.00	$7.00	$9.00	$16.00	$50.00	$525.00
1853, 3 over 4		25.00	60.00	150.00	200.00	450.00	—
1853O	1,332,000	5.00	7.00	11.00	22.00	70.00	600.00

Arrows at Date, No Rays 1854-1855

	Quan. Minted	G-4	VG-8	F-12	VF-20	EF-40	MS-60
1854	12,380,000	4.00	5.00	7.00	15.00	35.00	500.00
1854O	1,484,000	4.00	5.00	7.00	15.00	35.00	525.00
1855	2,857,000	4.00	5.00	7.00	15.00	35.00	525.00
1855O	176,000	22.00	35.00	50.00	100.00	170.00	1,000
1855S	396,400	22.00	35.00	50.00	90.00	150.00	1,000

No Motto Above Eagle 1856-1865

	Quan. Minted	G-4	VG-8	F-12	VF-20	EF-40	MS-60	Proof-60
1856	7,264,000	$4.00	$5.00	$7.00	$10.00	$21.00	$300.00	$750.00
1856O	968,000	5.00	7.00	11.00	16.00	30.00	310.00	
1856S	286,000	10.00	14.00	21.00	50.00	100.00	1,100	
1857	9,644,000	4.00	5.00	7.00	10.00	21.00	300.00	600.00
1857O	1,180,000	4.00	6.00	8.00	11.00	21.00	310.00	
1857S	82,000	20.00	32.00	45.00	120.00	225.00	1,250	
1858	7,368,000	4.00	5.00	7.00	10.00	20.00	300.00	450.00
1858O	520,000	4.00	6.00	8.00	11.00	22.00	325.00	
1858S	121,000	16.00	18.00	30.00	75.00	115.00	600.00	
1859 .... (800)	1,344,000	4.00	5.00	7.00	10.00	21.00	300.00	325.00
1859O	260,000	6.00	10.00	16.00	25.00	40.00	500.00	
1859S	80,000	25.00	40.00	75.00	125.00	250.00	1,000	
1860 .. (1,000)	805,400	4.00	5.00	7.00	10.00	21.00	300.00	325.00
1860O	388,000	5.00	7.00	10.00	14.00	30.00	310.00	
1860S	56,000	40.00	65.00	120.00	210.00	450.00	1,250	
1861 .. (1,000)	4,854,600	4.00	5.00	7.00	10.00	21.00	300.00	325.00
1861S	96,000	10.00	14.00	21.00	45.00	150.00	1,100	
1862 .... (550)	932,550	4.00	5.00	7.00	10.00	21.00	300.00	325.00
1862S	67,000	11.00	15.00	22.00	50.00	150.00	1,100	
1863 .... (460)	192,060	7.00	9.00	14.00	20.00	40.00	400.00	350.00
1864 .... (470)	94,070	11.00	15.00	22.00	40.00	80.00	500.00	350.00
1864S	20,000	50.00	85.00	150.00	225.00	500.00	—	
1865 .... (500)	59,300	16.00	21.00	35.00	50.00	90.00	475.00	350.00
1865S	41,000	15.00	20.00	30.00	60.00	135.00	1,700	

Motto Above Eagle 1866-1873

1866 .... (725)	17,525	45.00	75.00	90.00	130.00	200.00	600.00	300.00
1866S	28,000	20.00	30.00	60.00	100.00	200.00	1,200	
1867 .... (625)	20,625	20.00	30.00	70.00	110.00	200.00	500.00	300.00
1867S	48,000	18.00	25.00	40.00	65.00	90.00	1,200	
1868 .... (600)	30,000	19.00	27.00	45.00	70.00	125.00	400.00	300.00

QUARTER DOLLARS

	Quan. Minted	G-4	VG-8	F-12	VF-20	EF-40	MS-60	Proof-60
1868S	96,000	$11.00	$17.00	$30.00	$40.00	$80.00	$600.00	
1869 .... (600)	16,600	20.00	30.00	75.00	110.00	185.00	550.00	$300.00
1869S	76,000	11.00	17.00	28.00	35.00	80.00	550.00	
1870 .. (1,000)	87,400	11.00	15.00	22.00	37.00	60.00	300.00	300.00
1870CC	8,340	375.00	650.00	900.00	1,200	2,100	2,750	
1871 .... (960)	119,160	4.00	6.00	10.00	18.00	30.00	285.00	
1871CC	10,890	200.00	300.00	450.00	750.00	1,250	—	
1871S	30,900	35.00	65.00	125.00	175.00	270.00	1,300	
1872 .... (950)	182,950	4.00	6.00	9.00	14.00	30.00	300.00	300.00
1872CC	22,850	90.00	125.00	190.00	350.00	800.00	2,250	
1872S	83,000	35.00	65.00	120.00	175.00	275.00	1,700	
1873 .... (600)	212,600	4.00	9.00	14.00	21.00	150.00	300.00	300.00
1873CC	4,000						—	

Arrows at Date 1873-1874

1873 .... (540)	1,271,700	6.00	8.00	14.00	35.00	100.00	625.00	600.00
1873CC	12,462	200.00	250.00	350.00	550.00	825.00	3,000	
1873S	156,000	9.00	10.00	18.00	40.00	115.00	700.00	
1874 .... (700)	471,900	6.00	8.00	14.00	35.00	100.00	625.00	600.00
1874S	392,000	9.00	10.00	18.00	40.00	115.00	700.00	

No Arrows at Date 1875-1891

  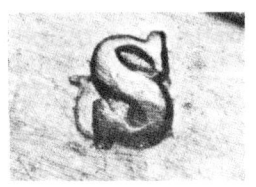

1877S, S over horizontal S

1875 .... (700)	4,293,500	3.00	4.00	5.00	10.00	20.00	275.00	275.00
1875CC	140,000	15.00	20.00	50.00	75.00	160.00	700.00	
1875S	680,000	4.00	6.00	10.00	18.00	30.00	300.00	
1876 .. (1,150)	17,817,150	3.00	4.00	5.00	10.00	20.00	275.00	275.00
1876CC	4,944,000	4.00	5.00	7.00	14.00	30.00	300.00	
1876S	8,596,000	3.00	4.00	5.00	10.00	20.00	275.00	
1877 .... (510)	10,911,710	3.00	4.00	5.00	10.00	20.00	250.00	275.00
1877CC	4,192,000	4.00	5.00	7.00	14.00	30.00	300.00	
1877S	} 8,996,000	3.00	4.00	5.00	10.00	20.00	250.00	
1877S over horizontal S		4.00	6.00	40.00	50.00	90.00	350.00	
1878 .... (800)	2,260,800	3.00	4.00	5.00	10.00	20.00	250.00	275.00
1878CC	996,000	4.00	5.00	7.00	11.00	25.00	350.00	
1878S	140,000	27.00	37.00	65.00	90.00	125.00	1,200	
1879 .. *(1,100)*	14,700	35.00	40.00	55.00	75.00	100.00	350.00	300.00

QUARTER DOLLARS

	Quan. Minted	G-4	VG-8	F-12	VF-20	EF-40	MS-60	Proof-60
1880 .. (1,355)	14,955	$35.00	$40.00	$55.00	$75.00	$100.00	$350.00	$285.00
1881 .... (975)	12,975	35.00	40.00	55.00	75.00	100.00	325.00	300.00
1882 .. (1,100)	16,300	35.00	40.00	55.00	75.00	100.00	325.00	300.00
1883 .. (1,039)	15,439	35.00	40.00	55.00	75.00	100.00	325.00	300.00
1884 .... (875)	8,875	40.00	50.00	65.00	90.00	125.00	375.00	300.00
1885 .... (930)	14,530	35.00	40.00	55.00	75.00	110.00	350.00	300.00
1886 .... (886)	5,886	45.00	60.00	70.00	100.00	150.00	375.00	300.00
1887 .... (710)	10,710	35.00	40.00	55.00	75.00	110.00	350.00	300.00
1888 .... (832)	10,833	35.00	40.00	55.00	75.00	110.00	350.00	300.00
1888S	1,216,000	4.00	5.00	6.00	11.00	20.00	250.00	
1889 .... (711)	12,711	33.00	37.00	50.00	65.00	90.00	350.00	300.00
1890 .... (590)	80,590	20.00	25.00	33.00	45.00	70.00	300.00	285.00
1891 .... (600)	3,920,600	3.00	4.00	5.00	10.00	20.00	275.00	275.00
1891O	68,000	50.00	65.00	100.00	150.00	275.00	1,500	
1891S	2,216,000	3.00	5.00	7.00	12.00	23.00	250.00	

BARBER or LIBERTY HEAD TYPE 1892-1916

Like other silver coins of this type the quarter dollars minted from 1892 to 1916 were designed by Charles E. Barber. His initial B is found at the truncation of the neck of Liberty.

G-4 GOOD—*Date and legends readable. LIBERTY worn off headband.*
VG-8 VERY GOOD—*Minimum of 3 letters in LIBERTY readable.*
F-12 FINE—*LIBERTY completely readable but not sharp.*
VF-20 VERY FINE—*All letters in LIBERTY evenly plain.*
EF-40 EXTREMELY FINE—*LIBERTY bold, and its ribbon distinct.*
MS-60 UNCIRCULATED—*No trace of wear. Light blemishes.*

Mint mark location is on the reverse below the eagle.

	Quan. Minted	G-4	VG-8	F-12	VF-20	EF-40	MS-60	Proof-63
1892 .. (1,245)	8,237,245	*$2.00*	*$2.00*	$3.50	$7.50	$26.00	$175.00	$500.00
1892O	2,640,000	*2.00*	3.00	4.50	9.00	30.00	200.00	
1892S	964,079	7.00	8.00	12.00	20.00	50.00	250.00	
1893 .... (792)	5,444,815	*2.00*	*2.00*	3.50	8.00	27.00	200.00	500.00
1893O	3,396,000	*2.00*	*2.00*	6.00	12.00	28.00	225.00	
1893S	1,454,535	*2.00*	3.50	8.00	14.00	35.00	225.00	
1894 .... (972)	3,432,972	*2.00*	*2.00*	3.50	11.00	27.00	190.00	500.00
1894O	2,852,000	*2.00*	*2.00*	6.00	9.00	30.00	225.00	
1894S	2,648,821	*2.00*	*2.00*	6.00	9.00	30.00	225.00	
1895 .... (880)	4,440,880	*2.00*	*2.00*	3.50	7.00	25.00	190.00	500.00
1895O	2,816,000	*2.00*	*2.00*	6.00	9.00	28.00	250.00	
1895S	1,764,681	?.00	2.00	7.00	12.00	25.00	235.00	
1896 .... (762)	3,874,762	*2.00*	*2.00*	3.50	9.00	28.00	190.00	500.00
1896O	1,484,000	*2.00*	3.00	7.00	20.00	60.00	525.00	
1896S	188,039	140.00	175.00	400.00	550.00	1,000	2,250	
1897 .... (731)	8,140,731	*2.00*	*2.00*	3.50	7.00	24.00	160.00	500.00
1897O	1,414,800	2.50	3.50	8.00	24.00	65.00	525.00	
1897S	542,229	5.00	7.00	14.00	28.00	60.00	250.00	
1898 .... (735)	11,100,735	*2.00*	*2.00*	3.50	7.00	24.00	160.00	500.00

Italic prices indicate unsettled values due to fluctuating bullion market. See Bullion Chart.

QUARTER DOLLARS

	Quan. Minted	G-4	VG-8	F-12	VF-20	EF-40	MS-60	Proof-63
1898O	1,868,000	*$2.00*	*$2.50*	$6.00	$14.00	$40.00	$350.00	
1898S	1,020,592	*2.00*	*2.50*	5.00	9.00	30.00	250.00	
1899 .... (846)	12,624,846	*2.00*	*2.00*	3.50	7.00	24.00	160.00	$500.00
1899O	2,644,000	*2.00*	*2.00*	5.00	12.00	25.00	275.00	
1899S	708,000	4.50	6.00	9.00	18.00	35.00	225.00	
1900 .... (912)	10,016,912	*2.00*	*2.00*	3.50	7.00	24.00	160.00	500.00
1900O	3,416,000	*2.00*	3.50	8.00	18.00	35.00	300.00	
1900S	1,858,585	*2.00*	*2.00*	5.00	11.00	25.00	210.00	
1901 .... (813)	8,892,813	*2.00*	*2.00*	3.50	7.00	24.00	160.00	500.00
1901O	1,612,000	5.00	8.00	18.00	35.00	75.00	525.00	
1901S	72,664	700.00	800.00	1,200	1,700	2,400	6,500	
1902 .... (777)	12,197,744	*2.00*	*2.00*	3.50	7.00	24.00	160.00	500.00
1902O	4,748,000	*2.00*	*2.00*	5.00	10.00	25.00	250.00	
1902S	1,524,612	*2.00*	4.00	6.00	16.00	38.00	240.00	
1903 .... (755)	9,670,064	*2.00*	*2.00*	3.50	7.00	24.00	160.00	500.00
1903O	3,500,000	*2.00*	*2.00*	7.00	12.00	27.00	220.00	
1903S	1,036,000	*2.00*	*2.50*	8.00	14.00	30.00	260.00	
1904 .... (670)	9,588,813	*2.00*	*2.00*	3.50	7.00	24.00	160.00	500.00
1904O	2,456,000	*2.00*	*2.50*	8.00	12.00	35.00	485.00	
1905 .... (727)	4,968,250	*2.00*	*2.00*	3.50	7.00	24.00	160.00	500.00
1905O	1,230,000	*2.00*	*2.50*	8.00	12.00	30.00	235.00	
1905S	1,884,000	*2.00*	*2.00*	5.00	11.00	25.00	220.00	
1906 .... (675)	3,656,435	*2.00*	*2.00*	3.50	7.00	24.00	160.00	500.00
1906D	3,280,000	*2.00*	*2.00*	3.50	7.00	24.00	200.00	
1906O	2,056,000	*2.00*	*2.00*	3.50	7.00	24.00	200.00	
1907 .... (575)	7,192,575	*2.00*	*2.00*	3.50	7.00	24.00	160.00	500.00
1907D	2,484,000	*2.00*	*2.00*	3.50	7.00	24.00	210.00	
1907O	4,560,000	*2.00*	*2.00*	3.50	7.00	24.00	200.00	
1907S	1,360,000	*2.00*	*2.00*	3.50	7.00	24.00	240.00	
1908 .... (545)	4,232,545	*2.00*	*2.00*	3.50	7.00	24.00	160.00	500.00
1908D	5,788,000	*2.00*	*2.00*	3.50	7.00	24.00	190.00	
1908O	6,244,000	*2.00*	*2.00*	3.50	7.00	24.00	190.00	
1908S	784,000	*2.00*	4.00	8.00	16.00	45.00	275.00	
1909 .... (650)	9,268,650	*2.00*	*2.00*	3.50	7.00	24.00	160.00	500.00
1909D	5,114,000	*2.00*	*2.00*	3.50	7.00	24.00	190.00	
1909O	712,000	4.00	6.00	18.00	25.00	75.00	400.00	
1909S	1,348,000	*2.00*	*2.00*	3.50	7.00	24.00	240.00	
1910 .... (551)	2,244,551	*2.00*	*2.00*	3.50	7.00	24.00	160.00	500.00
1910D	1,500,000	*2.00*	*2.00*	3.50	7.00	24.00	210.00	
1911 .... (543)	3,720,543	*2.00*	*2.00*	3.50	7.00	24.00	160.00	500.00
1911D	933,600	*2.00*	*2.00*	5.00	10.00	30.00	190.00	
1911S	988,000	*2.00*	*2.00*	5.00	10.00	30.00	220.00	
1912 .... (700)	4,400,700	*2.00*	*2.00*	3.50	7.00	24.00	160.00	500.00
1912S	708,000	*2.00*	*2.00*	5.00	10.00	30.00	235.00	
1913 .... (613)	484,613	5.00	8.00	25.00	65.00	225.00	825.00	800.00
1913D	1,450,800	*2.00*	*2.00*	3.50	7.00	24.00	190.00	
1913S	40,000	190.00	235.00	400.00	650.00	1,000	2,250	
1914 .... (380)	6,244,610	*2.00*	*2.00*	3.50	7.00	24.00	160.00	550.00
1914D	3,046,000	*2.00*	*2.00*	3.50	7.00	24.00	185.00	
1914S	264,000	7.00	11.00	20.00	50.00	135.00	475.00	
1915 .... (450)	3,480,450	*2.00*	*2.00*	3.50	7.00	24.00	160.00	550.00
1915D	3,694,000	*2.00*	*2.00*	3.50	7.00	24.00	160.00	
1915S	704,000	*2.00*	*2.00*	5.00	10.00	30.00	190.00	
1916	1,788,000	*2.00*	*2.00*	3.50	7.00	24.00	160.00	
1916D	6,540,888	*2.00*	*2.00*	3.50	7.00	24.00	160.00	

Italic prices indicate unsettled values due to fluctuating bullion market. See Bullion Chart.

QUARTER DOLLARS
STANDING LIBERTY TYPE 1916-1930

This design is by Hermon A. MacNeil, whose initial M is above and to the right of the date. Liberty bears a shield of protection in her left arm, while the right hand holds the olive branch of peace. There was a modification in 1917. The reverse has a new arrangement of stars and the eagle is higher. After 1924 the date was "recessed," thereby giving it greater protection from the effects of circulation.

G-4 GOOD—*Date and lettering readable. Top of date worn. Liberty's right leg and toes worn off. Left leg and drapery lines show much wear.*
VG-8 VERY GOOD—*Distinct date. Toes show faintly. Drapery lines visible above her left leg.*
F-12 FINE—*High curve of right leg flat from thigh to ankle. Left leg shows only slight wear. Drapery lines over right thigh seen only at sides of leg.*
VF-20 VERY FINE—*Garment line across right leg will be worn but show at sides.*
EF-40 EXTREMELY FINE—*Flattened only at high spots. Her toes are sharp. Drapery lines across right leg are evident.*
MS-60 UNCIRCULATED—*No trace of wear. Light blemishes.*

No stars below eagle 1916-1917

	Quan. Minted	G-4	VG-8	F-12	VF-20	EF-40	MS-60
1916	52,000	$650.00	$750.00	$1,000	$1,250	$1,500	$2,400
1917	8,740,000	3.00	6.00	7.50	15.00	25.00	90.00
1917D	1,509,200	6.00	9.00	13.00	30.00	60.00	100.00
1917S	1,952,000	5.00	8.00	12.00	30.00	60.00	110.00

Stars below eagle 1917-1930

1918S, 8 over 7

Mint mark position is on obverse at left of date.

1917	13,880,000	5.00	7.00	9.00	12.00	20.00	70.00
1917D	6,224,400	9.00	11.00	20.00	30.00	60.00	100.00
1917S	5,552,000	9.00	11.00	14.00	22.00	40.00	100.00
1918	14,240,000	5.00	7.00	10.00	18.00	30.00	90.00
1918D	7,380,000	13.00	15.00	22.00	30.00	55.00	130.00
1918S Norm. date	11,072,000	7.00	11.00	12.00	14.00	30.00	85.00
1918S 8 over 7		600.00	800.00	1,100	1,600	2,600	5,000
1919	11,324,000	15.00	18.00	20.00	25.00	35.00	100.00
1919D	1,944,000	25.00	35.00	60.00	80.00	150.00	345.00
1919S	1,836,000	25.00	35.00	50.00	65.00	135.00	280.00
1920	27,860,000	3.00	4.00	5.00	10.00	18.00	85.00
1920D	3,586,400	15.00	20.00	30.00	50.00	65.00	140.00
1920S	6,380,000	6.00	8.00	12.00	15.00	20.00	90.00

QUARTER DOLLARS

	Quan. Minted	G-4	VG-8	F-12	VF-20	EF-40	MS-60
1921	1,916,000	$35.00	$45.00	$65.00	$85.00	$130.00	$275.00
1923	9,716,000	3.00	4.00	5.00	10.00	18.00	80.00
1923S	1,360,000	60.00	85.00	115.00	165.00	250.00	400.00
1924	10,920,000	3.00	4.00	5.00	10.00	18.00	80.00
1924D	3,112,000	10.00	15.00	25.00	35.00	55.00	85.00
1924S	2,860,000	8.00	10.00	12.00	15.00	28.00	100.00

Recessed Date 1925-1930

	Quan. Minted	G-4	VG-8	F-12	VF-20	EF-40	MS-60
1925	12,280,000	2.00	2.00	3.00	5.00	10.00	75.00
1926	11,316,000	2.00	2.00	3.00	5.00	10.00	75.00
1926D	1,716,000	2.00	2.00	6.00	10.00	15.00	75.00
1926S	2,700,000	2.00	2.00	4.00	8.00	20.00	100.00
1927	11,912,000	2.00	2.00	3.00	5.00	10.00	75.00
1927D	976,000	2.00	2.00	6.00	12.00	18.00	90.00
1927S	396,000	3.00	5.00	20.00	50.00	200.00	900.00
1928	6,336,000	2.00	2.00	3.00	5.00	10.00	75.00
1928D	1,627,600	2.00	2.00	3.00	5.00	10.00	75.00
1928S	2,644,000	2.00	2.00	3.00	5.00	10.00	75.00
1929	11,140,000	2.00	2.00	3.00	5.00	10.00	75.00
1929D	1,358,000	2.00	2.00	3.00	5.00	10.00	75.00
1929S	1,764,000	2.00	2.00	3.00	5.00	10.00	75.00
1930	5,632,000	2.00	2.00	3.00	5.00	10.00	75.00
1930S	1,556,000	2.00	2.00	3.00	5.00	10.00	75.00

WASHINGTON TYPE 1932 to Date

This type was intended to be a commemorative issue marking the two-hundredth anniversary of Washington's birth. John Flannagan, a New York sculptor, was the designer. The initials JF are found at the base of the neck. Mint mark is on reverse below wreath, 1932 to 1964. Starting in 1968 mint mark is on obverse at right of ribbon.

VG-8 VERY GOOD—*Wing tips outlined. Rims are fine and even. Tops of letters at rim are flattened.*
F-12 FINE—*Hairlines about ear are visible. Tiny feathers on eagle's breast are faintly visible.*
VF-20 VERY FINE—*Hair details worn but plain. Feathers at sides of eagle's breast are plain.*
EF-40 EXTREMELY FINE—*Hairlines sharp. Wear spots confined to top of eagle's legs and center of breast.*
MS-60 UNCIRCULATED—*No trace of wear. Light blemishes.*
MS-65 CHOICE UNCIRCULATED—*No trace of wear. Barely noticeable blemishes.*

1976 Bicentennial reverse design

Starting in 1968 mint mark is on obverse at right of ribbon.

	Quan. Minted	VG-8	F-12	VF-20	EF-40	MS-60	MS-65
1932	5,404,000	$2.00	$2.00	$2.00	$3.00	$12.00	$65.00
1932D	436,800	20.00	25.00	35.00	50.00	200.00	1,200
1932S	408,000	18.00	23.00	30.00	35.00	100.00	600.00
1934	31,912,052	2.00	2.00	2.00	3.00	15.00	30.00
1934D	3,527,200	2.00	2.00	2.00	5.00	40.00	250.00
1935	32,484,000	2.00	2.00	2.00	3.00	8.00	25.00
1935D	5,780,000	2.00	2.00	2.00	5.00	40.00	250.00
1935S	5,660,000	2.00	2.00	2.00	4.00	35.00	100.00

Italic prices indicate unsettled values due to fluctuating bullion market. See Bullion Chart.

QUARTER DOLLARS

	Quan. Minted	F-12	VF-20	EF-40	MS-60	MS-65	Proof-65
1936 .... (3,837)	41,303,837	$2.00	$2.00	$2.00	$8.00	$25.00	$375.00
1936D	5,374,000	2.00	3.00	8.00	90.00	400.00	
1936S	3,828,000	2.00	2.00	3.00	30.00	100.00	
1937 .... (5,542)	19,701,542	2.00	2.00	2.00	8.00	25.00	100.00
1937D	7,189,600	2.00	2.00	2.00	12.00	60.00	
1937S	1,652,000	2.00	2.00	5.00	35.00	150.00	
1938 .... (8,045)	9,480,045	2.00	2.00	4.00	20.00	65.00	125.00
1938S	2,832,000	2.00	2.00	3.00	19.00	65.00	
1939 .... (8,795)	33,548,795	2.00	2.00	2.00	5.00	12.00	65.00
1939D	7,092,000	2.00	2.00	2.00	10.00	45.00	
1939S	2,628,000	2.00	2.00	3.00	20.00	65.00	
1940 ...... (11,246)	35,715,246	2.00	2.00	2.00	2.50	8.00	45.00
1940D	2,797,600	2.00	2.00	3.50	20.00	65.00	
1940S	8,244,000	2.00	2.00	2.00	5.00	18.00	
1941 ...... (15,287)	79,047,287	2.00	2.00	2.00	2.25	6.00	40.00
1941D	16,714,800	2.00	2.00	2.00	6.00	14.00	
1941S	16,080,000	2.00	2.00	2.00	6.50	15.00	
1942 ...... (21,123)	102,117,123	2.00	2.00	2.00	2.25	4.50	40.00
1942D	17,487,200	2.00	2.00	2.00	3.50	9.00	
1942S	19,384,000	2.00	2.00	2.00	18.00	40.00	
1943	99,700,000	2.00	2.00	2.00	2.25	6.00	
1943D	16,095,600	2.00	2.00	2.00	4.00	9.00	
1943S	21,700,000	2.00	2.00	2.00	12.00	30.00	
1944	104,956,000	2.00	2.00	2.00	2.25	3.00	
1944D	14,600,800	2.00	2.00	2.00	3.00	9.00	
1944S	12,560,000	2.00	2.00	2.00	2.50	8.00	
1945	74,372,000	*2.00*	*2.00*	*2.00*	*2.25*	*4.00*	
1945D	12,341,600	*2.00*	*2.00*	*2.00*	*2.25*	*7.00*	
1945S	17,004,001	*2.00*	*2.00*	*2.00*	*2.25*	*5.00*	
1946	53,436,000	*2.00*	*2.00*	*2.00*	*2.25*	*2.50*	
1946D	9,072,800	*2.00*	*2.00*	*2.00*	*2.25*	*3.00*	
1946S	4,204,000	*2.00*	*2.00*	*2.00*	*2.25*	*3.25*	
1947	22,556,000	*2.00*	*2.00*	*2.00*	*2.25*	*3.75*	
1947D	15,338,400	*2.00*	*2.00*	*2.00*	*2.25*	*5.00*	
1947S	5,532,000	*2.00*	*2.00*	*2.00*	*2.25*	*4.00*	
1948	35,196,000	*2.00*	*2.00*	*2.00*	*2.25*	*2.50*	
1948D	16,766,800	*2.00*	*2.00*	*2.00*	*2.25*	*4.00*	
1948S	15,960,000	*2.00*	*2.00*	*2.00*	*2.25*	*4.50*	
1949	9,312,000	*2.00*	*2.00*	*2.00*	5.00	14.00	
1949D	10,068,400	*2.00*	*2.00*	*2.00*	*2.50*	5.00	
1950 ...... (51,386)	24,971,512	*2.00*	*2.00*	*2.00*	*2.25*	*2.50*	50.00
1950D	} 21,075,600	*2.00*	*2.00*	*2.00*	*2.25*	*2.50*	
1950D, D over S			15.00	40.00	90.00	200.00	
1950S	} 10,284,004	*2.00*	*2.00*	*2.00*	*2.50*	5.00	
1950S, S over D			15.00	45.00	120.00	250.00	
1951 ...... (57,500)	43,505,602	*2.00*	*2.00*	*2.00*	*2.25*	*2.50*	25.00
1951D	35,354,800	*2.00*	*2.00*	*2.00*	*2.25*	*2.50*	
1951S	9,048,000	*2.00*	*2.00*	*2.00*	*2.50*	5.00	
1952 ...... (81,980)	38,862,073	*2.00*	*2.00*	*2.00*	*2.25*	*2.50*	17.50
1952D	49,795,200	*2.00*	*2.00*	*2.00*	*2.25*	*2.50*	
1952S	13,707,800	*2.00*	*2.00*	*2.00*	*2.25*	4.00	
1953 ..... (122,800)	18,664,920	*2.00*	*2.00*	*2.00*	*2.25*	*2.50*	8.00
1953D	56,112,400	*2.00*	*2.00*	*2.00*	*2.25*	*2.50*	
1953S	14,016,000	*2.00*	*2.00*	*2.00*	*2.25*	*2.50*	

	Quan. Minted	F-12	EF-40	MS-65	Proof-65
1954 .... (233,300)	54,645,503	*$2.00*	*$2.00*	*$2.25*	$5.00
1954D	46,305,500	*2.00*	*2.00*	*2.25*	
1954S	11,834,722	*2.00*	*2.00*	*2.50*	

Italic prices indicate unsettled values due to fluctuating bullion market. See Bullion Chart.

QUARTER DOLLARS

	Quan. Minted	F-12	EF-40	MS-65	Proof-65
1955 .... (378,200)	18,558,381	*$2.00*	*$2.00*	*$2.25*	$4.00
1955D................................	3,182,400	*2.00*	*2.00*	*2.25*	
1956 .... (669,384)	44,813,384	*2.00*	*2.00*	*2.00*	3.00
1956D................................	32,334,500	*2.00*	*2.00*	*2.00*	
1957 .... (1,247,952)	47,779,952	*2.00*	*2.00*	*2.00*	2.75
1957D................................	77,924,160	*2.00*	*2.00*	*2.00*	
1958 .... (875,652)	7,235,652	*2.00*	*2.00*	*2.25*	3.00
1958D................................	78,124,900	*2.00*	*2.00*	*2.00*	
1959 .... (1,149,291)	25,533,291	*2.00*	*2.00*	*2.00*	2.25
1959D................................	62,054,232	*2.00*	*2.00*	*2.00*	
1960 .... (1,691,602)	30,855,602	*2.00*	*2.00*	*2.00*	2.25
1960D................................	63,000,324	*2.00*	*2.00*	*2.00*	
1961 .... (3,028,244)	40,064,244	*2.00*	*2.00*	*2.00*	2.25
1961D................................	83,656,928	*2.00*	*2.00*	*2.00*	
1962 .... (3,218,019)	39,374,019	*2.00*	*2.00*	*2.00*	2.25
1962D................................	127,554,756	*2.00*	*2.00*	*2.00*	
1963 .... (3,075,645)	77,391,645	*2.00*	*2.00*	*2.00*	2.25
1963D................................	135,288,184	*2.00*	*2.00*	*2.00*	
1964 .... (3,950,762)	564,341,347	*2.00*	*2.00*	*2.00*	2.25
1964D................................	704,135,528	*2.00*	*2.00*	*2.00*	

Clad Coinage—1965 to Date

	Quan. Minted	MS-65	Proof-65
1965	1,819,717,540	$.25	
1966	821,101,500	.25	
1967	1,524,031,848	.25	
1968	220,731,500	.25	
1968D........	101,534,000	.25	
1968S Proof	(3,041,506)		$.35
1969	176,212,000	.25	
1969D........	114,372,000	.30	
1969S Proof	(2,934,631)		.35
1970	136,420,000	.25	
1970D........	417,341,364	.25	
1970S Proof	(2,632,810)		.40
1971	109,284,000	.25	
1971D........	258,634,428	.25	
1971S Proof	(3,220,733)		.35
1972	215,048,000	.25	
1972D........	311,067,732	.25	
1972S Proof	(3,260,996)		.35
1973	346,924,000	.25	
1973D........	232,977,400	.25	
1973S Proof	(2,760,339)		.35
1974.........	801,456,000	.25	
1974D	353,160,300	.25	
1974S Proof....	(2,612,568)		.40
Eagle Reverse Resumed			
(Dies slightly modified to lower relief)			
1977.........	468,556,000	.25	
1977D	256,524,978	.25	
1977S Proof....	(3,251,152)		.30
1978.........	521,452,000	$.25	
1978D	287,373,152	.25	
1978S Proof....	(3,127,781)		$.30
1979.........	515,708,000	.25	
1979D	489,789,780	.25	
1979S Proof....	(3,677,175)		
Filled S................			.40
Clear S................			2.00
1980P	635,832,000	.25	
1980D	518,327,487	.25	
1980S Proof....	(3,554,806)		.30
1981P	601,716,000	.25	
1981D	575,722,833	.25	
1981S Proof....	(4,063,083)		.35
1982P	500,931,000	.25	
1982D	480,042,788	.25	
1982S Proof....	(3,857,479)		.50
1983P		.25	
1983D		.25	
1983S Proof.............			.35

Italic prices indicate unsettled values due to fluctuating bullion market. See Bullion Chart.

QUARTER DOLLARS
BICENTENNIAL COINAGE DATED 1776-1976

	Quan. Minted	MS-65	Proof-65
1776-1976 Copper-nickel clad	809,784,016	$.25	
1776-1976D Copper-nickel clad	860,118,839	.25	
1776-1976S Copper-nickel clad	(7,059,099)		$.55
1776-1976S Silver clad	*11,000,000	1.00	
1776-1976S Silver clad	(*4,000,000)		1.50

*Approximate mintage. Not all released.

HALF DOLLARS — 1794 to Date

The half dollar, authorized by the Act of April 2, 1792, was not minted until December, 1794.

The weight of the half dollar was 208 grains and its fineness .8924 when first issued. This standard was not changed until 1837 when the law of January 18, 1837 specified 206¼ grains, .900 fine.

Arrows at the date in 1853 indicate the reduction of weight to 192 grains. During that year only, rays were added to the field on the reverse side. Arrows remained in 1854 and 1855.

In 1873 the weight was raised to 192.9 grains and arrows were again placed at the date.

FLOWING HAIR TYPE 1794-1795

AG-3 ABOUT GOOD—*Clear enough to identify.*
G-4 GOOD—*Date and letters sufficient to be readable. Main devices outlined, but lack details.*
VG-8 VERY GOOD—*Major details discernible. Letters well formed but worn.*
F-12 FINE—*Hair ends distinguishable. Top hairlines show, but otherwise worn smooth.*
VF-20 VERY FINE—*Hair in center shows some detail. Other details more bold.*
EF-40 EXTREMELY FINE—*Hair above head and down neck detailed with slight wear.*

2 Leaves under wings   3 Leaves under wings

	Quan. Minted	AG-3	G-4	VG-8	F-12	VF-20	EF-40
1794	23,464	$200.00	$400.00	$550.00	$800.00	$1,500	$2,800
1795 All kinds	299,680	125.00	250.00	350.00	450.00	750.00	1,500
1795 Recut date		125.00	250.00	375.00	475.00	800.00	1,600
1795 3 leaves under each wing		150.00	300.00	425.00	600.00	1,000	2,000

DRAPED BUST TYPE, SMALL EAGLE REVERSE 1796-1797

Grading same as above for About Good to Fine.

VF-20 VERY FINE—*Right side of drapery slightly worn. Left side to curls is smooth.*
EF-40 EXTREMELY FINE—*All lines in drapery on bust will show distinctly around to hair curls.*

HALF DOLLARS

1796, 15 Stars   1796, 16 Stars

	Quan. Minted	AG-3	G-4	VG-8	F-12	VF-20	EF-40
1796, 15 Stars	} 3,918	$3,500	$6,000	$8,000	$11,000	$15,000	$20,000
1796, 16 stars		3,500	6,000	8,000	11,000	15,000	20,000
1797, 15 stars		3,500	6,000	8,000	11,000	15,000	20,000

DRAPED BUST TYPE, HERALDIC EAGLE REVERSE 1801-1807

	Quan. Minted	G-4	VG-8	F-12	VF-20	EF-40	MS-60
1801	30,289	$75.00	$100.00	$200.00	$400.00	$700.00	$5,500
1802	29,890	65.00	95.00	175.00	300.00	550.00	4,500
1803	188,234	40.00	55.00	125.00	250.00	450.00	4,250

1805, 5 over 4   1806, 6 over 5

1805, 5 over 4	} 211,722	50.00	65.00	130.00	275.00	550.00	4,750
1805 Normal date		40.00	50.00	80.00	225.00	400.00	3,750
1806		40.00	50.00	80.00	225.00	400.00	3,750
1806, 6 over 5	} 839,576	40.00	50.00	90.00	250.00	425.00	3,750
1806, 6 over inverted 6		45.00	55.00	100.00	275.00	450.00	4,000
1807	301,076	35.00	45.00	75.00	200.00	400.00	3,750

CAPPED BUST TYPE, Lettered Edge 1807-1836

John Reich designed this Capped Head concept of Liberty. The head of Liberty facing left was used on all U.S. coin denominations for the next thirty years.

HALF DOLLARS

G-4 GOOD—*Date and letters readable. Bust worn smooth with outline distinct.*
VG-8 VERY GOOD—*LIBERTY visible but faint. Legends distinguishable. Clasp at shoulder visible. Curl above it nearly smooth.*
F-12 FINE—*Clasp and adjacent curl clearly outlined with slight details.*
VF-20 VERY FINE—*Clasp at shoulder clear. Curl has wear only on highest point. Hair over brow distinguishable.*
EF-40 EXTREMELY FINE—*Clasp and adjacent curl fairly sharp. Brow and hair above distinct. Curls well defined.*
MS-60 UNCIRCULATED—*No trace of wear. Light blemishes.*

First style 1807-1808

	Quan. Minted	G-4	VG-8	F-12	VF-20	EF-40	MS-60
1807	750,500	$16.00	$21.00	$35.00	$75.00	$150.00	$600.00
1808, 8 over 7	} 1,368,600	16.00	20.00	30.00	50.00	90.00	500.00
1808		16.00	20.00	25.00	40.00	70.00	410.00

Remodeled Portrait and Eagle 1809-1834

1809	1,405,810	14.00	17.00	20.00	30.00	65.00	350.00
1810	1,276,276	13.00	16.00	19.00	25.00	55.00	375.00
1811	1,203,644	13.00	15.00	18.00	25.00	55.00	350.00

 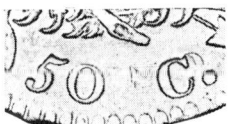 

1812, 2 over 1   1813, 50 C. over UNI   1814, 4 over 3

1812, 2 over 1	} 1,628,059	14.00	16.00	25.00	50.00	100.00	400.00
1812 Normal		13.00	15.00	18.00	25.00	55.00	350.00
1813	} 1,241,903	13.00	15.00	18.00	25.00	55.00	335.00
1813, 50C over UNI		15.00	18.00	32.00	50.00	90.00	410.00
1814, 4 over 3	} 1,039,075	13.00	16.00	21.00	30.00	65.00	335.00
1814 Normal		13.00	15.00	18.00	25.00	55.00	335.00

HALF DOLLARS

1817, 7 over 3   1817, 7 over 4   1817 Punctuated Date

	Quan. Minted	G-4	VG-8	F-12	VF-20	EF-40	MS-60
1815, 5 over 2	47,150	$150.00	$200.00	$275.00	$400.00	$600.00	$1,800
1817, 7 over 3		14.00	25.00	75.00	125.00	210.00	600.00
1817, 7 over 4				1,500	—	—	
1817 dated 181.7	1,215,567	13.00	16.00	22.00	40.00	80.00	375.00
1817 Normal		13.00	15.00	18.00	25.00	55.00	335.00

1818, 2nd 8 over 7   1819, 9 over 8   1820, 20 over 19

1818, 8 over 7	1,960,322	13.00	15.00	18.00	25.00	55.00	375.00
1818 Normal		13.00	15.00	18.00	25.00	55.00	335.00
1819 9 over 8	2,208,00	13.00	15.00	18.00	25.00	55.00	350.00
1819 Normal		13.00	15.00	18.00	25.00	55.00	350.00
1820, 20 over 19	751,122	13.00	15.00	18.00	25.00	55.00	375.00
1820 Normal		12.00	14.00	17.00	24.00	50.00	375.00
1821	1,305,797	12.00	14.00	17.00	24.00	50.00	350.00
1822, 2 over 1	1,559,573	18.00	25.00	40.00	50.00	90.00	400.00
1822 Normal		12.00	14.00	17.00	24.00	50.00	350.00
1823 Normal	1,694,200	12.00	14.00	17.00	24.00	50.00	335.00

"Various Dates"   1824, 4 over 1   1828 Curl Base, Knob 2   1828 Square Base 2
1828 Square Base 2
(probably 4 over
2 over 0)

1824 over various dates	3,504,954	12.00	14.00	17.00	24.00	50.00	335.00
1824, 4 over 1		12.00	14.00	17.00	24.00	50.00	335.00
1824 Normal		12.00	14.00	17.00	24.00	50.00	350.00
1825	2,943,166	12.00	14.00	17.00	24.00	50.00	335.00
1826	4,004,180	12.00	14.00	17.00	24.00	50.00	335.00
1827, 7 over 6	5,493,400	12.00	14.00	17.00	24.00	50.00	350.00
1827 Normal		12.00	14.00	17.00	24.00	50.00	335.00
1828 All kinds	3,075,200						
1828 Curl base no knob 2		12.00	14.00	17.00	24.00	50.00	335.00
1828 Curl base knob 2		16.00	20.00	27.00	40.00	60.00	400.00
1828 Sq. base		12.00	14.00	17.00	24.00	50.00	350.00

HALF DOLLARS

	Quan. Minted	G-4	VG-8	F-12	VF-20	EF-40	MS-60
1829, 9 over 7	} 3,712,156	$12.00	$14.00	$17.00	$24.00	$50.00	$350.00
1829 Normal		12.00	14.00	17.00	24.00	50.00	350.00
1830	4,764,800	12.00	14.00	17.00	24.00	50.00	335.00
1831	5,873,660	12.00	14.00	17.00	24.00	50.00	335.00
1832	4,797,000	12.00	14.00	17.00	24.00	50.00	335.00
1833	5,206,000	12.00	14.00	17.00	24.00	50.00	335.00
1834	6,412,004	12.00	14.00	17.00	24.00	50.00	350.00
1835	5,352,006	12.00	14.00	17.00	24.00	50.00	335.00
1836	} 6,545,000	12.00	14.00	17.00	24.00	50.00	335.00
1836, 50 over 00		15.00	20.00	25.00	40.00	70.00	425.00

Reeded Edge, Reverse "50 CENTS" 1836-1837

G-4 GOOD—*LIBERTY discernible on headband.*
VG-8 VERY GOOD—*Minimum of 3 letters in LIBERTY must be clear.*
F-12 FINE—*LIBERTY complete.*
VF-20 VERY FINE—*LIBERTY is sharp. Shoulder clasp is clear.*
EF-40 EXTREMELY FINE—*LIBERTY sharp and strong. Hair details show.*
MS-60 UNCIRCULATED—*No trace of wear. Light blemishes.*

| 1836 | 1,200 | 175.00 | 225.00 | 300.00 | 500.00 | 900.00 | 2,200 |
| 1837 | 3,629,820 | 18.00 | 20.00 | 25.00 | 45.00 | 100.00 | 600.00 |

Reeded Edge, Reverse "HALF DOL." 1838-1839

In 1838-39 the mint mark appears on the obverse; thereafter it is on the reverse below the eagle.

1838	3,546,000	18.00	20.00	25.00	45.00	100.00	650.00
1838O	(20)						30,000
1839	1,392,976	18.00	20.00	25.00	45.00	100.00	650.00
1839O	178,976	55.00	80.00	125.00	185.00	275.00	2,400

LIBERTY SEATED TYPE 1839-1891
No Motto Above Eagle 1839-1853

G-4 GOOD—*Scant rim. LIBERTY on shield worn off. Date and letters readable.*
VG-8 VERY GOOD—*Rim fairly defined. At least 3 letters in LIBERTY are evident.*
F-12 FINE—*LIBERTY complete, but weak.*
VF-20 VERY FINE—*LIBERTY mostly sharp.*
EF-40 EXTREMELY FINE—*LIBERTY entirely sharp. Scroll edges and clasp distinct.*
MS-60 UNCIRCULATED—*No trace of wear. Light blemishes.*

HALF DOLLARS

	Quan. Minted	G-4	VG-8	F-12	VF-20	EF-40	MS-60
1839 No drapery from elbow		$17.00	$25.00	$40.00	$75.00	$250.00	$3,600

Drapery from Elbow starting 1839   1842 Small Date

Date	Quan. Minted	G-4	VG-8	F-12	VF-20	EF-40	MS-60
1839	1,972,400	9.00	11.00	16.00	22.00	40.00	375.00
1840	1,435,008	8.00	10.00	15.00	20.00	37.00	375.00
1840O	855,100	8.00	10.00	15.00	20.00	37.00	375.00
1841	310,000	8.00	10.00	15.00	20.00	45.00	400.00
1841O	401,000	8.00	10.00	15.00	20.00	37.00	375.00
1842 Sm. date	} 2,012,764	8.00	10.00	15.00	21.00	37.00	375.00
1842 Med. date		8.00	10.00	15.00	21.00	37.00	375.00
1842O Small date	203,000	55.00	100.00	150.00	250.00	500.00	—
1842O Med. date	754,000	8.00	9.00	13.00	20.00	35.00	375.00
1843	3,844,000	8.00	9.00	13.00	20.00	35.00	375.00
1843O	2,268,000	8.00	9.00	13.00	20.00	35.00	375.00
1844	1,766,000	8.00	9.00	13.00	20.00	35.00	375.00
1844O	2,005,000	8.00	9.00	13.00	20.00	35.00	375.00
1845	589,000	8.00	9.00	13.00	20.00	35.00	375.00
1845O	2,094,000	8.00	9.00	13.00	20.00	35.00	375.00
1846 All kinds	2,210,000	8.00	9.00	13.00	18.00	35.00	375.00
1846 over horizontal 6 (error)		15.00	30.00	45.00	75.00	100.00	550.00
1846O	2,304,000	8.00	9.00	13.00	18.00	35.00	375.00
1847	1,156,000	8.00	9.00	13.00	18.00	35.00	375.00
1847O	2,584,000	8.00	9.00	13.00	18.00	35.00	375.00
1848	580,000	12.00	17.00	25.00	35.00	60.00	450.00
1848O	3,180,000	8.00	9.00	13.00	18.00	35.00	375.00
1849	1,252,000	8.00	9.00	13.00	18.00	35.00	375.00
1849O	2,310,000	8.00	9.00	13.00	18.00	35.00	375.00
1850	227,000	15.00	21.00	35.00	45.00	80.00	450.00
1850O	2,456,000	8.00	9.00	13.00	18.00	35.00	375.00
1851	200,750	15.00	21.00	35.00	45.00	80.00	450.00
1851O	402,000	8.00	9.00	13.00	18.00	35.00	375.00
1852	77,130	25.00	35.00	60.00	110.00	200.00	600.00
1852O	144,000	15.00	21.00	35.00	45.00	80.00	450.00
1853O		2,000	4,000	10,000	15,000		

HALF DOLLARS

Arrows at Date, Rays Around Eagle 1853 Only

	Quan. Minted	G-4	VG-8	F-12	VF-20	EF-40	MS-60
1853	3,532,708	$7.00	$9.00	$15.00	$45.00	$135.00	$1,400
1853O All kinds	1,328,000	7.00	9.00	15.00	45.00	135.00	1,600

Arrows at Date, No Rays 1854-1855

1854	2,982,000	6.00	7.00	12.00	21.00	50.00	650.00
1854O	5,240,000	6.00	7.00	12.00	21.00	50.00	650.00
1855 over 1854	} 759,500		25.00	50.00	100.00	200.00	900.00
1855 Normal date		6.00	7.00	12.00	21.00	50.00	650.00
1855O	3,688,000	6.00	7.00	12.00	21.00	50.00	650.00
1855S	129,950	50.00	70.00	120.00	250.00	350.00	1,900

No Arrows at Date 1856-1866

1856	938,000	7.00	8.00	12.00	17.00	35.00	350.00
1856O	2,658,000	7.00	8.00	12.00	17.00	35.00	350.00
1856S	211,000	9.00	11.00	17.00	40.00	80.00	500.00
1857	1,988,000	7.00	8.00	12.00	17.00	35.00	350.00
1857O	818,000	7.00	8.00	12.00	17.00	35.00	350.00
1857S	158,000	11.00	16.00	20.00	45.00	90.00	525.00

	Quan. Minted	G-4	VG-8	F-12	VF-20	EF-40	MS-60	Proof-60
1858	4,226,000	$7.00	$8.00	$12.00	$17.00	$35.00	$350.00	$600.00
1858O	7,294,000	7.00	8.00	12.00	17.00	35.00	350.00	
1858S	476,000	9.00	11.00	15.00	24.00	45.00	550.00	
1859 (800)	748,000	7.00	8.00	12.00	17.00	35.00	350.00	450.00
1859O	2,834,000	7.00	8.00	12.00	17.00	35.00	350.00	
1859S	566,000	9.00	11.00	15.00	25.00	70.00	500.00	
1860 (1,000)	303,700	9.00	11.00	14.00	22.00	40.00	400.00	375.00
1860O	1,290,000	7.00	8.00	12.00	17.00	35.00	350.00	
1860S	472,000	9.00	11.00	14.00	20.00	35.00	375.00	
1861 (1,000)	2,888,400	7.00	8.00	12.00	17.00	35.00	350.00	375.00
1861O	2,532,633	7.00	8.00	12.00	17.00	35.00	350.00	
1861S	939,500	7.00	8.00	12.00	17.00	35.00	350.00	
1862 (550)	253,550	10.00	14.00	18.00	35.00	50.00	450.00	375.00
1862S	1,352,000	7.00	8.00	12.00	17.00	35.00	350.00	
1863 (460)	503,660	9.00	11.00	14.00	22.00	40.00	400.00	375.00
1863S	916,000	7.00	8.00	12.00	17.00	35.00	350.00	
1864 (470)	379,570	9.00	11.00	14.00	22.00	40.00	400.00	375.00
1864S	658,000	7.00	8.00	12.00	17.00	35.00	350.00	
1865 (500)	511,900	9.00	11.00	14.00	22.00	40.00	400.00	375.00
1865S	675,000	7.00	8.00	12.00	17.00	35.00	350.00	
1866S No motto	60,000	23.00	39.00	70.00	120.00	175.00	2,000	

HALF DOLLARS

Motto "In God We Trust" Added Above Eagle 1866-1873

	Quan. Minted	G-4	VG-8	F-12	VF-20	EF-40	MS-60	Proof-60
1866 .... (725)	745,625	$5.00	$6.00	$10.00	$15.00	$30.00	$350.00	$350.00
1866S	994,000	5.00	6.00	10.00	15.00	30.00	375.00	
1867 .... (625)	449,925	6.00	7.00	11.00	16.00	35.00	400.00	350.00
1867S	1,196,000	5.00	6.00	10.00	15.00	30.00	375.00	
1868 .... (600)	418,200	5.00	6.00	10.00	15.00	30.00	350.00	350.00
1868S	1,160,000	5.00	6.00	10.00	15.00	30.00	375.00	
1869 .... (600)	795,900	5.00	6.00	10.00	15.00	30.00	350.00	350.00
1869S	656,000	5.00	6.00	10.00	15.00	30.00	375.00	
1870 .... (1,000)	634,900	5.00	6.00	10.00	15.00	30.00	350.00	350.00
1870CC	54,617	70.00	125.00	275.00	450.00	850.00	———	
1870S	1,004,000	5.00	6.00	10.00	15.00	30.00	375.00	
1871 .... (960)	1,204,560	5.00	6.00	10.00	15.00	30.00	350.00	350.00
1871CC	153,950	24.00	35.00	65.00	120.00	250.00	1,700	
1871S	2,178,000	5.00	6.00	10.00	15.00	30.00	375.00	
1872 .... (950)	881,550	5.00	6.00	10.00	15.00	30.00	325.00	350.00
1872CC	257,000	15.00	25.00	40.00	90.00	150.00	1,100	
1872S	580,000	6.00	7.00	11.00	15.00	30.00	400.00	
1873 .... (600)	801,800	5.00	6.00	10.00	15.00	30.00	400.00	350.00
1873CC	122,500	23.00	37.00	80.00	135.00	200.00	1,500	

Arrows at Date 1873-1874

1873 .... (550)	1,815,700	10.00	14.00	18.00	45.00	125.00	700.00	650.00
1873CC	214,560	16.00	25.00	50.00	90.00	150.00	2,250	
1873S	228,000	14.00	20.00	30.00	50.00	125.00	700.00	
1874 .... (700)	2,360,300	10.00	14.00	18.00	45.00	125.00	700.00	650.00
1874CC	59,000	21.00	38.00	100.00	150.00	300.00	1,400	
1874S	394,000	14.00	20.00	35.00	60.00	125.00	1,300	

No Arrows at Date 1875-1891

1875 .... (700)	6,027,500	5.00	6.00	10.00	15.00	27.00	325.00	350.00
1875CC	1,008,000	5.00	7.00	11.00	20.00	35.00	375.00	

[106]

HALF DOLLARS

	Quan. Minted	G-4	VG-8	F-12	VF-20	EF-40	MS-60	Proof-60
1875S	3,200,000	$5.00	$6.00	$10.00	$15.00	$27.00	$325.00	
1876 (1,150)	8,419,150	5.00	6.00	10.00	15.00	27.00	325.00	$350.00
1876CC	1,956,000	5.00	6.00	10.00	16.00	30.00	400.00	
1876S	4,528,000	5.00	6.00	10.00	15.00	27.00	325.00	
1877 (510)	8,304,510	5.00	6.00	10.00	15.00	27.00	325.00	350.00
1877CC	1,420,000	5.00	6.00	10.00	16.00	32.00	375.00	
1877S	5,356,000	5.00	6.00	10.00	15.00	27.00	325.00	
1878 (800)	1,378,400	5.00	6.00	10.00	15.00	27.00	325.00	350.00
1878CC	62,000	60.00	120.00	175.00	270.00	450.00	1,800	
1878S	12,000	800.00	1,200	1,800	2,750	4,000	7,000	
1879 (1,100)	5,900	60.00	75.00	100.00	125.00	180.00	550.00	450.00
1880 (1,355)	9,755	50.00	65.00	90.00	110.00	150.00	500.00	450.00
1881 (975)	10,975	50.00	65.00	90.00	110.00	150.00	500.00	450.00
1882 (1,100)	5,500	60.00	75.00	100.00	125.00	180.00	550.00	450.00
1883 (1,039)	9,039	50.00	65.00	90.00	110.00	150.00	500.00	450.00
1884 (875)	5,275	60.00	75.00	100.00	125.00	180.00	600.00	450.00
1885 (930)	6,130	50.00	65.00	90.00	110.00	150.00	600.00	450.00
1886 (886)	5,886	50.00	65.00	90.00	110.00	150.00	600.00	450.00
1887 (710)	5,710	50.00	65.00	90.00	110.00	150.00	600.00	450.00
1888 (832)	12,833	45.00	60.00	75.00	100.00	140.00	500.00	450.00
1889 (711)	12,711	45.00	60.00	75.00	100.00	140.00	500.00	450.00
1890 (590)	12,590	45.00	60.00	75.00	100.00	140.00	500.00	450.00
1891 (600)	200,600	5.00	6.00	10.00	16.00	30.00	325.00	450.00

BARBER or LIBERTY HEAD TYPE 1892-1915

Like the dime and quarter dollar, this type was designed by Charles E. Barber, whose initial B is on the truncation of the neck.

G-4 GOOD—*Date and legends readable. LIBERTY worn off headband.*
VG-8 VERY GOOD—*Minimum of 3 letters readable in LIBERTY.*
F-12 FINE—*LIBERTY completely readable, but not sharp.*
VF-20 VERY FINE—*All letters in LIBERTY evenly plain.*
EF-40 EXTREMELY FINE—*LIBERTY bold, and its ribbon distinct.*
MS-60 UNCIRCULATED—*No trace of wear. Light blemishes.*

Mint mark location on reverse below eagle.

	Quan. Minted	G-4	VG-8	F-12	VF-20	EF-40	MS-60	Proof-63
1892 (1,245)	935,245	$6.00	$9.00	$12.00	$25.00	$85.00	$350.00	$700.00
1892O	390,000	45.00	55.00	80.00	135.00	225.00	550.00	
1892S	1,029,028	45.00	55.00	80.00	135.00	225.00	550.00	
1893 (792)	1,826,792	5.00	6.50	12.00	25.00	85.00	325.00	700.00
1893O	1,389,000	8.00	12.00	20.00	45.00	140.00	400.00	
1893S	740,000	22.50	30.00	45.00	110.00	180.00	550.00	
1894 (972)	1,148,972	5.00	6.50	12.00	27.00	85.00	325.00	700.00
1894O	2,138,000	5.00	6.50	12.00	27.00	90.00	350.00	
1894S	4,048,690	5.00	6.50	12.00	27.00	90.00	350.00	

Italic prices indicate unsettled values due to fluctuating bullion market. See Bullion Chart.

HALF DOLLARS

	Quan. Minted	G-4	VG-8	F-12	VF-20	EF-40	MS-60	Proof-63
1895 ...... (880)	1,835,218	$5.00	$6.50	$12.00	$27.00	$85.00	$325.00	$700.00
1895O	1,766,000	5.00	6.50	12.00	27.00	90.00	425.00	
1895S	1,108,086	7.50	11.00	19.00	40.00	90.00	325.00	
1896 ...... (762)	950,762	5.00	6.50	12.00	27.00	85.00	325.00	700.00
1896O	924,000	7.50	12.00	20.00	50.00	140.00	600.00	
1896S	1,140,948	25.00	30.00	42.50	95.00	175.00	675.00	
1897 ...... (731)	2,480,731	*4.00*	*4.25*	8.00	17.00	65.00	325.00	700.00
1897O	632,000	25.00	30.00	42.50	110.00	240.00	850.00	
1897S	933,900	45.00	50.00	65.00	120.00	225.00	750.00	
1898 ...... (735)	2,956,735	*4.00*	*4.25*	8.00	17.00	65.00	325.00	700.00
1898O	874,000	6.50	9.00	15.00	40.00	120.00	425.00	
1898S	2,358,550	*4.50*	5.00	12.00	25.00	85.00	400.00	
1899 ...... (846)	5,538,846	*4.00*	*4.25*	8.00	17.00	65.00	325.00	700.00
1899O	1,724,000	*4.50*	5.00	12.00	25.00	110.00	425.00	
1899S	1,686,411	*4.50*	5.00	12.00	25.00	85.00	325.00	
1900 ...... (912)	4,762,912	*4.00*	*4.25*	8.00	17.00	65.00	325.00	700.00
1900O	2,744,000	*4.50*	5.00	12.00	25.00	110.00	425.00	
1900S	2,560,322	*4.50*	5.00	12.00	25.00	85.00	325.00	
1901 ...... (813)	4,268,813	*4.00*	*4.25*	8.00	17.00	65.00	325.00	700.00
1901O	1,124,000	*4.75*	6.00	15.00	30.00	150.00	700.00	
1901S	847,044	7.00	10.00	20.00	70.00	225.00	800.00	
1902 ...... (777)	4,922,777	*4.00*	*4.25*	8.00	17.00	65.00	325.00	700.00
1902O	2,526,000	*4.50*	5.00	12.00	25.00	90.00	425.00	
1902S	1,460,670	*4.50*	5.00	12.00	25.00	90.00	400.00	
1903 ...... (755)	2,278,755	*4.00*	*4.25*	8.00	17.00	65.00	325.00	700.00
1903O	2,100,000	*4.50*	5.00	12.00	25.00	95.00	385.00	
1903S	1,920,772	*4.50*	5.00	12.00	25.00	95.00	385.00	
1904 ...... (670)	2,992,670	*4.00*	*4.25*	8.00	17.00	65.00	325.00	700.00
1904O	1,117,600	5.00	6.50	14.00	30.00	160.00	650.00	
1904S	553,038	6.50	8.00	20.00	65.00	175.00	625.00	
1905 ...... (727)	662,727	*4.00*	*4.25*	8.00	17.00	65.00	325.00	700.00
1905O	505,000	5.50	6.50	16.00	40.00	135.00	450.00	
1905S	2,494,000	*4.50*	5.00	12.00	25.00	85.00	400.00	
1906 ...... (675)	2,638,675	*4.00*	*4.25*	8.00	17.00	65.00	325.00	700.00
1906D	4,028,000	*4.25*	5.00	12.00	20.00	70.00	325.00	
1906O	2,446,000	*4.25*	*4.50*	10.00	18.00	70.00	350.00	
1906S	1,740,154	*4.25*	*4.50*	10.00	22.00	85.00	370.00	
1907 ...... (575)	2,598,575	*4.00*	*4.25*	8.00	17.00	65.00	325.00	700.00
1907D	3,856,000	*4.25*	*4.50*	10.00	18.00	70.00	325.00	
1907O	3,946,600	*4.25*	*4.50*	10.00	18.00	70.00	325.00	
1907S	1,250,000	*4.25*	*4.50*	12.00	20.00	100.00	400.00	
1908 ...... (545)	1,354,545	*4.00*	*4.25*	8.00	17.00	65.00	325.00	700.00
1908D	3,280,000	*4.25*	*4.50*	9.00	18.00	65.00	325.00	
1908O	5,360,000	*4.25*	*4.50*	9.00	18.00	65.00	325.00	
1908S	1,644,828	*4.25*	*4.50*	10.00	18.00	90.00	350.00	
1909 ...... (650)	2,368,650	*4.00*	*4.25*	8.00	17.00	65.00	325.00	700.00
1909O	925,400	*4.50*	5.00	14.00	27.50	110.00	425.00	
1909S	1,764,000	*4.25*	*4.50*	10.00	19.00	85.00	350.00	
1910 ...... (551)	418,551	*4.50*	6.00	15.00	30.00	120.00	385.00	750.00
1910S	1,948,000	*4.25*	*4.50*	10.00	19.00	85.00	350.00	
1911 ...... (543)	1,406,543	*4.00*	*4.25*	8.00	17.00	65.00	325.00	700.00
1911D	695,080	*4.25*	*4.50*	10.00	18.00	70.00	350.00	
1911S	1,272,000	*4.25*	*4.50*	10.00	18.00	70.00	350.00	
1912 ...... (700)	1,550,700	*4.00*	*4.25*	8.00	17.00	65.00	325.00	700.00
1912D	2,300,800	*4.25*	*4.50*	9.00	18.00	70.00	325.00	
1912S	1,370,000	*4.25*	*4.50*	9.00	18.00	70.00	325.00	

Italic prices indicate unsettled values due to fluctuating bullion market. See Bullion Chart.

HALF DOLLARS

	Quan. Minted	G-4	VG-8	F-12	VF-20	EF-40	MS-60	Proof-63
1913 (627)	188,627	$9.00	$11.00	$18.00	$45.00	$120.00	$500.00	$800.00
1913D	534,000	*4.50*	5.00	12.00	22.00	80.00	350.00	
1913S	604,000	*4.50*	5.00	13.00	35.00	70.00	350.00	
1914 (380)	124,610	11.00	13.50	25.00	70.00	160.00	500.00	850.00
1914S	992,000	*4.25*	*4.50*	12.00	22.00	70.00	350.00	
1915 (450)	138,450	10.00	12.50	22.50	50.00	125.00	500.00	850.00
1915D	1,170,400	*4.00*	*4.25*	8.00	17.00	65.00	325.00	
1915S	1,604,000	*4.00*	*4.25*	8.00	17.00	65.00	325.00	

LIBERTY WALKING TYPE 1916-1947

This type was designed by A. A. Weinman. The designer's monogram AAW appears under the tip of the wing feathers. On the 1916 coins and some of the 1917 coins the mint mark is located on the obverse below the motto.

G-4 GOOD—*Rims are defined. Motto IN GOD WE TRUST readable.*
VG-8 VERY GOOD—*Motto is distinct. About half of skirt lines at left are clear.*
F-12 FINE—*All skirt lines evident, but worn in spots. Details in sandal below motto are clear.*
VF-20 VERY FINE—*Skirt lines sharp including leg area. Little wear on breast and right arm.*
EF-40 EXTREMELY FINE—*All skirt lines bold.*
MS-60 UNCIRCULATED—*No trace of wear. Light blemishes.*
MS-65 CHOICE UNCIRCULATED—*No trace of wear. Barely noticeable blemishes.*

  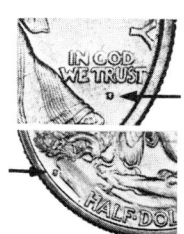

Mint mark location.

Choice uncirculated well struck specimens are worth more than values listed.

	Quan. Minted	G-4	VG-8	F-12	VF-20	EF-40	MS-60	Proof-65
1916	608,000	$12.00	$14.00	$33.00	$65.00	$120.00	$240.00	
1916D (Obv.)	1,014,400	8.00	12.00	16.00	35.00	75.00	225.00	
1916S (Obv.)	508,000	17.00	25.00	65.00	135.00	225.00	450.00	
1917	12,292,000	*4.00*	*4.00*	5.00	9.00	18.00	85.00	
1917D (Obv.)	765,400	5.00	6.50	16.00	45.00	85.00	300.00	
1917D (Rev.)	1,940,000	*4.00*	*4.25*	10.00	25.00	70.00	310.00	
1917S (Obv.)	952,000	5.00	7.00	20.00	80.00	215.00	625.00	
1917S (Rev.)	5,554,000	*4.00*	*4.25*	5.00	14.00	25.00	150.00	
1918	6,634,00	*4.00*	*4.00*	5.00	24.00	70.00	225.00	
1918D	3,853,040	*4.00*	*4.00*	5.00	25.00	75.00	425.00	
1918S	10,282,000	*4.00*	*4.00*	5.00	15.00	27.50	150.00	
1919	962,000	5.00	7.00	10.00	60.00	210.00	625.00	

Italic prices indicate unsettled values due to fluctuating bullion market. See Bullion Chart.

HALF DOLLARS

	Quan. Minted	G-4	VG-8	F-12	VF-20	EF-40	MS-60	Proof-65
1919D	1,165,000	$4.50	$6.00	$9.00	$75.00	$225.00	$1,300	
1919S	1,552,000	4.00	5.00	8.00	55.00	200.00	1,100	
1920	6,372,000	4.00	4.00	4.25	12.00	30.00	150.00	
1920D	1,551,000	4.00	4.00	12.00	60.00	150.00	625.00	
1920S	4,624,000	4.00	4.00	7.50	20.00	62.50	500.00	
1921	246,000	30.00	50.00	100.00	225.00	575.00	1,250	
1921D	208,000	50.00	65.00	135.00	300.00	625.00	1,400	
1921S	548,000	7.00	12.00	20.00	115.00	625.00	4,000	
1923S	2,178,000	4.00	4.00	5.00	22.50	80.00	550.00	
1927S	2,392,000	4.00	4.00	4.50	13.00	45.00	435.00	
1928S	1,940,000	4.00	4.00	4.50	15.00	55.00	475.00	
1929D	1,001,200	4.00	4.00	4.50	9.00	40.00	225.00	
1929S	1,902,000	4.00	4.00	4.50	8.50	35.00	225.00	
1933S	1,786,000	4.00	4.00	4.50	6.00	21.00	195.00	
1934	6,964,000	4.00	4.00	4.00	4.00	7.00	50.00	
1934D	2,361,400	4.00	4.00	4.00	4.00	16.50	100.00	
1934S	3,652,000	4.00	4.00	4.00	4.00	12.50	195.00	
1935	9,162,000	4.00	4.00	4.00	4.00	6.00	37.50	
1935D	3,003,800	4.00	4.00	4.00	4.00	15.00	110.00	
1935S	3,854,000	4.00	4.00	4.00	4.00	12.00	125.00	
1936 .... (3,901)	12,617,901	4.00	4.00	4.00	4.00	6.00	35.00	$900.00
1936D	4,252,400	4.00	4.00	4.00	4.00	12.00	70.00	
1936S	3,884,000	4.00	4.00	4.00	4.00	12.00	85.00	
1937 ..... (5,728)	9,527,728	4.00	4.00	4.00	4.00	6.00	37.50	750.00
1937D	1,676,000	4.00	4.00	4.00	4.00	15.00	135.00	
1937S	2,090,000	4.00	4.00	4.00	4.00	12.00	95.00	
1938 ..... (8,152)	4,118,152	4.00	4.00	4.00	4.00	7.00	60.00	500.00
1938D	491,600	12.50	13.50	17.50	22.50	55.00	250.00	
1939 ..... (8,808)	6,820,808	4.00	4.00	4.00	4.00	7.00	50.00	450.00
1939D	4,267,800	4.00	4.00	4.00	4.00	8.00	45.00	
1939S	2,552,000	4.00	4.00	4.00	4.00	9.00	70.00	

	Quan. Minted	VG-8	F-12	VF-20	EF-40	MS-60	MS-65	Proof-65
1940 ... (11,279)	9,167,279	$4.00	$4.00	$4.00	$5.00	$27.50	$150.00	$400.00
1940S	4,550,000	4.00	4.00	4.00	6.00	55.00	375.00	
1941 .. (15,412)	24,207,412	4.00	4.00	4.00	4.00	20.00	115.00	350.00
1941D	11,248,400	4.00	4.00	4.00	4.00	32.50	175.00	
1941S	8,098,000	4.00	4.00	4.00	4.00	90.00	400.00	
1942 .. (21,120)	47,839,120	4.00	4.00	4.00	4.00	20.00	115.00	350.00
1942D	10,973,800	4.00	4.00	4.00	4.00	40.00	210.00	
1942S	12,708,000	4.00	4.00	4.00	4.00	50.00	300.00	
1943	53,190,000	4.00	4.00	4.00	4.00	20.00	115.00	
1943D	11,346,000	4.00	4.00	4.00	4.00	42.50	225.00	
1943S	13,450,000	4.00	4.00	4.00	4.00	55.00	250.00	
1944	28,206,000	4.00	4.00	4.00	4.00	20.00	115.00	
1944D	9,769,000	4.00	4.00	4.00	4.00	30.00	150.00	
1944S	8,904,000	4.00	4.00	4.00	4.00	45.00	225.00	
1945	31,502,000	4.00	4.00	4.00	4.00	20.00	115.00	
1945D	9,966,800	4.00	4.00	4.00	4.00	30.00	150.00	
1945S	10,156,000	4.00	4.00	4.00	4.00	40.00	200.00	
1946	12,118,000	4.00	4.00	4.00	4.00	22.50	165.00	
1946D	2,151,000	4.00	4.00	4.00	4.00	30.00	125.00	
1946S	3,724,000	4.00	4.00	4.00	4.00	30.00	125.00	
1947	4,094,000	4.00	4.00	4.00	4.00	45.00	225.00	
1947D	3,900,600	4.00	4.00	4.00	4.00	40.00	225.00	

Italic prices indicate unsettled values due to fluctuating bullion market. See Bullion Chart.

HALF DOLLARS
FRANKLIN-LIBERTY BELL TYPE 1948-1963

The Benjamin Franklin half dollar and the Roosevelt dime were both designed by John R. Sinnock. His initials appear below the shoulder.

VF-20 VERY FINE—*At least half of the lower and upper incused lines on the rim of the bell must show.*
EF-40 EXTREMELY FINE—*Wear spots appear at top of end curls and hair back of ears. On reverse, Liberty Bell will show wear at top and on lettering.*
MS-63 SELECT UNCIRCULATED—*No trace of wear. Light blemishes. Attractive mint luster.*
MS-65 CHOICE UNCIRCULATED—*No trace of wear. Barely noticeable blemishes.*

Mint mark location

Choice, well struck uncirculated halves command higher prices.

	Quan. Minted	VF-20	EF-40	MS-63	MS-65	Proof-65
1948	3,006,814	$4.00	$4.00	$10.00	$20.00	
1948D	4,028,600	4.00	4.00	8.00	20.00	
1949	5,614,000	4.00	4.00	35.00	75.00	
1949D	4,120,600	4.00	4.00	32.50	70.00	
1949S	3,744,000	4.00	4.00	110.00	225.00	
1950	(51,386) 7,793,509	4.00	4.00	40.00	55.00	$200.00
1950D	8,031,600	4.00	4.00	20.00	35.00	
1951	(57,500) 16,859,602	4.00	4.00	8.00	18.00	125.00
1951D	9,475,200	4.00	4.00	32.50	65.00	
1951S	13,696,000	4.00	4.00	22.50	45.00	
1952	(81,980) 21,274,073	4.00	4.00	8.00	20.00	70.00
1952D	25,395,600	4.00	4.00	8.00	20.00	
1952S	5,526,000	4.00	4.00	22.50	55.00	
1953	(128,800) 2,796,920	4.00	4.00	20.00	40.00	45.00
1953D	20,900,400	4.00	4.00	6.50	15.00	
1953S	4,148,000	4.00	4.00	10.00	30.00	
1954	(233,300) 13,421,503	4.00	4.00	6.00	12.00	32.00
1954D	25,445,580	4.00	4.00	6.00	12.00	
1954S	4,993,400	4.00	4.00	6.50	20.00	
1955	(378,200) 2,876,381	4.00	4.00	7.50	13.00	25.00
1956	(669,384) 4,701,384	4.00	4.00	7.50	13.00	12.00
1957	(1,247,952) 6,361,952	4.00	4.00	5.50	11.00	9.00
1957D	19,966,850	4.00	4.00	5.00	6.00	
1958	(875,652) 4,917,652	*4.00*	*4.00*	6.00	9.00	11.00
1958D	23,962,412	*4.00*	*4.00*	*4.25*	*4.50*	
1959	(1,149,291) 7,349,291	*4.00*	*4.00*	*4.25*	*4.50*	9.00
1959D	13,053,750	*4.00*	*4.00*	*4.25*	*4.50*	
1960	(1,691,602) 7,715,602	*4.00*	*4.00*	*4.25*	*4.50*	7.00
1960D	18,215,812	*4.00*	*4.00*	*4.25*	*4.50*	

Italic prices indicate unsettled values due to fluctuating bullion market. See Bullion Chart.

HALF DOLLARS

	Quan. Minted		VF-20	EF-40	MS-63	MS-65	Proof-65
1961	(3,028,244)	11,318,244	$4.00	$4.00	$4.25	$4.50	$5.50
1961D		20,276,442	4.00	4.00	4.25	4.50	
1962	(3,218,019)	12,932,019	4.00	4.00	4.25	4.50	5.50
1962D		35,473,281	4.00	4.00	4.25	4.50	
1963	(3,075,645)	25,239,645	4.00	4.00	4.25	4.50	5.50
1963D		67,069,292	4.00	4.00	4.25	4.50	

KENNEDY TYPE 1964 to Date

Gilroy Roberts, former Chief Engraver of the Mint, designed the obverse of this coin. His stylized initials are on the truncation of the forceful bust of President John F. Kennedy. The reverse, which uses the presidential coat of arms for the motif, is the work of Chief Engraver Frank Gasparro.

1964 Mint mark location

1968 Mint mark location

Silver Coinage 1964

	Quan. Minted	MS-65	Proof-65
1964	(3,950,762) 277,254,766	$4.00	$5.00
1964D	156,205,446	4.00	

Silver Clad Coinage 1965-1970

	Quan. Minted	MS-65	Proof-65
1965	65,879,366	1.00	
1966	108,984,932	1.00	
1967	295,046,978	1.00	
1968D	246,951,930	1.00	
1968S Proof	(3,041,506)		2.00
1969D	129,881,800	1.00	
1969S Proof	(2,934,631)		2.00
1970D (Issued only in mint sets)	2,150,000	18.00	
1970S Proof	(2,632,810)		5.00

Copper-Nickel Clad Coinage 1971-

	Quan. Minted	MS-65	Proof-65		Quan. Minted	MS-65	Proof-65
1971	155,164,000	$.50		1973S Proof	(2,760,339)		$1.00
1971D	302,097,424	.50		1974	201,596,000	$.50	
1971S Proof	(3,220,733)		$1.00	1974D	79,066,300	.50	
1972	153,180,000	.50		1974S Proof	(2,612,568)		1.50
1972D	141,890,000	.50		1977	43,598,000	.50	
1972S Proof	(3,260,996)		1.00	1977D	31,449,106	.50	
1973	64,964,000	.50		1977S Proof	(3,251,152)		.90
1973D	83,171,400	.50		1978	14,350,000	.70	

Italic prices indicate unsettled values due to fluctuating bullion market. See Bullion Chart.

HALF DOLLARS

	Quan. Minted	MS-65	Proof-65
1978D	13,765,799	$.70	
1978S Proof	(3,127,781)		$1.50
1979	68,312,000	.50	
1979D	15,815,422	.50	
1979S Proof	(3,677,175)		
Filled S			1.00
Clear S			15.00
1980P	44,134,000	.50	
1980D	33,456,449	.50	
1980S Proof	(3,554,806)		.85
1981P	29,544,000	$.50	
1981D	27,839,533	.50	
1981S Proof	(4,063,083)		$1.00
1982P	10,819,000	.50	
1982D	13,140,102	.50	
1982S Proof	(3,857,479)		5.50
1983P		.50	
1983D		.50	
1983S Proof			1.50

BICENTENNIAL COINAGE DATED 1776—1976

	Quan. Minted	MS-65	Proof-65
1776-1976 Copper-nickel clad	234,308,000	$.50	
1776-1976D Copper-nickel clad	287,565,248	.50	
1776-1976S Copper-nickel clad	(7,059,099)		$.75
1776-1976S Silver clad	*11,000,000	1.50	
1776-1976S Silver clad	*(4,000,000)		2.75

*Approximate mintage. Not all released.

SILVER DOLLARS — 1794 to Date

The silver dollar was authorized by Congress April 2, 1792. Weight and fineness were specified at 416 grains and 892.4 fine. The first issues appeared in 1794 and until 1804 all silver dollars had the value stamped on the edge: HUNDRED CENTS, ONE DOLLAR OR UNIT. After a lapse in coinage of the silver dollar during the period 1804 to 1839, these coins had reeded edges and the value was placed on the reverse side.

The weight was changed by the law of January 18, 1837 to 412½ grains, fineness .900. The coinage was discontinued by the Act of February 12, 1873 and reauthorized by the Act of February 28, 1878. The dollar was again discontinued after 1935, and since then only the copper-nickel pieces first authorized in 1971 have been coined for circulation.

FLOWING HAIR TYPE 1794-1795

AG-3 ABOUT GOOD—*Clear enough to identify.*
G-4 GOOD—*Date and letters readable. Main devices outlined, but lack details.*
VG-8 VERY GOOD—*Major details discernible. Letters well formed but worn.*
F-12 FINE—*Hair ends distinguishable. Top hairlines show, but otherwise worn smooth.*
VF-20 VERY FINE—*Hair in center shows some detail. Other details more bold.*
EF-40 EXTREMELY FINE—*Hair well defined but will show some wear.*
MS-60 UNCIRCULATED—*No trace of wear. Light blemishes.*

SILVER DOLLARS

	Quan. Minted	AG-3	G-4	VG-8	F-12	VF-20	EF-40	MS-60
1794	1,758	$1,600	$3,000	$4,500	$7,000	$12,000	$20,000	—
1795	160,295	350.00	850.00	1,200	1,600	2,100	3,750	$14,000

DRAPED BUST TYPE, SMALL EAGLE REVERSE 1795-1798

AG-3 ABOUT GOOD—*Clear enough to identify.*
G-4 GOOD—*Bust outlined, no detail. Date readable, some leaves evident.*
VG-8 VERY GOOD—*Drapery worn except deepest folds. Hairlines smooth.*
F-12 FINE—*All drapery lines distinguishable. Hairlines near cheek and neck show some detail.*
VF-20 VERY FINE—*Left side of drapery worn smooth.*
EF-40 EXTREMELY FINE—*Drapery shows distinctly. Hair well outlined and detailed.*
MS-60 UNCIRCULATED—*No trace of wear. Light blemishes.*

1975 Bust Type	42,738	$325.00	$700.00	$1,000	$1,400	$1,850	$2,600	$10,000
1796	72,920	200.00	500.00	750.00	1,000	1,300	2,100	7,500
1797	7,776	200.00	500.00	750.00	1,000	1,300	2,100	7,500
1798 All kinds	327,536	200.00	500.00	750.00	1,000	1,300	2,100	7,500

HERALDIC EAGLE REVERSE 1798-1804

G-4 GOOD—*Letters and date readable. E PLURIBUS UNUM obliterated.*
VG-8 VERY GOOD—*Motto partially readable. Only deepest drapery details visible. All other lines smooth.*
F-12 FINE—*All drapery lines distinguishable. Hairlines near cheek and neck show some detail.*
VF-20 VERY FINE—*Left side of drapery worn smooth.*
EF-40 EXTREMELY FINE—*Drapery is distinct. Hair well detailed.*
MS-60 UNCIRCULATED—*No trace of wear. Light blemishes.*

SILVER DOLLARS

	Quan. Minted	G-4	VG-8	F-12	VF-20	EF-40	MS-60
1798 Heraldic eagle		$180.00	$225.00	$300.00	$475.00	$775.00	$5,000
1799	423,515	180.00	225.00	300.00	475.00	775.00	5,000
1800	220,920	180.00	225.00	300.00	475.00	775.00	5,000
1801	54,454	180.00	225.00	300.00	475.00	775.00	5,000
1802	41,650	180.00	225.00	300.00	475.00	775.00	5,000
1803	85,634	180.00	225.00	300.00	475.00	775.00	5,000
1804 Variety 1, letter O in "OF" above cloud							Proof $125,000
1804 Variety 2, letter O above space between clouds							Proof $100,000

GOBRECHT SILVER DOLLARS

Silver dollars of 1836, 1838 and 1839 were mostly made as trial pieces, but some were made in quantities for general circulation. There was no regular issue of dollars 1805 to 1835 inclusive.

	VF-20	EF-40	Proof-60
1836 C. GOBRECHT F. on base. Rev. Eagle flying left amid stars. Plain edge. Although scarce, this is the most common variety and was issued for circulation as regular coinage	$1,000	$1,500	$3,500
1838 Similar obv., designer's name omitted, stars added around border. Rev. Eagle flying left in plain field. Reeded edge	1,500	2,500	4,500
1839 Obv. as above. Rev. Eagle in plain field. Reeded edge. Issued for circulation as regular coinage	1,500	2,500	4,500

SILVER DOLLARS
LIBERTY SEATED TYPE — REGULAR ISSUES 1840-1873

In 1840 silver dollars were again issued for general circulation, and the seated figure of Liberty device was adopted for the obverse.

VG-8 VERY GOOD—*Any 3 letters of LIBERTY at least two-thirds complete.*
F-12 FINE—*All 7 letters of LIBERTY visible though weak.*
VF-20 VERY FINE—*LIBERTY is strong but its ribbon shows slight wear.*
EF-40 EXTREMELY FINE—*Horizontal lines of shield complete. Eagle's eye plain.*
MS-60 UNCIRCULATED—*No trace of wear. Light marks or blemishes.*

Mint mark location is on the reverse below eagle.

	Quan. Minted	VG-8	F-12	VF-20	EF-40	MS-60	Proof-60
1840	61,005	$55.00	$85.00	$125.00	$185.00	$500.00	$1,500
1841	173,000	55.00	80.00	120.00	175.00	450.00	1,500
1842	184,618	55.00	80.00	120.00	175.00	450.00	1,500
1843	165,100	55.00	80.00	120.00	175.00	450.00	1,500
1844	20,000	65.00	90.00	135.00	200.00	700.00	1,500
1845	24,500	65.00	90.00	135.00	200.00	700.00	1,500
1846	110,600	55.00	80.00	120.00	175.00	450.00	1,500
1846O	59,000	70.00	100.00	135.00	225.00	1,000	
1847	140,750	55.00	80.00	120.00	175.00	450.00	1,500
1848	15,000	65.00	90.00	135.00	225.00	700.00	1,500
1849	62,600	55.00	80.00	120.00	175.00	450.00	1,500
1850	7,500	65.00	90.00	135.00	200.00	1,300	2,500
1850O	40,000	70.00	100.00	160.00	270.00	1,200	
1851	1,300	450.00	600.00	1,000	2,000	6,000	6,000
1852	1,100					4,500	4,500
1853	46,110	55.00	80.00	120.00	175.00	575.00	2,500
1854	33,140	60.00	100.00	150.00	250.00	725.00	1,700
1855	26,000	100.00	125.00	175.00	300.00	725.00	2,750
1856	63,500	65.00	100.00	140.00	200.00	650.00	2,600
1857	94,000	60.00	90.00	135.00	185.00	650.00	1,500
1858 ...... Est. (80)	80						2,000
1859 .... (800)	256,500	55.00	80.00	120.00	175.00	500.00	650.00
1859O	360,000	55.00	80.00	120.00	175.00	500.00	
1859S	20,000	60.00	90.00	135.00	225.00	850.00	
1860 ...... (1,330)	218,930	55.00	80.00	120.00	175.00	450.00	650.00
1860O	515,000	55.00	80.00	120.00	175.00	450.00	
1861 ...... (1,000)	78,500	57.50	85.00	125.00	185.00	550.00	650.00
1862 .... (550)	12,090	100.00	125.00	225.00	325.00	900.00	650.00
1863 .... (460)	27,660	65.00	100.00	140.00	235.00	650.00	650.00
1864 .... (470)	31,170	65.00	100.00	140.00	235.00	650.00	650.00
1865 .... (500)	47,000	65.00	100.00	140.00	235.00	650.00	650.00

SILVER DOLLARS
Motto "In God We Trust" Added to Reverse

	Quan. Minted	VG-8	F-12	VF-20	EF-40	MS-60	Proof-60
1866 .... (725)	49,625	$55.00	$80.00	$120.00	$175.00	$475.00	$650.00
1867 .... (625)	47,525	55.00	80.00	120.00	175.00	475.00	650.00
1868 .... (600)	162,700	55.00	80.00	120.00	175.00	475.00	650.00
1869 .... (600)	424,300	55.00	80.00	120.00	175.00	475.00	650.00
1870 ...... (1,000)	416,000	55.00	80.00	120.00	175.00	475.00	650.00
1870CC	12,462	70.00	100.00	150.00	275.00	1,100	
1870S					17,500	30,000	
1871 .... (960)	1,074,760	55.00	80.00	120.00	175.00	475.00	650.00
1871CC	1,376	350.00	500.00	750.00	1,200	4,200	
1872 .... (950)	1,106,450	55.00	80.00	120.00	175.00	475.00	650.00
1872CC	3,150	200.00	300.00	400.00	600.00	2,100	
1872S	9,000	65.00	100.00	150.00	375.00	1,400	
1873 .... (600)	293,600	55.00	80.00	120.00	175.00	475.00	650.00
1873CC	2,300	400.00	600.00	900.00	1,600	6,500	

TRADE DOLLARS 1873-1885

This coin was issued for circulation in the Orient to compete with dollar-size coins of other countries. It weighed 420 grains compared to 412½ grains, the weight of the regular silver dollar.

VG-8 VERY GOOD—*About half of mottoes IN GOD WE TRUST and E PLURIBUS UNUM will show. Rim on both sides well defined.*
F-12 FINE—*Mottoes and LIBERTY readable but worn.*
EF-40 EXTREMELY FINE—*Mottoes and LIBERTY are sharp. Only slight wear on rims.*
MS-60 UNCIRCULATED—*No trace of wear. Light blemishes.*

1875S
S over CC

TRADE DOLLARS 1873 - 1885

	Quan. Minted	VG-8	F-12	EF-40	MS-60	Proof-63
1873 .... (865)	397,500	$30.00	$40.00	$80.00	$400.00	$1,000
1873CC	124,500	35.00	45.00	85.00	600.00	
1873S	703,000	30.00	40.00	80.00	400.00	
1874 .... (700)	987,800	30.00	40.00	80.00	335.00	1,000
1874CC	1,373,200	35.00	45.00	85.00	500.00	
1874S	2,549,000	30.00	40.00	80.00	335.00	
1875 .... (700)	218,900	40.00	60.00	125.00	600.00	1,000
1875CC	1,573,700	35.00	45.00	85.00	425.00	
1875S	4,487,000	30.00	40.00	80.00	335.00	
1875S, S over CC		40.00	70.00	150.00	700.00	
1876 .... (1,150)	456,150	30.00	40.00	80.00	335.00	1,000
1876CC	509,000	35.00	45.00	85.00	425.00	
1876S	5,227,000	30.00	40.00	80.00	335.00	
1877 .... (510)	3,039,710	30.00	40.00	80.00	335.00	1,000
1877CC	534,000	35.00	50.00	100.00	600.00	
1877S	9,519,000	30.00	40.00	80.00	335.00	
1878 .... (900)	900					1,200
1878CC	97,000	65.00	100.00	275.00	1,500	
1878S	4,162,000	30.00	40.00	80.00	335.00	
1879 .... (1,541)	1,541					1,000
1880 .... (1,987)	1,987					1,000
1881 .... (960)	960					1,000
1882 .... (1,097)	1,097					1,000
1883 .... (979)	979					1,000

LIBERTY HEAD OR MORGAN TYPE 1878-1921

George T. Morgan, formerly a pupil of Wyon in the Royal Mint in London, designed the new dollar. His initial M is found at the truncation of the neck, at the last tress. It also appears on the reverse on the left-hand loop of the ribbon.

Sharply struck "proof-like" coins have a highly reflective surface and usually command substantial premiums.

VF-20 VERY FINE—*Two-thirds of hairlines from top of forehead to ear must show. Ear well defined. Feathers on eagle's breast worn.*

EF-40 EXTREMELY FINE—*All hairlines strong and ear bold. Eagle's feathers all plain but slight wear on breast and wing tips.*

AU-50 ABOUT UNCIRCULATED—*Slight trace of wear. Most of mint luster is present although marred by bag marks.*

MS-60 UNCIRCULATED—*No trace of wear. Has full mint luster, but may be noticeably marred by scuff marks or bag abrasions.*

MS-63 SELECT UNCIRCULATED—*No trace of wear, full mint luster, few noticeable surface marks.*

Most uncirculated silver dollars have scratches or nicks because of handling of mint bags. Choice sharply struck coins with full brilliance and without blemishes are worth more than listed values.

8 Tail Feathers, 1878 Philadelphia Only
Mint mark location on the reverse below wreath

SILVER DOLLARS

	Quan. Minted	VF-20	EF-40	AU-50	MS-60	MS-63
1878, 8 tail feathers. (500)	750,000	$14.00	$15.00	$19.00	$40.00	$70.00
1878, 7 tail feathers. (500)	} 9,759,550	*12.00*	*12.50*	14.00	36.00	47.50
1878, 7 over 8 feathers...		15.00	20.00	27.50	50.00	80.00
1878CC	2,212,000	22.00	25.00	37.50	80.00	100.00
1878S	9,774,000	*12.00*	*12.50*	16.00	36.00	50.00
1879 .... (1,100)	14,807,100	*12.00*	*12.50*	14.00	35.00	45.00
1879CC	756,000	45.00	150.00	270.00	450.00	800.00
1879O	2,887,000	*12.00*	*13.00*	15.00	40.00	85.00
1879S	9,110,000	*12.00*	*12.50*	14.00	36.00	55.00
1880 .... (1,355)	12,601,355	*12.00*	*12.50*	14.CJ	35.00	48.00
1880CC	591,000	40.00	55.00	80.00	130.00	160.00
1880O	5,305,000	*12.00*	*12.50*	14.00	50.00	110.00
1880S	8,900,000	*12.00*	*12.50*	14.00	38.00	50.00
1881 .... (975)	9,163,975	*12.00*	*12.50*	14.00	35.00	47.50
1881CC	296,000	50.00	65.00	85.00	125.00	150.00
1881O	5,708,000	*12.00*	*12.50*	14.00	35.00	47.50
1881S	12,760,000	*12.00*	*12.50*	14.00	40.00	55.00
1882 .... (1,100)	11,101,100	*12.00*	*12.50*	14.00	35.00	47.50
1882CC	1,133,000	22.00	27.00	36.00	60.00	75.00
1882O	6,090,000	*12.00*	*12.50*	14.00	35.00	50.00
1882S	9,250,000	*12.00*	*12.50*	14.00	40.00	55.00
1883 .... (1,039)	12,291,039	*12.00*	*12.50*	14.00	35.00	47.50
1883CC	1,204,000	21.00	26.00	35.00	55.00	75.00
1883O	8,725,000	*12.00*	*12.50*	*13.00*	30.00	40.00
1883S	6,250,000	14.00	17.00	85.00	275.00	400.00
1884 .... (875)	14,070,875	*12.00*	*12.50*	14.00	40.00	60.00
1884CC	1,136,000	24.00	30.00	38.00	60.00	75.00
1884O	9,730,000	*12.00*	*12.50*	*13.00*	30.00	40.00
1884S	3,200,000	15.00	22.00	170.00	800.00	1,750
1885 .... (930)	17,787,767	*12.00*	*12.50*	*13.00*	30.00	40.00
1885CC	228,000	80.00	100.00	110.00	125.00	150.00
1885O	9,185,000	*12.00*	*12.50*	14.00	30.00	40.00
1885S	1,497,000	*12.00*	*13.00*	35.00	75.00	125.00
1886 .... (886)	19,963,886	*12.00*	*12.50*	14.00	30.00	40.00
1886O	10,710,000	*12.00*	15.00	30.00	230.00	450.00
1886S	750,000	16.00	21.00	30.00	75.00	125.00
1887 .... (710)	20,290,710	*12.00*	*12.50*	*13.00*	30.00	40.00
1887O	11,550,000	*12.00*	*12.50*	14.00	35.00	60.00
1887S	1,771,000	*12.00*	*12.50*	14.00	45.00	75.00
1888 .... (832)	19,183,333	*12.00*	*12.50*	14.00	35.00	45.00
1888O	12,150,000	*12.00*	*12.50*	14.00	35.00	45.00
1888S	657,000	20.00	25.00	35.00	80.00	140.00
1889 .... (811)	21,726,811	*12.00*	*12.50*	14.00	35.00	45.00
1889CC	350,000	200.00	450.00	950.00	2,750	5,400
1889O	11,875,000	*12.00*	*12.50*	16.00	60.00	150.00
1889S	700,000	20.00	25.00	35.00	48.00	80.00
1890 .... (590)	16,802,590	*12.00*	*12.50*	14.00	37.50	48.00
1890CC	2,309,041	22.00	27.00	45.00	150.00	200.00
1890O	10,701,000	*12.00*	*12.50*	14.00	45.00	70.00

Proof Morgan Dollars where indicated in mintage record (quantity shown in parenthesis) are valued approximately as follows:

Proof-60 $450.00   Proof-63 $900.00   Proof-65 $2,800

Italic prices indicate unsettled values due to fluctuating bullion market. See Bullion Chart.

SILVER DOLLARS

	Quan. Minted	VF-20	EF-40	AU-50	MS-60	MS-63
1890S	8,230,373	*$12.00*	*$13.00*	$17.00	$38.00	$55.00
1891 (650)	8,694,206	*12.00*	15.00	20.00	55.00	90.00
1891CC	1,618,000	20.00	25.00	40.00	115.00	150.00
1891O	7,954,529	*12.00*	14.00	20.00	45.00	110.00
1891S	5,296,000	*12.00*	*13.00*	17.00	38.00	55.00
1892 (1,245)	1,037,245	*13.00*	15.00	25.00	90.00	230.00
1892CC	1,352,000	30.00	45.00	110.00	200.00	275.00
1892O	2,744,000	14.00	16.00	27.50	80.00	185.00
1892S	1,200,000	27.50	90.00	500.00	2,500	5,000
1893 (792)	389,792	35.00	60.00	115.00	200.00	375.00
1893CC	677,000	90.00	210.00	300.00	500.00	800.00
1893O	300,000	65.00	150.00	225.00	650.00	1,300
1893S	100,000	1,200	2,300	6,000	12,000	19,000
1894 (972)	110,972	225.00	275.00	475.00	625.00	900.00
1894O	1,723,000	14.00	20.00	45.00	300.00	700.00
1894S	1,260,000	25.00	45.00	100.00	215.00	400.00
1895 (880)	12,880				†8,000	†11,000
1895O	450,000	70.00	175.00	350.00	1,200	3,000
1895S	400,000	90.00	250.00	375.00	525.00	850.00
1896 (762)	9,976,762	*12.00*	*12.50*	14.00	35.00	45.00
1896O	4,900,000	*13.00*	15.00	50.00	400.00	900.00
1896S	5,000,000	20.00	45.00	140.00	270.00	450.00
1897 (731)	2,822,731	*12.00*	*12.50*	14.00	35.00	47.50
1897O	4,004,000	*12.00*	*13.00*	25.00	250.00	600.00
1897S	5,825,000	*13.00*	14.00	15.00	40.00	60.00
1898 (735)	5,884,735	*12.00*	*12.50*	14.00	35.00	45.00
1898O	4,440,000	*12.00*	*12.50*	14.00	34.00	42.00
1898S	4,102,000	*13.00*	15.00	35.00	90.00	185.00
1899 (846)	330,846	22.00	36.00	45.00	65.00	95.00
1899O	12,290,000	*13.00*	14.00	15.00	35.00	42.00
1899S	2,562,000	*13.00*	16.00	35.00	90.00	190.00
1900 (912)	8,830,912	*12.00*	*12.50*	14.00	33.00	40.00
1900O	12,590,000	*13.00*	14.00	15.00	35.00	45.00
1900S	3,540,000	*13.00*	15.00	28.00	80.00	175.00
1901 (813)	6,962,813	22.00	35.00	140.00	575.00	1,300
1901O	13,320,000	*13.00*	15.00	17.00	35.00	45.00
1901S	2,284,000	14.00	20.00	40.00	175.00	325.00
1902 (777)	7,994,777	*12.00*	14.00	18.00	40.00	65.00
1902O	8,636,000	*12.00*	*13.00*	16.00	30.00	40.00
1902S	1,530,000	35.00	57.50	95.00	145.00	250.00
1903 (755)	4,652,755	*12.00*	14.00	18.00	35.00	65.00
1903O	4,450,000	115.00	120.00	135.00	170.00	200.00
1903S	1,241,000	30.00	110.00	375.00	1,000	1,700
1904 (650)	2,788,650	*12.00*	14.00	25.00	75.00	170.00
1904O	3,720,000	*12.00*	14.00	17.00	28.00	40.00
1904S	2,304,000	35.00	65.00	225.00	525.00	925.00
1921	44,690,000	*12.00*	*12.50*	*13.00*	20.00	30.00
1921D	20,345,000	*12.00*	*12.50*	*13.00*	21.00	40.00
1921S	21,695,000	*12.00*	*12.50*	*13.00*	23.00	55.00

†Values are for proofs.

Proof Morgan Dollars where indicated in mintage record (quantity shown in parenthesis) are valued approximately as follows:

Proof-60 $450.00   Proof-63 $900.00   Proof-65 $2,800

Italic prices indicate unsettled values due to fluctuating bullion market. See Bullion Chart.

SILVER DOLLARS

PEACE TYPE 1921-1935

Anthony De Francisci, a medalist, designed this dollar. His monogram is located in the field of the coin under the neck of Liberty.

VF-20 VERY FINE—*Hair over eye well worn. Some strands over ear well defined. Some eagle feathers on top and outside edge of right wing will show.*

EF-40 EXTREMELY FINE—*Hairlines over brow and ear are strong though slightly worn. Outside wing feathers at right and those at top are visible but faint.*

AU-50 ABOUT UNCIRCULATED—*Slight trace of wear. Most of mint luster is present although marred by contact marks.*

MS-60 UNCIRCULATED—*No trace of wear. Has full mint luster but may be noticeably marred by stains, surface marks or bag abrasions.*

MS-63 SELECT UNCIRCULATED—*No trace of wear, full mint luster, few noticeable surface marks.*

Most uncirculated silver dollars have scratches or nicks because of handling of mint bags. Choice sharply struck coins with full brilliance and without blemishes are worth more than listed values.

	Quan. Minted	VF-20	EF-40	AU-50	MS-60	MS-63
1921	1,006,473	$18.00	$25.00	$45.00	$125.00	$250.00
1922	51,737,000	*12.00*	*12.50*	*13.00*	20.00	28.00
1922D	15,063,000	*12.00*	*12.50*	*13.00*	25.00	45.00
1922S	17,475,000	*12.00*	*12.50*	*13.00*	28.00	60.00
1923	30,800,000	*12.00*	*12.50*	*13.00*	20.00	28.00
1923D	6,811,000	*12.00*	*12.50*	*13.00*	28.00	52.00
1923S	19,020,000	*12.00*	*12.50*	*13.00*	28.00	70.00
1924	11,811,000	*12.00*	*12.50*	*13.00*	24.00	35.00
1924S	1,728,000	*12.00*	14.00	20.00	100.00	215.00
1925	10,198,000	*12.00*	*12.50*	*13.00*	23.00	30.00
1925S	1,610,000	*12.00*	14.00	17.00	70.00	150.00
1926	1,939,000	*12.00*	*13.00*	16.00	30.00	65.00
1926D	2,348,700	*12.00*	*13.00*	18.00	45.00	90.00
1926S	6,980,000	*12.00*	*13.00*	16.00	30.00	65.00
1927	848,000	*13.00*	14.00	25.00	75.00	125.00
1927D	1,268,900	*12.00*	14.00	55.00	150.00	350.00
1927S	866,000	*12.00*	14.00	30.00	110.00	190.00
1928	360,649	60.00	80.00	90.00	135.00	250.00
1928S	1,632,000	*13.00*	14.00	25.00	80.00	185.00
1934	954,057	14.00	16.00	27.50	60.00	115.00
1934D	1,569,500	*13.00*	15.00	27.50	75.00	180.00
1934S	1,011,000	20.00	85.00	275.00	750.00	1,250
1935	1,576,000	*12.00*	*13.00*	17.00	45.00	85.00
1935S	1,964,000	*12.00*	*13.00*	25.00	100.00	250.00

Italic prices indicate unsettled values due to fluctuating bullion market. See Bullion Chart.

EISENHOWER DOLLARS 1971-1978

Honoring both President Dwight D. Eisenhower and the first landing of man on the moon, this design is the work of Chief Engraver Frank Gasparro, whose initials are on the truncation and below the eagle. The reverse is an adaptation of the official Apollo 11 insignia.

Mint mark location is above the date.

	Quan. Minted Proof	Regular	MS-65	Proof-65
1971 Copper-nickel clad		47,799,000	$1.00	
1971D Copper-nickel clad		68,587,424	1.00	
1971S Silver clad	(4,265,234)	6,868,530	4.00	$5.00
1972 Copper-nickel clad		75,890,000	1.00	
1972D Copper-nickel clad		92,548,511	1.00	
1972S Silver clad	(1,811,631)	2,193,056	5.00	7.50
1973 Copper-nickel clad		*2,000,056	5.00	
1973D Copper-nickel clad		*2,000,000	5.00	
1973S Copper-nickel clad	(2,760,339)			2.50
1973S Silver clad	(1,013,646)	1,883,140	6.00	40.00
1974 Copper-nickel clad		27,366,000	1.00	
1974D Copper-nickel clad		45,517,000	1.00	
1974S Copper-nickel clad	(2,612,568)			2.50
1974S Silver clad	(1,306,579)	1,900,000	5.00	10.00

*1,769,258 of each sold only in sets and not released for circulation. Unissued coins destroyed at mint.

BICENTENNIAL COINAGE DATED 1776-1976

Obverse and Reverse Variety II   Reverse Var. I

Variety I: Design in low relief, bold lettering on reverse. Variety II: Sharp design, delicate lettering on reverse.

[122]

BICENTENNIAL DOLLARS

	Quan. Minted	MS-65	Proof-65
1776-1976 Copper-nickel clad, variety I	4,019,000	$1.00	
1776-1976 Copper-nickel clad, variety II	113,318,000	1.00	
1776-1976D Copper-nickel clad, variety I	21,048,710	1.00	
1776-1976D Copper-nickel clad, variety II	82,179,564	1.00	
1776-1976S Copper-nickel clad, variety I	(2,845,450)		$2.50
1776-1976S Copper-nickel clad, variety II	(4,149,730)		2.00
1776-1976S Silver clad, variety I	* 11,000,000	4.00	
1776-1976S Silver clad, variety I	*(4,000,000)		5.00

*Approximate mintage. Not all released.

EAGLE REVERSE RESUMED

	Quan. Minted	MS-65	Proof-65
1977 Copper-nickel clad	12,596,000	1.00	
1977D Copper-nickel clad	32,983,006	1.00	
1977S Copper-nickel clad	(3,251,152)		1.50
1978 Copper-nickel clad	25,702,000	1.00	
1978D Copper-nickel clad	23,012,890	1.00	
1978S Copper-nickel clad	(3,127,781)		2.75

SUSAN B. ANTHONY DOLLARS 1979-1981

Clear S Filled S

	Quan. minted	MS-65	Proof-65
1979P	360,222,000	$1.00	
1979D	288,015,744	1.00	
1979S	109,576,000	1.00	
1979S Proof	(3,677,175)		
Filled S			$5.00
Clear S			50.00
1980P	27,610,000	1.00	

	Quan. minted	MS-65	Proof-65
1980D	41,628,708	$1.00	
1980S	20,422,000	1.25	
1980S Proof	(3,554,806)		$3.00
1981P	3,000,000	2.25	
1981D	3,250,000	2.25	
1981S	3,492,000	2.25	
1981S Proof	(4,063,083)		3.00

GOLD
GOLD DOLLARS 1849-1889

Coinage of the gold dollar was authorized by the Act of March 3, 1849. The weight was 25.8 grains, fineness .900. The first type, struck until 1854, is known as the Liberty Head or small-sized type.

In 1854 the piece was made larger in diameter and thinner. The design was changed to a feather headdress on a female, generally referred to as the Indian Head or large-sized type. In 1856 the type was changed slightly by enlarging the size of the head.

LIBERTY HEAD TYPE 1849-1854

VF-20 VERY FINE—*LIBERTY on headband complete and readable. Knobs on coronet are defined.*

EF-40 EXTREMELY FINE—*Slight wear on Liberty's hair. Knobs on coronet sharp.*

AU-50 ABOUT UNCIRCULATED—*Trace of wear over eye and on coronet.*

MS-60 UNCIRCULATED—*No trace of wear. Light marks and blemishes.*

Mint mark is below wreath.

	Quan. Minted	VF-20	EF-40	AU-50	MS-60
1849	688,567	$85.00	$100.00	$125.00	$410.00
1849C	11,634	125.00	225.00	325.00	1,000
1849D	21,588	125.00	225.00	325.00	1,000
1849O	215,000	85.00	100.00	125.00	450.00
1850	481,953	85.00	100.00	125.00	410.00
1850C	6,966	125.00	225.00	325.00	1,000
1850D	8,382	125.00	225.00	325.00	850.00
1850O	14,000	110.00	140.00	185.00	700.00
1851	3,317,671	85.00	100.00	125.00	410.00
1851C	41,267	125.00	225.00	325.00	800.00
1851D	9,882	125.00	225.00	325.00	800.00
1851O	290,000	85.00	100.00	125.00	450.00
1852	2,045,351	85.00	100.00	125.00	410.00
1852C	9,434	125.00	225.00	325.00	900.00
1852D	6,360	125.00	225.00	325.00	900.00
1852O	140,000	85.00	100.00	125.00	450.00
1853	4,076,051	85.00	100.00	125.00	410.00
1853C	11,515	125.00	225.00	325.00	1,000
1853D	6,583	125.00	225.00	325.00	1,000
1853O	290,000	85.00	100.00	125.00	450.00
1854	855,502	85.00	100.00	125.00	410.00
1854D	2,935	200.00	275.00	600.00	1,500
1854S	14,632	125.00	225.00	325.00	850.00

INDIAN HEAD TYPE, Small Head 1854-1856

VF-20 VERY FINE—*Feather curl tips outlined but details worn.*

EF-40 EXTREMELY FINE—*Slight wear on tips of feather curls on headdress.*

AU-50 ABOUT UNCIRCULATED—*Trace of wear on headdress.*

MS-60 UNCIRCULATED—*No trace of wear. Light marks and blemishes.*

	Quan. Minted	VF-20	EF-40	AU-50	MS-60	Proof-63
1854	783,943	$175.00	$275.00	$500.00	$1,400	—
1855	758,269	175.00	275.00	500.00	1,400	—
1855C	9,803	275.00	400.00	800.00	3,200	
1855D	1,811	1,400	1,900	2,750	7,500	
1855O	55,000	190.00	300.00	650.00	2,000	
1856S	24,600	190.00	300.00	650.00	1,800	

GOLD DOLLARS

INDIAN HEAD TYPE, Large Head 1856-1889

VF-20 VERY FINE—*Curled feathers have slight detail. Details worn smooth at eyebrow, hair below headdress and behind ear and bottom curl.*

EF-40 EXTREMELY FINE—*Slight wear above and to right of eye and on top of curled feathers.*

AU-50 ABOUT UNCIRCULATED—*Trace of wear on headdress.*

MS-60 UNCIRCULATED—*No trace of wear. Light marks and blemishes.*

	Quan. Minted	VF-20	EF-40	AU-50	MS-60	Proof-63
1856	1,762,936	$85.00	$100.00	$125.00	$400.00	$3,000
1856D	1,460	1,200	2,200	3,000	7,500	
1857	774,789	85.00	100.00	125.00	400.00	3,000
1857C	13,280	170.00	230.00	350.00	800.00	
1857D	3,533	250.00	350.00	600.00	2,000	
1857S	10,000	100.00	150.00	225.00	700.00	
1858	117,995	85.00	100.00	125.00	400.00	3,000
1858D	3,477	300.00	400.00	650.00	1,800	
1858S	10,000	100.00	150.00	225.00	700.00	
1859 (80)	168,244	85.00	100.00	125.00	400.00	2,900
1859C	5,235	160.00	250.00	350.00	1,300	
1859D	4,952	200.00	300.00	450.00	1,500	
1859S	15,000	100.00	150.00	225.00	700.00	
1860 (154)	36,668	85.00	100.00	125.00	400.00	2,500
1860D	1,566	1,000	2,200	4,000	6,500	
1860S	13,000	100.00	150.00	225.00	700.00	
1861 (349)	527,499	85.00	100.00	125.00	400.00	2,500
1861D		3,000	5,000	7,000	14,000	
1862 (35)	1,361,390	85.00	100.00	125.00	400.00	2,500
1863 (50)	6,250	150.00	200.00	375.00	1,600	4,200
1864 (50)	5,950	140.00	175.00	350.00	1,500	4,200
1865 (25)	3,725	140.00	175.00	350.00	1,500	4,200
1866 (30)	7,130	100.00	175.00	325.00	700.00	3,000
1867 (50)	5,250	130.00	180.00	300.00	850.00	3,000
1868 (25)	10,525	90.00	170.00	250.00	600.00	3,000
1869 (25)	5,925	100.00	175.00	325.00	700.00	3,000
1870 (35)	6,335	100.00	175.00	325.00	700.00	3,000
1870S	3,000	250.00	375.00	600.00	1,800	
1871 (30)	3,930	100.00	170.00	250.00	700.00	3,000
1872 (30)	3,530	100.00	170.00	250.00	700.00	3,000
1873 Closed 3 (25)	1,825	120.00	180.00	300.00	800.00	4,000
1873 Open 3	123,300	85.00	100.00	125.00	400.00	
1874 (20)	198,820	85.00	100.00	125.00	400.00	3,000
1875 (20)	420	1,000	1,500	2,500	5,000	12,000
1876 (45)	3,245	100.00	150.00	200.00	750.00	2,500
1877 (20)	3,920	100.00	150.00	200.00	750.00	2,500
1878 (20)	3,020	100.00	150.00	200.00	750.00	2,500
1879 (30)	3,030	100.00	150.00	200.00	750.00	2,500
1880 (36)	1,636	100.00	150.00	200.00	750.00	2,500
1881 (87)	7,707	85.00	100.00	125.00	400.00	2,400
1882 (125)	5,125	85.00	100.00	125.00	400.00	2,400
1883 (207)	11,007	85.00	100.00	125.00	400.00	2,400
1884 (1,006)	6,236	85.00	100.00	125.00	400.00	2,000
1885 (1,105)	12,261	85.00	100.00	125.00	400.00	2,000
1886 (1,016)	6,016	85.00	100.00	125.00	400.00	2,000
1887 (1,043)	8,543	85.00	100.00	125.00	400.00	2,000
1888 (1,079)	16,580	85.00	100.00	125.00	400.00	2,000
1889 (1,779)	30,729	85.00	100.00	125.00	400.00	2,000

QUARTER EAGLES—1796-1929
($2.50 GOLD PIECES)

Although authorized by the Act of April 2, 1792, coinage of quarter eagles was not begun until 1796.

CAPPED BUST TO RIGHT 1796-1807
No Stars on Obverse 1796 Only

F-12 FINE—*Hair worn smooth on high spots. E PLURIBUS UNUM weak but readable.*
VF-20 VERY FINE—*Some wear on high spots.*
EF-40 EXTREMELY FINE—*Only slight wear on hair and cheek.*
MS-60 UNCIRCULATED—*No trace of wear. Light blemishes.*

Stars on Obverse 1796-1807

	Quan. Minted	F-12	VF-20	EF-40	MS-60
1796 No stars on obverse	963	$5,000	$7,000	$12,000	$22,000
1796 Stars on obverse	432	3,500	6,000	8,000	17,500
1797	427	2,500	4,000	7,000	12,000
1798	1,094	1,800	2,600	3,600	8,000
1802, 2 over 1	3,035	1,000	1,600	2,750	7,500
1804, 13-Star reverse	} 3,327	2,000	4,000	6,000	10,000
1804, 14-Star reverse		1,000	1,600	2,750	7,500
1805	1,781	1,000	1,600	2,750	7,500
1806, 6 over 4, stars 8+5	1,136	1,000	1,600	2,750	7,500
1806, 6 over 5, stars 7+6	480	1,500	3,000	4,500	10,000
1807	6,812	1,000	1,600	2,750	7,500

CAPPED BUST TO LEFT, Large Size 1808

F-12 FINE—*E PLURIBUS UNUM and LIBERTY on headband readable but weak.*
VF-20 VERY FINE—*Motto and LIBERTY clear.*
EF-40 EXTREMELY FINE—*All details of hair are plain.*
MS-60 UNCIRCULATED—*No trace of wear. Light blemishes.*

1808	2,710	4,500	7,000	10,000	27,500

CAPPED HEAD TO LEFT 1821-1834
Those dated 1829-1834 are smaller in diameter than the 1821-1827 pieces.

1821	6,448	1,200	2,000	3,000	8,500
1824, 4 over 1	2,600	1,200	2,000	3,000	8,500
1825	4,434	1,200	2,000	3,000	8,500
1826, 6 over 5	760	2,200	3,300	5,000	16,000

QUARTER EAGLES

	Quan. Minted	F-12	VF-20	EF-40	MS-60
1827	2,800	$1,200	$2,000	$3,000	$8,500
1829	3,403	1,200	2,000	3,000	7,500
1830	4,540	1,000	1,500	2,500	7,500
1831	4,520	1,000	1,500	2,500	7,500
1832	4,400	1,000	1,500	2,500	7,500
1833	4,160	1,000	1,500	2,500	7,500
1834 (Motto)	4,000	2,600	4,300	6,750	14,000

CLASSIC HEAD TYPE, No Motto on Reverse 1834-1839

In 1834 the quarter eagle was redesigned. A ribbon binding the hair, bearing the word LIBERTY, replaces the Liberty cap. The motto was omitted from the reverse.

F-12 FINE—*LIBERTY readable and complete. Curl under ear oulined but no detail.*
VF-20 VERY FINE—*LIBERTY plain. Hair curl has detail.*
EF-40 EXTREMELY FINE—*Small amount of wear on top of hair and below L in LIBERTY. Wear evident on wing.*
AU-50 ABOUT UNCIRCULATED—*Trace of wear on coronet and hair above ear.*
MS-60 UNCIRCULATED—*No trace of wear. Light blemishes.*

  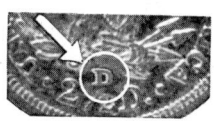

Mint mark location.

	Quan. Minted	F-12	VF-20	EF-40	AU-50	MS-60
1834 No motto	112,234	$125.00	$150.00	$225.00	$400.00	$1,100
1835	131,402	125.00	150.00	225.00	400.00	1,100
1836	547,986	125.00	150.00	225.00	400.00	1,100
1837	45,080	125.00	160.00	250.00	450.00	1,750
1838	47,030	125.00	160.00	250.00	450.00	1,750
1838C	7,880	175.00	250.00	500.00	600.00	2,500
1839	27,021	125.00	160.00	250.00	450.00	1,750
1839C	18,140	175.00	250.00	500.00	600.00	2,400
1839D	13,674	175.00	250.00	500.00	650.00	2,500
1839O	17,781	150.00	200.00	300.00	500.00	2,300

CORONET TYPE 1840-1907

  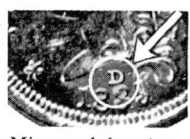

Mint mark location.

4 Plain 4

4 Crosslet 4

	Quan. Minted	VF-20	EF-40	AU-50	MS-60
1840	18,859	$150.00	$175.00	$225.00	$450.00
1840C	12,822	200.00	300.00	450.00	1,200
1840D	3,532	350.00	475.00	700.00	1,750
1840O	33,580	150.00	175.00	225.00	450.00
1841 Proofs only		6,000	12,500	17,500	32,500
1841C	10,281	275.00	450.00	525.00	850.00
1841D	4,164	300.00	475.00	600.00	1,600
1842	2,823	275.00	450.00	525.00	1,200
1842C	6,729	275.00	450.00	525.00	850.00
1842D	4,643	300.00	475.00	600.00	1,400
1842O	19,800	150.00	175.00	225.00	450.00
1843	100,546	150.00	175.00	225.00	400.00

QUARTER EAGLES

	Quan. Minted	VF-20	EF-40	AU-50	MS-60
1843D	36,209	$275.00	$450.00	$525.00	$1,000
1843O	364,002	150.00	175.00	225.00	450.00
1844	6,784	160.00	200.00	350.00	700.00
1844C	11,622	200.00	250.00	400.00	1,000
1844D	17,332	200.00	300.00	450.00	1,100
1845	91,051	150.00	175.00	200.00	400.00
1845D	19,460	200.00	250.00	400.00	1,000
1845O	4,000	250.00	350.00	600.00	—
1846	21,598	150.00	175.00	200.00	400.00
1846C	4,808	250.00	350.00	550.00	1,200
1846D	19,303	200.00	250.00	400.00	1,000
1846O	62,000	150.00	175.00	200.00	400.00
1847	29,814	150.00	175.00	200.00	400.00
1847C	23,226	200.00	225.00	375.00	850.00
1847D	15,784	200.00	225.00	375.00	1,000
1847O	124,000	150.00	175.00	200.00	400.00
1848	7,497	250.00	400.00	600.00	1,200

CAL. Above Eagle on Reverse

California Gold Quarter Eagle

In 1848 about two hundred and thirty ounces of gold were sent to Secretary of War Marcy by Col. R. B. Mason, Military Governor of California. The gold was turned over to the mint and made into quarter eagles. The distinguishing mark "CAL." was punched above the eagle on the reverse side, while the coins were in the die.

	Quan. Minted	VF-20	EF-40	AU-50	MS-60
1848 CAL. above eagle	1,389	3,000	5,000	7,000	14,000
1848C	16,788	200.00	285.00	400.00	1,000
1848D	13,771	250.00	350.00	550.00	1,150
1849	23,294	150.00	165.00	200.00	400.00
1849C	10,220	200.00	300.00	450.00	1,000
1849D	10,945	200.00	300.00	500.00	1,100
1850	252,923	125.00	150.00	175.00	375.00
1850C	9,148	200.00	285.00	400.00	1,000
1850D	12,148	200.00	300.00	450.00	1,100
1850O	84,000	125.00	150.00	175.00	400.00
1851	1,372,748	125.00	150.00	175.00	375.00
1851C	14,923	200.00	250.00	400.00	1,000
1851D	11,264	200.00	275.00	450.00	1,100
1851O	148,000	125.00	150.00	175.00	375.00
1852	1,159,681	125.00	150.00	175.00	375.00
1852C	9,772	200.00	300.00	450.00	1,000
1852D	4,078	300.00	450.00	700.00	1,800
1852O	140,000	125.00	150.00	175.00	450.00
1853	1,404,668	125.00	150.00	175.00	375.00
1853D	3,178	350.00	600.00	850.00	2,200
1854	596,258	125.00	150.00	175.00	375.00
1854C	7,295	200.00	300.00	450.00	1,000
1854D	1,760	1,200	1,800	2,200	4,000
1854O	153,000	125.00	150.00	175.00	375.00
1854S	246		10,000	17,000	—
1855	235,480	125.00	150.00	175.00	375.00
1855C	3,677	350.00	600.00	850.00	2,250

QUARTER EAGLES

	Quan. Minted	VF-20	EF-40	AU-50	MS-60	Proof-63
1855D	1,123	$800.00	$1,500	$2,250	$5,500	
1856	384,240	125.00	150.00	175.00	375.00	
1856C	7,913	200.00	300.00	450.00	1,300	
1856D	874	1,500	3,000	4,500	9,500	
1856O	21,100	150.00	165.00	250.00	500.00	
1856S	72,120	150.00	165.00	250.00	500.00	
1857	214,130	125.00	150.00	175.00	375.00	
1857D	2,364	300.00	450.00	800.00	2,000	
1857O	34,000	125.00	150.00	175.00	450.00	
1857S	69,200	125.00	150.00	200.00	600.00	
1858	47,377	125.00	150.00	175.00	400.00	
1858C	9,056	180.00	250.00	400.00	1,000	
1859	(80) 39,444	125.00	150.00	175.00	425.00	$5,000
1859D	2,244	250.00	500.00	850.00	2,000	
1859S	15,200	150.00	170.00	225.00	600.00	
1860	(112) 22,675	125.00	150.00	175.00	400.00	3,500
1860C	7,469	185.00	350.00	450.00	1,200	
1860S	35,600	150.00	165.00	225.00	600.00	
1861	(90) 1,283,878	125.00	150.00	175.00	375.00	3,500
1861S	24,000	150.00	165.00	225.00	500.00	
1862, 2 over 1	(35) 98,543		700.00	1,000	—	
1862		125.00	150.00	175.00	375.00	4,000
1862S	8,000	150.00	165.00	225.00	800.00	
1863 Proofs only	(30) 30					—
1863S	10,800	150.00	165.00	225.00	800.00	
1864	(50) 2,874	300.00	500.00	1,000	1,800	5,500
1865	(25) 1,545	350.00	550.00	1,100	2,000	5,500
1865S	23,376	150.00	165.00	225.00	450.00	
1866	(30) 3,110	175.00	225.00	400.00	900.00	4,000
1866S	38,960	150.00	160.00	225.00	600.00	
1867	(50) 3,250	165.00	,200.00	350.00	750.00	3,200
1867S	28,000	150.00	165.00	225.00	600.00	
1868	(25) 3,625	150.00	190.00	350.00	700.00	3,200
1868S	34,000	150.00	165.00	225.00	500.00	
1869	(25) 4,345	150.00	165.00	300.00	600.00	3,200
1869S	29,500	150.00	165.00	200.00	500.00	
1870	(35) 4,555	150.00	165.00	225.00	600.00	3,200
1870S	16,000	150.00	165.00	200.00	500.00	
1871	(30) 5,350	150.00	165.00	225.00	600.00	3,200
1871S	22,000	125.00	150.00	175.00	400.00	
1872	(30) 3,030	150.00	175.00	275.00	550.00	3,200
1872S	18,000	125.00	150.00	175.00	375.00	
1873	(25) 178,025	125.00	150.00	175.00	375.00	3,200
1873S	27,000	125.00	150.00	175.00	400.00	
1874	(20) 3,940	160.00	175.00	275.00	500.00	4,000
1875	(20) 420	900.00	1,800	2,750	5,500	13,000
1875S	11,600	125.00	150.00	175.00	400.00	
1876	(45) 4,221	150.00	185.00	300.00	600.00	3,000
1876S	5,000	150.00	165.00	225.00	500.00	
1877	(20) 1,652	250.00	325.00	425.00	1,000	4,000
1877S	35,400	125.00	150.00	175.00	375.00	
1878	(20) 286,260	125.00	150.00	175.00	375.00	3,000
1878S	178,000	125.00	150.00	175.00	375.00	
1879	(30) 88,990	125.00	150.00	175.00	375.00	3,000
1879S	43,500	125.00	150.00	175.00	375.00	
1880	(36) 2,996	150.00	165.00	225.00	500.00	3,000
1881	(51) 691	350.00	500.00	1,000	1,750	4,500
1882	(67) 4,067	150.00	165.00	200.00	500.00	3,000

[129]

QUARTER EAGLES

	Quan. Minted	VF-20	EF-40	AU-50	MS-60	Proof-63
1883	(82) 2,002	$150.00	$175.00	$225.00	$500.00	$3,000
1884	(73) 2,023	150.00	175.00	225.00	500.00	3,000
1885	(87) 887	350.00	500.00	900.00	1,500	4,000
1886	(88) 4,088	150.00	175.00	225.00	475.00	2,750
1887	(122) 6,282	150.00	165.00	200.00	450.00	2,500
1888	(97) 16,098	125.00	150.00	175.00	400.00	2,500
1889	(48) 17,648	125.00	150.00	175.00	400.00	2,500
1890	(93) 8,813	125.00	150.00	175.00	400.00	2,500
1891	(80) 11,040	125.00	150.00	175.00	400.00	2,500
1892	(105) 2,545	150.00	175.00	225.00	600.00	2,400
1893	(106) 30,106	125.00	150.00	175.00	375.00	2,400
1894	(122) 4,122	150.00	165.00	200.00	450.00	2,200
1895	(119) 6,119	125.00	150.00	175.00	400.00	2,200
1896	(132) 19,202	125.00	150.00	175.00	375.00	2,200
1897	(136) 29,904	125.00	150.00	175.00	375.00	2,200
1898	(165) 24,165	125.00	150.00	175.00	375.00	2,000
1899	(150) 27,350	125.00	150.00	175.00	375.00	2,000
1900	(205) 67,205	125.00	150.00	175.00	375.00	2,000
1901	(223) 91,323	125.00	150.00	175.00	375.00	2,000
1902	(193) 133,733	125.00	150.00	175.00	375.00	2,000
1903	(197) 201,257	125.00	150.00	175.00	375.00	2,000
1904	(170) 160,960	125.00	150.00	175.00	375.00	2,000
1905	(144) 217,944	125.00	150.00	175.00	375.00	2,000
1906	(160) 176,490	125.00	150.00	175.00	375.00	2,000
1907	(154) 336,448	125.00	150.00	175.00	375.00	2,000

INDIAN HEAD TYPE 1908-1929

Bela Lyon Pratt was the designer of this and the half eagle piece. The coin has no raised milling and the main devices and legends are incuse.

VF-20 VERY FINE—*Hair cord knot distinct. Feathers at top of head clear. Cheekbone worn.*

EF-40 EXTREMELY FINE—*Cheekbone, war bonnet and headband feathers slightly worn.*

AU-50 ABOUT UNCIRCULATED—*Trace of wear on cheekbone and headdress.*

MS-60 UNCIRCULATED—*No trace of wear. Light blemishes.*

Mint mark location is on reverse left of fasces.

	Quan. Minted	VF-20	EF-40	AU-50	MS-60	Matte Proof-63
1908	(236) 565,057	$110.00	$120.00	$135.00	$185.00	$2,500
1909	(139) 441,899	110.00	120.00	135.00	185.00	2,500
1910	(682) 492,682	110.00	120.00	135.00	185.00	2,500
1911	(191) 704,191	110.00	120.00	135.00	185.00	2,500
1911D	55,680	450.00	650.00	900.00	1,800	
1912	(197) 616,197	110.00	120.00	135.00	185.00	2,500
1913	(165) 722,165	110.00	120.00	135.00	185.00	2,500
1914	(117) 240,117	110.00	120.00	135.00	185.00	2,500
1914D	448,000	110.00	120.00	135.00	185.00	
1915	(100) 606,100	110.00	120.00	135.00	185.00	2,500
1925D	578,000	110.00	120.00	135.00	185.00	
1926	446,000	110.00	120.00	135.00	185.00	
1927	388,000	110.00	120.00	135.00	185.00	
1928	416,000	110.00	120.00	135.00	185.00	
1929	532,000	110.00	120.00	135.00	185.00	

THREE DOLLAR GOLD PIECES

THREE DOLLAR GOLD PIECES — 1854-1889

The three dollar gold piece was authorized by the Act of February 21, 1853. The coin was first struck in 1854. It was never popular and saw very little circulation.

VF-20 VERY FINE—*Eyebrow, hair about forehead and ear and bottom curl are worn smooth. Curled feather-ends have faint details showing.*

EF-40 EXTREMELY FINE—*Light wear above and to right of eye and on top of curled feathers.*

AU-50 ABOUT UNCIRCULATED—*Trace of wear on top of curled feathers and in hair above and to right of eye.*

MS-60 UNCIRCULATED—*No trace of wear. Light blemishes.*

Mint mark location is on reverse below wreath

	Quan. Minted	VF-20	EF-40	AU-50	MS-60	Proof-63
1854	138,618	$300.00	$450.00	$600.00	$1,400	$12,000
1854D	1,120	2,500	5,000	7,500	12,000	
1854O	24,000	300.00	450.00	600.00	1,400	
1855	50,555	300.00	450.00	600.00	1,400	15,000
1855S	6,600	300.00	450.00	600.00	2,350	
1856	26,010	300.00	450.00	600.00	1,400	9,000
1856S	34,500	300.00	450.00	600.00	1,500	
1857	20,891	300.00	450.00	600.00	1,400	7,500
1857S	14,000	300.00	450.00	600.00	1,500	
1858	2,133	375.00	500.00	700.00	2,200	7,000
1859 (80)	15,638	300.00	450.00	600.00	1,400	6,000
1860 (119)	7,155	300.00	450.00	600.00	1,400	4,000
1860S (2,592 melted at Mint)	7,000	400.00	550.00	700.00	1,800	
1861 (113)	6,072	300.00	450.00	600.00	1,400	4,000
1862 (35)	5,785	300.00	450.00	600.00	1,400	4,000
1863 (39)	5,039	300	450.00	600.00	1,400	4,000
1864 (50)	2,680	300.00	450.00	600.00	1,400	4,000
1865 (25)	1,165	450.00	575.00	800.00	3,000	6,500
1866 (30)	4,030	300.00	450.00	600.00	1,400	4,000
1867 (50)	2,650	300.00	450.00	600.00	1,400	4,000
1868 (25)	4,875	300.00	450.00	600.00	1,400	4,000
1869 (25)	2,525	300.00	450.00	600.00	1,400	4,000
1870 (35)	3,535	300.00	450.00	600.00	1,400	4,000
1870S	1	(Unique)				
1871 (30)	1,330	375.00	500.00	700.00	1,700	4,000
1872 (30)	2,030	300.00	450.00	600.00	1,400	4,000
1873 Open 3 (original) (25)	25					16,000
1873 Closed 3		1,200	1,800	2,300	4,000	8,000
1874 (20)	41,820	300.00	450.00	600.00	1,400	5,000
1875 Proofs only (20)	20					—
1876 Proofs only (45)	45					—
1877 (20)	1,488	450.00	700.00	1,100	2,500	6,000
1878 (20)	82,324	300.00	450.00	600.00	1,400	5,000
1879 (30)	3,030	300.00	450.00	600.00	1,400	4,000
1880 (36)	1,036	400.00	500.00	700.00	1,500	4,000
1881 (54)	554	500.00	750.00	1,100	2,000	5,000
1882 (76)	1,576	300.00	450.00	600.00	1,400	3,500
1883 (89)	989	400.00	500.00	700.00	1,500	3,500
1884 (106)	1,106	400.00	500.00	700.00	1,500	3,000
1885 (109)	910	400.00	500.00	700.00	1,500	3,000
1886 (142)	1,142	400.00	500.00	650.00	1,700	3,000
1887 (160)	6,160	400.00	450.00	600.00	1,400	3,000
1888 (291)	5,291	400.00	450.00	600.00	1,400	3,000
1889 (129)	2,429	400.00	450.00	600.00	1,400	3,000

FOUR DOLLAR GOLD OR "STELLA"

These pattern coins were first suggested by the Hon. John A. Kasson, then U.S. Minister to Austria; and it was through the efforts of Dr. W. W. Hubbell, who patented the goloid metal used in making the goloid metric dollars, that we have these beautiful and interesting pieces. Only those struck in gold are listed.

	Quan. Minted	VF-20	EF-40	Proof-60
1879 Flowing hair	415	$7,000	$10,000	$15,000
1879 Coiled hair	10	15,000	20,000	35,000
1880 Flowing hair	15	10,000	12,000	20,000
1880 Coiled hair	10	15,000	20,000	35,000

HALF EAGLES — 1795-1929
($5.00 GOLD PIECES)

The half eagle was the first gold coin struck for the United States. The $5.00 piece was authorized to be coined by the Act of April 2, 1792, and the first type weighed 135 grains, 916 2/3 fine. The weight was changed by the Act of June 28, 1834 to 129 grains, 899.225 fine. Fineness became .900 by the Act of January 18, 1837.

CAPPED BUST TO RIGHT, SMALL EAGLE 1795-1798

F-12 FINE—*Hair worn smooth but with distinct outline. For heraldic type, E PLURIBUS UNUM is faint but readable.*
VF-20 VERY FINE—*Slight to noticeable wear on high spots such as hair, turban, eagle's head and wings.*
EF-40 EXTREMELY FINE—*Slight wear on hair and highest part of cheek.*
MS-60 UNCIRCULATED—*No trace of wear. Light blemishes.*

	Quan. Minted	F-12	VF-20	EF-40	MS-60
1795 Small eagle	8,707	$2,500	$3,500	$5,000	$16,000

1796, 6 over 5   1797, 15 Stars   1797, 16 Stars

1796, 6 over 5	6,196	2,500	3,500	5,000	15,000
1797, 15 stars		3,500	4,500	7,500	16,500

HALF EAGLES

	Quan. Minted	F-12	VF-20	EF-40	MS-60
1797, 16 stars All kinds	3,609	$3,500	$4,500	$7,500	$16,500
1798 Small eagle (7 known)		—	—	—	—

CAPPED BUST TO RIGHT, HERALDIC EAGLE 1795-1807

1795 Heraldic eagle		3,500	4,000	8,000	17,000
1797, 7 over 5		3,000	3,500	7,000	15,000
1798 13 star reverse	} 24,867	650.00	900.00	1,500	4,500
1798 14 star reverse		800.00	1,500	2,000	6,000
1799	7,451	650.00	900.00	1,500	4,500
1800	37,628	650.00	900.00	1,500	4,500
1802, 2 over 1	53,176	650.00	900.00	1,500	4,500
1803, 3 over 2	33,506	650.00	900.00	1,500	4,500
1804	30,475	650.00	900.00	1,500	4,500
1805	33,183	650.00	900.00	1,500	4,500
1806	64,093	650.00	900.00	1,500	4,500
1807	32,488	650.00	900.00	1,500	4,500

CAPPED DRAPED BUST TO LEFT 1807-1812

F-12 FINE—*LIBERTY readable but partly weak.*
VF-20 VERY FINE—*Headband edges slightly worn. LIBERTY is bold.*
EF-40 EXTREMELY FINE—*Slight wear on highest portions of hair. 80% of major curls are plain.*
MS-60 UNCIRCULATED—*No trace of wear. Light blemishes.*

1807	51,605	650.00	900.00	1,500	4,000
1808, 8 over 7	} 55,578	600.00	800.00	1,250	3,750
1808		600.00	800.00	1,250	3,750
1809, 9 over 8	33,875	600.00	800.00	1,250	3,750
1810	100,287	600.00	800.00	1,250	3,750
1811	99,581	600.00	800.00	1,250	3,750
1812	58,087	600.00	800.00	1,250	3,750

CAPPED HEAD TO LEFT 1813-1829

1813	95,428	650.00	1,000	1,500	4,250
1814, 4 over 3	15,454	750.00	1,300	1,800	5,000
1815	635				70,000
1818	48,588	700.00	1,100	1,600	4,500
1819	51,723			20,000	45,000
1820	263,806	700.00	1,100	1,750	5,000
1821	34,641	1,600	3,250	4,250	13,000
1822	17,796	—	—	—	

HALF EAGLES

	Quan. Minted	F-12	VF-20	EF-40	MS-60
1823	14,485	$1,000	$1,700	$2,300	$8,000
1824	17,340	3,000	4,500	9,000	18,000
1825, 5 over 1	} 29,060	1,500	2,500	4,000	12,000
1825, 5 over 4					
1826	18,069	1,800	3,100	4,500	13,500
1827	24,913	3,000	5,000	13,000	
1828, 8 over 7	} 28,029	2,400	3,500	7,500	12,000
1828		3,000	4,500	9,000	
1829 Large date	57,442				

CAPPED HEAD TO LEFT (reduced diameter) 1829-1834

	Quan. Minted	F-12	VF-20	EF-40	MS-60
1829 Small date	inc. above		10,000	15,000	30,000
1830	126,351	1,200	2,000	3,000	7,500
1831	140,594	1,200	2,000	3,000	7,500
1832 Curved-base 2, 12 stars (4 known)	} 157,487				
1832 Square-base 2, 13 stars		2,000	3,500	5,000	10,000
1833	193,630	1,200	2,000	3,000	7,250
1834	50,141	1,200	2,000	3,000	7,250

CLASSIC HEAD TYPE 1834-1838

	Quan. Minted	F-12	VF-20	EF-40	MS-60
1834	657,460	135.00	175.00	275.00	1,500
1835	371,534	135.00	175.00	275.00	1,500
1836	553,147	135.00	175.00	275.00	1,500
1837	207,121	135.00	175.00	275.00	1,500
1838	286,588	135.00	175.00	275.00	1,500
1838C	17,179	400.00	500.00	1,000	4,200
1838D	20,583	400.00	500.00	1,000	4,200

CORONET TYPE, No Motto Above Eagle 1839-1866

VF-20 VERY FINE—*LIBERTY bold. Major lines show in neck hair.*

EF-40 EXTREMELY FINE—*Neck hair details clear. Slight wear on top and lower part of coronet, and hair.*

AU-50 ABOUT UNCIRCULATED—*Trace of wear on coronet and hair above eye.*

MS-60 UNCIRCULATED—*No trace of wear. Light blemishes.*

Mint mark above date 1839 only, below eagle 1840-1908.

HALF EAGLES

	Quan. Minted	VF-20	EF-40	AU-50	MS-60
1839	118,143	$100.00	$125.00	$275.00	$600.00
1839C	17,205	150.00	300.00	500.00	1,200
1839D	18,939	150.00	300.00	500.00	1,200
1840	137,382	100.00	120.00	225.00	600.00
1840C	18,992	150.00	300.00	500.00	1,200
1840D	22,896	150.00	300.00	500.00	1,200
1840O	40,120	125.00	200.00	400.00	700.00
1841	15,833	125.00	200.00	400.00	700.00
1841C	21,467	150.00	300.00	500.00	1,200
1841D	29,392	150.00	300.00	500.00	1,200

1842 Large Date   Large letters   Small Letters

	Quan. Minted	VF-20	EF-40	AU-50	MS-60
1842 Small Letters	27,578	100.00	120.00	185.00	600.00
1842 Large letters		100.00	120.00	185.00	600.00
1842C Small date	27,432	350.00	500.00	900.00	1,750
1842C Large date		125.00	200.00	400.00	1,000
1842D Small date	59,608	125.00	200.00	400.00	1,200
1842D Large date		150.00	300.00	500.00	1,400
1842O	16,400	100.00	150.00	300.00	625.00
1843	611,205	100.00	120.00	175.00	500.00
1843C	44,277	125.00	200.00	400.00	1,000
1843D	98,452	125.00	200.00	400.00	1,000
1843O Small letters	19,075	100.00	150.00	300.00	625.00
1843O Large letters	82,000	100.00	120.00	200.00	900.00
1844	340,330	100.00	120.00	175.00	500.00
1844C	23,631	125.00	250.00	500.00	1,400
1844D	88,982	125.00	200.00	400.00	1,000
1844O	364,600	100.00	120.00	200.00	600.00
1845	417,099	100.00	120.00	175.00	500.00
1845D	90,629	125.00	200.00	250.00	900.00
1845O	41,000	100.00	120.00	200.00	600.00
1846	395,942	100.00	120.00	175.00	500.00
1846C	12,995	150.00	300.00	500.00	1,200
1846D	80,294	125.00	200.00	400.00	900.00
1846O	58,000	100.00	120.00	200.00	600.00
1847	915,981	100.00	120.00	175.00	500.00
1847C	84,151	125.00	200.00	400.00	1,000
1847D	64,405	125.00	200.00	400.00	1,000
1847O	12,000	125.00	225.00	450.00	1,000
1848	260,775	100.00	120.00	175.00	500.00
1848C	64,472	125.00	200.00	400.00	900.00
1848D	47,465	125.00	200.00	400.00	1,000
1849	133,070	100.00	120.00	175.00	500.00
1849C	64,823	125.00	200.00	400.00	1,000
1849D	39,036	125.00	200.00	400.00	1,000
1850	64,491	100.00	120.00	175.00	500.00

Values of common gold coins are based on the prevailing price of gold bullion, and will vary according to current market price. See Bullion Chart.

HALF EAGLES

	Quan. Minted	VF-20	EF-40	AU-50	MS-60	Proof-60
1850C	63,591	$125.00	$200.00	$400.00	$1,000	
1850D	43,984	125.00	200.00	400.00	1,000	
1851	377,505	100.00	120.00	175.00	500.00	
1851C	49,176	125.00	200.00	400.00	1,000	
1851D	62,710	125.00	200.00	400.00	1,000	
1851O	41,000	100.00	125.00	250.00	600.00	
1852	573,901	100.00	120.00	175.00	500.00	
1852C	72,574	125.00	200.00	400.00	1,000	
1852D	91,584	125.00	200.00	400.00	1,000	
1853	305,770	100.00	120.00	175.00	500.00	
1853C	65,571	125.00	200.00	400.00	1,000	
1853D	89,678	125.00	200.00	400.00	1,000	
1854	160,675	100.00	120.00	175.00	500.00	
1854C	39,283	125.00	200.00	400.00	1,000	
1854D	56,413	125.00	200.00	400.00	1,000	
1854O	46,000	100.00	125.00	250.00	600.00	
1854S	268	—	—	—		
1855	117,098	100.00	120.00	175.00	500.00	
1855C	39,788	125.00	200.00	400.00	1,000	
1855D	22,432	125.00	200.00	400.00	1,000	
1855O	11,100	125.00	200.00	400.00	1,000	
1855S	61,000	100.00	120.00	175.00	600.00	
1856	197,990	100.00	120.00	175.00	500.00	
1856C	28,457	125.00	200.00	400.00	1,000	
1856D	19,786	125.00	200.00	400.00	1,000	
1856O	10,000	150.00	300.00	500.00	1,200	
1856S	105,100	100.00	120.00	175.00	500.00	
1857	98,188	100.00	120.00	175.00	500.00	
1857C	31,360	125.00	200.00	400.00	1,000	
1857D	17,046	125.00	200.00	400.00	1,000	
1857O	13,000	125.00	200.00	400.00	1,000	
1857S	87,000	100.00	120.00	175.00	500.00	
1858	15,136	100.00	125.00	250.00	600.00	
1858C	38,856	125.00	200.00	400.00	1,000	
1858D	15,362	125.00	200.00	400.00	1,000	
1858S	18,600	100.00	125.00	275.00	550.00	
1859 (80)	16,814	100.00	125.00	250.00	550.00	$4,500
1859C	31,847	125.00	200.00	400.00	1,000	
1859D	10,366	150.00	250.00	500.00	1,250	
1859S	13,220	100.00	125.00	275.00	550.00	
1860 (62)	19,825	100.00	125.00	250.00	550.00	3,500
1860C	14,813	125.00	200.00	400.00	1,000	
1860D	14,635	125.00	200.00	400.00	1,200	
1860S	21,200	100.00	125.00	250.00	—	
1861 (66)	688,150	100.00	120.00	175.00	500.00	3,500
1861C	6,879	700.00	1,000	1,700	3,250	
1861D	1,597	1,750	2,500	4,000	10,000	
1861S	18,000	100.00	125.00	185.00	—	
1862 (35)	4,465	100.00	150.00	275.00	—	3,500
1862S	9,500	125.00	225.00	350.00	—	
1863 (30)	2,472	150.00	350.00	500.00	1,250	3,500
1863S	17,000	100.00	150.00	275.00	625.00	
1864 (50)	4,220	125.00	200.00	400.00	1,400	3,500

Values of common gold coins are based on the prevailing price of gold bullion, and will vary according to current market price. See Bullion Chart.

HALF EAGLES

	Quan. Minted	VF-20	EF-40	AU-50	MS-60	Proof-63
1864S	3,888	$350.00	$700.00	$1,200	—	
1865	(25) 1,295	300.00	400.00	650.00	$1,500	$3,500
1865S	27,612	100.00	125.00	185.00	—	
1866S	9,000	125.00	200.00	400.00	—	

Motto Above Eagle 1866-1908

VF-20 VERY FINE—*Half of hairlines above coronet missing. Hair curls under ear evident, but worn. Motto and its ribbon sharp.*

EF-40 EXTREMELY FINE—*Small amount of wear on top of hair and below L in LIBERTY. Wear evident on wing tips and neck of eagle.*

AU-50 ABOUT UNCIRCULATED—*Trace of wear on tip of coronet and hair above eye.*

MS-60 UNCIRCULATED—*No trace of wear. Light blemishes.*

	Quan. Minted	VF-20	EF-40	AU-50	MS-60	Proof-63
1866	(30) 6,730	120.00	170.00	300.00	750.00	4,500
1866S	34,920	100.00	150.00	275.00	500.00	
1867	(50) 6,920	120.00	170.00	300.00	700.00	4,500
1867S	29,000	100.00	150.00	250.00	—	
1868	(25) 5,725	120.00	170.00	300.00	700.00	4,500
1868S	52,000	100.00	150.00	250.00	—	
1869	(25) 1,785	150.00	275.00	400.00	1,000	4,500
1869S	31,000	100.00	120.00	175.00	400.00	
1870	(35) 4,035	100.00	150.00	275.00	500.00	4,500
1870CC	7,675	650.00	1,200	2,000		
1870S	17,000	100.00	120.00	200.00	—	
1871	(30) 3,230	120.00	170.00	300.00	—	4,500
1871CC	20,770	150.00	275.00	500.00	1,100	
1871S	25,000	100.00	120.00	200.00	600.00	
1872	(30) 1,690	200.00	275.00	500.00	1,100	4,500
1872CC	16,980	200.00	275.00	500.00	1,100	
1872S	36,400	100.00	120.00	175.00	350.00	
1873	(25) 112,505	100.00	110.00	120.00	175.00	
1873CC	7,416	200.00	400.00	700.00	1,500	
1873S	31,000	100.00	120.00	200.00	500.00	
1874	(20) 3,508	120.00	170.00	300.00	750.00	4,500
1874CC	21,198	120.00	170.00	300.00	850.00	
1874S	16,000	100.00	120.00	175.00	—	
1875	(20) 220		—	—	—	—
1875CC	11,828	150.00	350.00	550.00	1,000	
1875S	9,000	125.00	275.00	400.00	850.00	
1876	(45) 1,477	200.00	350.00	600.00	1,250	4,500
1876CC	6,887	150.00	275.00	500.00	1,100	
1876S	4,000	150.00	275.00	500.00	1,000	
1877	(20) 1,152	175.00	325.00	600.00	1,500	4,500
1877CC	8,680	150.00	275.00	500.00	1,100	
1877S	26,700	100.00	110.00	125.00	200.00	
1878	(20) 131,740	100.00	110.00	120.00	185.00	4,500
1878CC	9,054	400.00	900.00	1,250		
1878S	144,700	100.00	110.00	120.00	185.00	
1879	(30) 301,950	100.00	110.00	120.00	185.00	4,500
1879CC	17,281	125.00	150.00	300.00	650.00	

Values of common gold coins are based on the prevailing price of gold bullion, and will vary according to current market price. See Bullion Chart.

HALF EAGLES

	Quan. Minted	VF-20	EF-40	AU-50	MS-60	Proof-63
1879S	426,200	$100.00	$110.00	$120.00	$185.00	
1880 (36)	3,166,436	100.00	110.00	120.00	175.00	$3,500
1880CC	51,017	120.00	170.00	225.00	450.00	
1880S	1,348,900	100.00	110.00	120.00	175.00	
1881 (42)	5,708,802	100.00	110.00	120.00	175.00	3,500
1881CC	13,886	125.00	150.00	300.00	600.00	
1881S	969,000	100.00	110.00	120.00	175.00	
1882 (48)	2,514,568	100.00	110.00	120.00	175.00	3,000
1882CC	82,817	100.00	120.00	175.00	350.00	
1882S	969,000	100.00	110.00	120.00	175.00	
1883 (61)	233,461	100.00	110.00	120.00	175.00	3,000
1883CC	12,958	125.00	150.00	300.00	450.00	
1883S	83,200	100.00	110.00	120.00	175.00	
1884 (48)	191,078	100.00	110.00	120.00	175.00	3,000
1884CC	16,402	125.00	150.00	300.00	450.00	
1884S	177,000	100.00	110.00	120.00	175.00	
1885 (66)	601,506	100.00	110.00	120.00	175.00	3,000
1885S	1,211,500	100.00	110.00	120.00	175.00	
1886 (72)	388,432	100.00	110.00	120.00	175.00	3,000
1886S	3,268,000	100.00	110.00	120.00	175.00	
1887 Proofs only (87)	87					10,000
1887S	1,912,000	100.00	110.00	120.00	175.00	
1888 (95)	18,296	110.00	130.00	140.00	200.00	2,750
1888S	293,900	100.00	110.00	120.00	175.00	
1889 (45)	7,565	100.00	125.00	200.00	500.00	2,750
1890 (88)	4,328	100.00	200.00	300.00	600.00	2,750
1890CC	53,800	100.00	120.00	175.00	250.00	
1891 (53)	61,413	100.00	110.00	120.00	175.00	2,750
1891CC	208,000	100.00	120.00	150.00	200.00	
1892 (92)	753,572	100.00	110.00	120.00	175.00	2,750
1892CC	82,968	100.00	120.00	150.00	200.00	
1892O	10,000	225.00	350.00	600.00	1,100	
1892S	298,400	100.00	110.00	120.00	175.00	
1893 (77)	1,528,197	100.00	110.00	120.00	175.00	2,750
1893CC	60,000	100.00	120.00	150.00	300.00	
1893O	110,000	100.00	120.00	175.00	350.00	
1893S	224,000	100.00	110.00	120.00	175.00	
1894 (75)	957,955	100.00	110.00	120.00	175.00	2,750
1894O	16,600	100.00	120.00	175.00	375.00	
1894S	55,900	100.00	110.00	120.00	190.00	
1895 (81)	1,345,936	100.00	110.00	120.00	175.00	2,750
1895S	112,000	100.00	110.00	120.00	175.00	
1896 (103)	59,063	100.00	110.00	120.00	175.00	2,750
1896S	155,400	100.00	110.00	120.00	175.00	
1897 (83)	867,883	100.00	110.00	120.00	175.00	2,750
1897S	354,000	100.00	110.00	120.00	175.00	
1898 (75)	633,495	100.00	110.00	120.00	175.00	2,750
1898S	1,397,400	100.00	110.00	120.00	175.00	
1899 (99)	1,710,729	100.00	110.00	120.00	175.00	2,750
1899S	1,545,000	100.00	110.00	120.00	175.00	
1900 (230)	1,405,730	100.00	110.00	120.00	175.00	2,750
1900S	329,000	100.00	110.00	120.00	175.00	
1901 (140)	616,040	100.00	110.00	120.00	175.00	2,750

Values of common gold coins are based on the prevailing price of gold bullion, and will vary according to current market price. See Bullion Chart.

HALF EAGLES

	Quan. Minted	VF-20	EF-40	AU-50	MS-60	Proof-63
1901S, 1 over 0	} 3,648,000	$100.00	$110.00	$125.00	$190.00	
1901S		100.00	110.00	120.00	175.00	
1902 (162)	172,562	100.00	110.00	120.00	175.00	$2,750
1902S	939,000	100.00	110.00	120.00	175.00	
1903 (154)	227,024	100.00	110.00	120.00	175.00	2,750
1903S	1,855,000	100.00	110.00	120.00	175.00	
1904 (136)	392,136	100.00	110.00	120.00	175.00	2,750
1904S	97,000	100.00	110.00	120.00	175.00	
1905 (108)	302,308	100.00	110.00	120.00	175.00	2,750
1905S	880,700	100.00	110.00	120.00	175.00	
1906 (85)	348,820	100.00	110.00	120.00	175.00	2,750
1906D	320,000	100.00	110.00	120.00	175.00	
1906S	598,000	100.00	110.00	120.00	175.00	
1907 (92)	626,192	100.00	110.00	120.00	175.00	2,750
1907D	888,000	100.00	110.00	120.00	175.00	
1908	421,874	100.00	110.00	120.00	175.00	

INDIAN HEAD TYPE 1908-1929

This type conforms to the quarter eagle of the same date. The incuse designs and lettering make this a unique series, along with the quarter eagle, in United States coinage.

VF-20 VERY FINE—*Noticeable wear on large middle feathers and tip of eagle's wing.*
EF-40 EXTREMELY FINE—*Cheekbone, war bonnet and headband feathers slightly worn. Feathers on eagle's upper wing show considerable wear.*
AU-50 ABOUT UNCIRCULATED—*Trace of wear on cheekbone and headdress.*
MS-60 UNCIRCULATED—*No trace of wear. Light blemishes.*

Scarcer coins with well struck mint marks command higher prices.

Mint mark location

						Matte Proof-63
1908 (167)	578,012	125.00	150.00	175.00	500.00	3,750
1908D	148,000	125.00	150.00	175.00	500.00	
1908S	82,000	150.00	175.00	280.00	1,500	
1909 (78)	627,138	125.00	150.00	175.00	500.00	3,750
1909D	3,423,560	125.00	150.00	175.00	500.00	
1909O	34,200	250.00	400.00	600.00	3,500	
1909S	297,200	125.00	150.00	200.00	1,000	
1910 (250)	604,250	125.00	150.00	175.00	500.00	3,750
1910D	193,600	125.00	150.00	175.00	600.00	
1910S	770,200	125.00	150.00	200.00	1,100	
1911 (139)	915,139	125.00	150.00	175.00	500.00	3,750
1911D	72,500	150.00	175.00	350.00	2,000	
1911S	1,416,000	125.00	150.00	200.00	650.00	
1912 (144)	790,144	125.00	150.00	175.00	500.00	3,750
1912S	392,000	125.00	150.00	200.00	800.00	
1913 (99)	916,000	125.00	150.00	175.00	500.00	3,750

Values of common gold coins are based on the prevailing price of gold bullion, and will vary according to current market price. See Bullion Chart.

HALF EAGLES

	Quan. Minted	VF-20	EF-40	AU-50	MS-60	Matte Proof-63
1913S	408,000	$125.00	$150.00	$275.00	$1,600	
1914 (125)	247,125	125.00	150.00	175.00	500.00	$3,750
1914D	247,000	125.00	150.00	175.00	500.00	
1914S	263,000	125.00	150.00	200.00	650.00	
1915 (75)	588,075	125.00	150.00	175.00	500.00	3,750
1915S	164,000	125.00	150.00	250.00	1,200	
1916S	240,000	125.00	150.00	200.00	800.00	
1929	662,000	1,200	1,800	2,200	3,500	

EAGLES ($10.00 Gold Pieces) — 1795-1933

Coinage authority including specified weights and fineness of the eagle conforms to that of the half eagle. The small eagle reverse was used until 1797 when the large, heraldic eagle replaced it.

CAPPED BUST TO RIGHT, SMALL EAGLE 1795-1797

F-12 FINE—*Details on turban and head obliterated.*

VF-20 VERY FINE—*Neck hairlines and details under turban and over forehead are worn but distinguishable.*

EF-40 EXTREMELY FINE—*Definite wear on hair to left of eye and strand of hair across and around turban, also on eagle's wing tips.*

MS-60 UNCIRCULATED—*No trace of wear. Light blemishes.*

	Quan. Minted	F-12	VF-20	EF-40	MS-60
1795	5,583	$3,000	$4,500	$7,000	$20,000
1796	4,146	3,000	4,500	7,000	20,000
1797 Small eagle	3,615	3,000	4,500	7,500	21,500

CAPPED BUST TO RIGHT, HERALDIC EAGLE 1797-1804

	Quan. Minted				
1797 Large eagle	10,940	1,000	1,800	3,000	9,000
1798, 8 over 7, 9 stars left, 4 right	900	2,500	4,000	7,000	14,000
1798, 8 over 7, 7 stars left, 6 right	842	7,000	14,000	—	—
1799	37,449	1,000	1,500	2,500	7,000
1800	5,999	1,100	1,600	2,600	7,500

EAGLES

	Quan. Minted	F-12	VF-20	EF-40	MS-60
1801	44,344	$1,000	$1,500	$2,500	$7,000
1803	15,017	1,100	1,600	2,600	7,500
1804	3,757	1,500	2,200	3,000	12,000

CORONET TYPE, No Motto Above Eagle 1838-1866

In 1838 the weight and diameter of the eagle were reduced and the obverse and reverse were redesigned. Liberty now faces left and the word LIBERTY is placed on the coronet.

VF-20 VERY FINE—*Hairlines above coronet partly worn. Curls under ear worn but defined.*

EF-40 EXTREMELY FINE—*Small amount of wear on top of hair and below L in LIBERTY. Wear evident on wing tips and neck of eagle.*

AU-50 ABOUT UNCIRCULATED—*Trace of wear on tip of coronet and hair above eye.*

MS-60 UNCIRCULATED—*No trace of wear. Light blemishes.*

Mint mark location on reverse below eagle

	Quan. Minted	VF-20	EF-40	AU-50	MS-60
1838	7,200	$300.00	$600.00	$1,000	$4,000
1839 Large letters	25,801	225.00	400.00	750.00	2,500
1839 Small letters	12,447	275.00	500.00	1,000	3,000
1840	47,338	200.00	225.00	350.00	1,700
1841	63,131	200.00	225.00	350.00	1,500
1841O	2,500	250.00	550.00	700.00	3,000
1842	81,507	200.00	225.00	325.00	1,100
1842O	27,400	200.00	225.00	350.00	1,900
1843	75,462	200.00	225.00	325.00	1,100
1843O	175,162	200.00	225.00	300.00	1,200
1844	6,361	225.00	400.00	550.00	2,000
1844O	118,700	200.00	225.00	300.00	1,200
1845	26,153	200.00	225.00	325.00	1,400
1845O	47,500	200.00	225.00	300.00	1,200
1846	20,095	200.00	225.00	325.00	1,500
1846O	81,780	200.00	225.00	300.00	1,200
1847	862,258	200.00	225.00	300.00	800.00
1847O	571,500	200.00	225.00	300.00	800.00
1848	145,484	200.00	225.00	300.00	800.00
1848O	35,850	200.00	225.00	300.00	1,200
1849	653,618	200.00	225.00	300.00	800.00
1849O	23,900	200.00	225.00	300.00	1,200
1850	291,451	200.00	225.00	300.00	800.00
1850O	57,500	200.00	225.00	300.00	1,100

EAGLES

	Quan. Minted	VF-20	EF-40	AU-50	MS-60	Proof-60
1851	176,328	$200.00	$225.00	$300.00	$800.00	
1851O	263,000	200.00	225.00	300.00	800.00	
1852	263,106	200.00	225.00	300.00	800.00	
1852O	18,000	220.00	250.00	350.00	1,400	
1853, 3 over 2	} 201,253	225.00	400.00			
1853		200.00	225.00	300.00	800.00	
1853O	51,000	200.00	225.00	300.00	1,000	
1854	54,250	200.00	225.00	300.00	850.00	
1854O	52,500	200.00	225.00	300.00	1,000	
1854S	123,826	200.00	225.00	300.00	800.00	
1855	121,701	200.00	225.00	300.00	800.00	——
1855O	18,000	220.00	250.00	350.00	1,400	
1855S	9,000	250.00	400.00	600.00	2,500	——
1856	60,490	200.00	225.00	300.00	800.00	
1856O	14,500	200.00	250.00	300.00	1,400	
1856S	68,000	200.00	225.00	300.00	800.00	
1857	16,606	200.00	225.00	300.00	1,000	——
1857O	5,500	300.00	600.00	800.00	2,500	
1857S	26,000	200.00	225.00	300.00	875.00	
1858	2,521	2,000	3,000	4,500	12,000	——
1858O	20,000	200.00	225.00	300.00	1,400	
1858S	11,800	200.00	250.00	350.00	1,600	
1859 (80)	16,093	200.00	225.00	300.00	1,300	$4,000
1859O	2,300	550.00	900.00	1,500	3,000	
1859S	7,000	300.00	550.00	700.00	2,000	
1860 (50)	15,105	200.00	225.00	300.00	1,300	4,000
1860O	11,100	200.00	250.00	300.00	1,500	
1860S	5,000	300.00	600.00	750.00	2,500	
1861 (69)	113,233	200.00	225.00	300.00	1,000	4,000
1861S	15,500	200.00	225.00	300.00	1,000	
1862 (35)	10,995	200.00	225.00	300.00	1,200	4,000
1862S	12,500	200.00	225.00	300.00	1,000	
1863 (30)	1,248	1,000	2,200	2,800	3,500	7,500
1863S	10,000	275.00	400.00	550.00	1,400	
1864 (50)	3,580	400.00	650.00	850.00	2,000	6,000
1864S	2,500	900.00	1,600			
1865 (25)	4,005	340.00	550.00	675.00	2,000	5,000
1865S	16,700	340.00	550.00	675.00	2,000	
1866S	8,500	400.00	750.00	1,100	2,400	

Motto Above Eagle 1866-1907

Mint mark location on the reverse below eagle.

Values of common gold coins are based on the prevailing price of gold bullion, and will vary according to current market price. See Bullion Chart.

EAGLES

VF-20 VERY FINE—*Half of hairlines over coronet visible. Curls under ear worn but defined. IN GOD WE TRUST and its ribbon are sharp.*

EF-40 EXTREMELY FINE—*Small amount of wear on top of hair and below L in LIBERTY. Wear evident on wing tips and neck of eagle.*

AU-50 ABOUT UNCIRCULATED—*Trace of wear on hair above eye and on coronet.*

MS-60 UNCIRCULATED—*No trace of wear. Light blemishes.*

	Quan. Minted	VF-20	EF-40	AU-50	MS-60	Proof-63
1866 (30)	3,780	$225.00	$275.00	$450.00	$1,000	$7,500
1866S	11,500	200.00	250.00	300.00	700.00	
1867 (50)	3,140	225.00	275.00	450.00	1,000	6,000
1867S	9,000	200.00	250.00	300.00	700.00	
1868 (25)	10,655	200.00	250.00	300.00	600.00	6,000
1868S	13,500	200.00	250.00	300.00	600.00	
1869 (25)	1,855	300.00	500.00	800.00	1,200	6,000
1869S	6,430	200.00	250.00	300.00	700.00	
1870 (35)	4,025	225.00	300.00	450.00	750.00	6,000
1870CC	5,908	500.00	1,200	2,200		
1870S	8,000	200.00	250.00	300.00	700.00	
1871 (30)	1,820	300.00	500.00	800.00	2,000	6,000
1871CC	8,085	300.00	500.00	800.00		
1871S	16,500	200.00	250.00	300.00	600.00	
1872 (30)	1,650	400.00	700.00	1,100	1,800	6,000
1872CC	4,600	275.00	475.00	600.00	1,800	
1872S	17,300	200.00	250.00	300.00	550.00	
1873 (25)	825	650.00	1,200	2,000	4,000	13,000
1873CC	4,543	425.00	800.00	1,500	3,000	
1873S	12,000	200.00	250.00	300.00	550.00	
1874 (20)	53,160	200.00	210.00	225.00	250.00	6,500
1874CC	16,767	200.00	225.00	250.00	700.00	
1874S	10,000	200.00	225.00	250.00	550.00	
1875 (20)	120	—	—	—	—	—
1875CC	7,715	250.00	275.00	550.00	1,200	
1876 (45)	732	500.00	1,100	1,800	4,000	8,000
1876CC	4,696	300.00	600.00	725.00	1,600	
1876S	5,000	200.00	250.00	425.00	900.00	
1877 (20)	817	600.00	1,100	1,800	4,500	10,000
1877CC	3,332	300.00	550.00	800.00	2,000	
1877S	17,000	200.00	210.00	225.00	315.00	
1878 (20)	73,800	200.00	210.00	225.00	250.00	5,000
1878CC	3,244	300.00	550.00	1,000	2,000	
1878S	26,100	200.00	210.00	225.00	250.00	
1879 (30)	384,770	200.00	210.00	225.00	250.00	4,000
1879CC	1,762	1,100	2,500	3,500	6,000	
1879O	1,500	500.00	900.00	1,500	4,000	
1879S	224,000	200.00	210.00	225.00	250.00	
1880	1,644,876	200.00	210.00	225.00	250.00	4,000
1880CC	11,190	200.00	225.00	275.00	600.00	
1880O	9,200	200.00	225.00	225.00	400.00	
1880S	506,250	200.00	210.00	225.00	250.00	
1881 (40)	3,877,260	200.00	210.00	225.00	250.00	4,000
1881CC	24,015	200.00	225.00	275.00	375.00	
1881O	8,350	200.00	250.00	300.00	550.00	
1881S	970,000	200.00	210.00	225.00	250.00	
1882 (40)	2,324,480	200.00	210.00	225.00	250.00	4,000
1882CC	6,764	200.00	250.00	300.00	600.00	
1882O	10,820	200.00	225.00	250.00	350.00	

Values of common gold coins are based on the prevailing price of gold bullion, and will vary according to current market price. See Bullion Chart.

EAGLES

	Quan. Minted	VF-20	EF-40	AU-50	MS-60	Proof-63
1882S	132,000	$200.00	$210.00	$225.00	$250.00	
1883 (40)	208,740	200.00	210.00	225.00	250.00	$4,000
1883CC	12,000	200.00	250.00	300.00	600.00	
1883O	800	800.00	1,800	2,500	5,000	
1883S	38,000	200.00	210.00	225.00	250.00	
1884 (15)	76,905	200.00	210.00	225.00	250.00	8,000
1884CC	9,925	200.00	250.00	300.00	600.00	
1884S	124,250	200.00	210.00	225.00	250.00	
1885 (65)	253,527	200.00	210.00	225.00	250.00	4,000
1885S	228,000	200.00	210.00	225.00	250.00	
1886 (60)	236,160	200.00	210.00	225.00	250.00	4,000
1886S	826,000	200.00	210.00	225.00	250.00	
1887 (80)	53,680	200.00	210.00	225.00	250.00	4,000
1887S	817,000	200.00	210.00	225.00	250.00	
1888 (75)	132,996	200.00	210.00	225.00	250.00	4,000
1888O	21,335	200.00	210.00	225.00	275.00	
1888S	648,700	200.00	210.00	225.00	250.00	
1889 (45)	4,485	200.00	250.00	300.00	550.00	4,000
1889S	425,400	200.00	210.00	225.00	250.00	
1890 (63)	58,043	200.00	210.00	225.00	375.00	4,000
1890CC	17,500	200.00	210.00	225.00	275.00	
1891 (48)	91,868	200.00	210.00	225.00	250.00	4,000
1891CC	103,732	200.00	210.00	225.00	275.00	
1892 (72)	797,552	200.00	210.00	225.00	250.00	4,000
1892CC	40,000	200.00	210.00	240.00	400.00	
1892O	28,688	200.00	210.00	225.00	250.00	
1892S	115,500	200.00	210.00	225.00	250.00	
1893 (55)	1,840,895	200.00	210.00	225.00	250.00	3,500
1893CC	14,000	200.00	250.00	300.00	450.00	
1893O	17,000	200.00	210.00	250.00	350.00	
1893S	141,350	200.00	210.00	225.00	250.00	
1894 (43)	2,470,778	200.00	210.00	225.00	250.00	3,500
1894O	107,500	200.00	210.00	225.00	250.00	
1894S	25,000	200.00	210.00	225.00	250.00	
1895 (56)	567,826	200.00	210.00	225.00	250.00	3,500
1895O	98,000	200.00	210.00	225.00	250.00	
1895S	49,000	200.00	210.00	225.00	250.00	
1896 (78)	76,348	200.00	210.00	225.00	250.00	3,500
1896S	123,750	200.00	210.00	225.00	250.00	
1897 (69)	1,000,159	200.00	210.00	225.00	250.00	3,500
1897O	42,500	200.00	210.00	225.00	250.00	
1897S	234,750	200.00	210.00	225.00	250.00	
1898 (67)	812,197	200.00	210.00	225.00	250.00	3,500
1898S	473,600	200.00	210.00	225.00	250.00	
1899 (86)	1,262,305	200.00	210.00	225.00	250.00	3,250
1899O	37,047	200.00	210.00	225.00	250.00	
1899S	841,000	200.00	210.00	225.00	250.00	
1900 (120)	293,960	200.00	210.00	225.00	250.00	3,250
1900S	81,000	200.00	210.00	225.00	250.00	
1901 (85)	1,718,825	200.00	210.00	225.00	250.00	3,250
1901O	72,041	200.00	210.00	225.00	250.00	
1901S	2,812,750	200.00	210.00	225.00	250.00	
1902 (113)	82,513	200.00	210.00	225.00	250.00	3,250
1902S	469,500	200.00	210.00	225.00	250.00	

Values of common gold coins are based on the prevailing price of gold bullion, and will vary according to current market price. See Bullion Chart.

EAGLES

	Quan. Minted	VF-20	EF-40	AU-50	MS-60	Proof-63
1903 .... (96)	125,926	$200.00	$210.00	$225.00	$250.00	$3,250
1903O	112,771	200.00	210.00	225.00	250.00	
1903S	538,000	200.00	210.00	225.00	250.00	
1904 .... (108)	162,038	200.00	210.00	225.00	250.00	3,250
1904O	108,950	200.00	210.00	225.00	250.00	
1905 .... (86)	201,078	200.00	210.00	225.00	250.00	3,250
1905S	369,250	200.00	210.00	225.00	250.00	
1906 .... (77)	165,497	200.00	210.00	225.00	250.00	3,250
1906D	981,000	200.00	210.00	225.00	250.00	
1906O	86,895	200.00	210.00	225.00	250.00	
1906S	457,000	200.00	210.00	225.00	250.00	
1907 .... (74)	1,203,973	200.00	210.00	225.00	250.00	3,250
1907D	1,030,000	200.00	210.00	225.00	250.00	
1907S	210,500	200.00	210.00	225.00	250.00	

INDIAN HEAD TYPE 1907-1933
No Motto on Reverse 1907-1908

With Motto
IN GOD WE TRUST

Mint mark location is above left tip of branch on 1908D no motto, and at left of arrow points thereafter.

VF-20 VERY FINE—*Bonnet feathers worn near band. Hair high points show wear.*
EF-40 EXTREMELY FINE—*Slight wear on cheekbone and headdress feathers. Eagle's eye and left wing will show slight wear.*
AU-50 ABOUT UNCIRCULATED—*Trace of wear on hair above eye and on forehead.*
MS-60 UNCIRCULATED—*No trace of wear. Light blemishes.*

Choice uncirculated (MS-65) coins are worth substantial premiums.

	Quan. Minted	VF-20	EF-40	AU-50	MS-60	Proof-63
1907 "Wire edge" (rim), periods.........	500			$3,000	$7,000	$10,000
1907 Rounded edge, periods before and after •E•PLURIBUS•UNUM•	42					15,000
1907 No periods	239,406	$250.00	$300.00	325.00	400.00	
1908 No motto	33,500	250.00	325.00	350.00	750.00	
1908D No motto	210,000	250.00	275.00	300.00	500.00	

Motto on Reverse 1908-1933

	Quan. Minted	VF-20	EF-40	AU-50	MS-60	Matte Proof-63
1908 .... (116)	341,486	250.00	275.00	300.00	375.00	6,000
1908D	836,500	250.00	275.00	300.00	425.00	
1908S	59,850	250.00	275.00	350.00	1,500	
1909 .... (74)	184,863	250.00	275.00	300.00	375.00	6,000
1909D	121,540	250.00	275.00	300.00	400.00	

Values of common gold coins are based on the prevailing price of gold bullion, and will vary according to current market price. See Bullion Chart.

EAGLES

	Quan. Minted	VF-20	EF-40	AU-50	MS-60	Matte Proof-63
1909S	292,350	$250.00	$275.00	$300.00	$700.00	
1910 (204)	318,704	250.00	275.00	300.00	375.00	$6,000
1910D	2,356,640	250.00	275.00	300.00	375.00	
1910S	811,000	250.00	275.00	300.00	700.00	
1911 (95)	505,595	250.00	275.00	300.00	375.00	6,000
1911D	30,100	275.00	350.00	500.00	2,250	
1911S	51,000	250.00	275.00	400.00	1,400	
1912 (83)	405,083	250.00	275.00	300.00	375.00	6,000
1912S	300,000	250.00	275.00	300.00	950.00	
1913 (71)	442,071	250.00	275.00	300.00	375.00	6,000
1913S	66,000	250.00	350.00	500.00	7,000	
1914 (50)	151,050	250.00	275.00	300.00	375.00	6,000
1914D	343,500	250.00	275.00	300.00	375.00	
1914S	208,000	250.00	275.00	300.00	850.00	
1915 (75)	351,075	250.00	275.00	300.00	375.00	6,000
1915S	59,000	250.00	275.00	350.00	1,400	
1916S	138,500	250.00	275.00	300.00	800.00	
1920S	126,500	2,200	3,500	6,000	15,000	
1926	1,014,000	250.00	275.00	300.00	375.00	
1930S	96,000	1,300	1,800	3,250	7,000	
1932	4,463,000	250.00	275.00	300.00	375.00	
1933	312,500				———	

DOUBLE EAGLES ($20.00 Gold Pieces) — 1849-1933

This largest denomination of all regular United States issues was authorized to be coined by the Act of March 3, 1849. Its weight was 516 grains, .900 fine.

Mint mark location is below the eagle

VF-20 VERY FINE—*LIBERTY is bold. Jewels on crown defined. Lower half worn flat. Hair worn about ear.*
EF-40 EXTREMELY FINE—*Trace of wear on rounded prongs of crown and down hair curls. Minor bag marks.*
AU-50 ABOUT UNCIRCULATED—*Trace of wear on hair over eye and on coronet.*
MS-60 UNCIRCULATED—*No trace of wear. Light blemishes.*

Without Motto on Reverse 1849-1866

	Quan. Minted	VF-20	EF-40	AU-50	MS-60	Proof-63
1850	1,170,261	$410.00	$435.00	$500.00	$1,200	
1850O	141,000	410.00	435.00	550.00	1,500	
1851	2,087,155	410.00	435.00	500.00	1,000	
1851O	315,000	410.00	435.00	550.00	1,500	
1852	2,053,026	410.00	435.00	500.00	1,000	
1852O	190,000	410.00	435.00	550.00	1,500	

Values of common gold coins are based on the prevailing price of gold bullion, and will vary according to current market price. See Bullion Chart.

DOUBLE EAGLES

	Quan. Minted	VF-20	EF-40	AU-50	MS-60	Proof-63
1853	1,261,326	$410.00	$435.00	$500.00	$900.00	
1853O	71,000	410.00	435.00	550.00	1,700	
1854	757,899	410.00	435.00	500.00	900.00	
1854O	3,250			20,000		
1854S	141,468	410.00	435.00	500.00	1,900	
1855	364,666	410.00	435.00	500.00	800.00	
1855O	8,000	600.00	900.00	1,800	4,250	
1855S	879,675	410.00	435.00	500.00	800.00	
1856	329,878	410.00	435.00	500.00	800.00	
1856O	2,250	10,000	15,000	20,000		
1856S	1,189,750	410.00	435.00	500.00	800.00	
1857	439,375	410.00	435.00	500.00	800.00	
1857O	30,000	410.00	435.00	550.00	1,600	
1857S	970,500	410.00	435.00	500.00	800.00	
1858	211,714	410.00	435.00	500.00	800.00	
1858O	35,250	410.00	400.00	700.00	2,500	
1858S	846,710	410.00	435.00	500.00	800.00	
1859 (80)	43,597	410.00	435.00	500.00	1,250	
1859O	9,100	800.00	1,200	2,000	3,500	
1859S	636,445	410.00	435.00	500.00	800.00	
1860 (59)	577,670	410.00	435.00	500.00	800.00	
1860O	6,600	800.00	1,500	2,000	3,500	
1860S	544,950	410.00	435.00	500.00	800.00	
1861 (66)	2,976,453	410.00	435.00	500.00	800.00	
1861O	17,741	500.00	900.00	1,400	3,000	
1861S	768,000	410.00	435.00	500.00	800.00	
1862 (35)	92,133	410.00	435.00	500.00	1,500	$12,000
1862S	854,173	410.00	435.00	500.00	800.00	
1863 (30)	142,790	410.00	435.00	500.00	1,200	12,000
1863S	966,570	410.00	435.00	500.00	800.00	
1864 (50)	204,285	410.00	435.00	500.00	1,000	12,000
1864S	793,660	410.00	435.00	500.00	800.00	
1865 (25)	351,200	410.00	435.00	500.00	800.00	12,000
1865S	1,042,500	410.00	435.00	500.00	800.00	
1866S		410.00	435.00	550.00	1,400	

Motto Above Eagle, Value TWENTY D. 1866-1876

	Quan. Minted	VF-20	EF-40	AU-50	MS-60	Proof-63
1866 (30)	698,775	400.00	415.00	450.00	700.00	9,000
1866S	842,250	400.00	415.00	450.00	650.00	
1867 (50)	251,065	400.00	415.00	450.00	650.00	9,000
1867S	920,750	400.00	415.00	450.00	650.00	

Values of common gold coins are based on the prevailing price of gold bullion, and will vary according to current market price. See Bullion Chart.

DOUBLE EAGLES

	Quan. Minted	VF-20	EF-40	AU-50	MS-60	Proof-63
1868	(25) 98,600	$400.00	$415.00	$450.00	$700.00	$9,000
1868S	837,500	400.00	415.00	450.00	650.00	
1869	(25) 175,155	400.00	415.00	450.00	650.00	9,000
1869S	686,750	400.00	415.00	450.00	650.00	
1870	(35) 155,185	400.00	415.00	450.00	650.00	9,000
1870CC	3,789	6,000	12,000	—	—	
1870S	982,000	400.00	415.00	450.00	600.00	
1871	(30) 80,150	400.00	415.00	450.00	650.00	9,000
1871CC	17,387	750.00	1,200	1,600		
1871S	928,000	400.00	415.00	450.00	550.00	
1872	(30) 251,880	400.00	415.00	450.00	550.00	9,000
1872CC	26,900	400.00	475.00	650.00	1,400	
1872S	780,000	400.00	415.00	450.00	550.00	
1873	(25) 1,709,825	400.00	415.00	450.00	550.00	9,000
1873CC	22,410	450.00	500.00	600.00	1,400	
1873S	1,040,600	400.00	415.00	450.00	550.00	
1874	(20) 366,800	400.00	415.00	450.00	550.00	9,500
1874CC	115,085	450.00	475.00	500.00	800.00	
1874S	1,214,000	400.00	415.00	450.00	550.00	
1875	(20) 295,740	400.00	415.00	450.00	550.00	—
1875CC	111,151	400.00	435.00	475.00	650.00	
1875S	1,230,000	400.00	415.00	450.00	550.00	
1876	(45) 583,905	400.00	415.00	450.00	550.00	9,000
1876CC	138,441	400.00	435.00	475.00	600.00	
1876S	1,597,000	400.00	415.00	450.00	550.00	

TWENTY DOLLARS 1877-1907

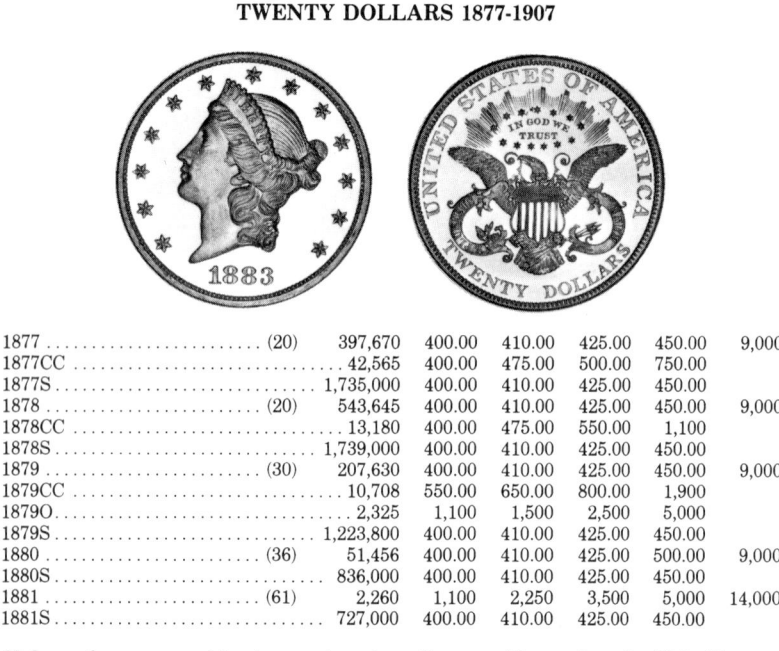

1877	(20) 397,670	400.00	410.00	425.00	450.00	9,000
1877CC	42,565	400.00	475.00	500.00	750.00	
1877S	1,735,000	400.00	410.00	425.00	450.00	
1878	(20) 543,645	400.00	410.00	425.00	450.00	9,000
1878CC	13,180	400.00	475.00	550.00	1,100	
1878S	1,739,000	400.00	410.00	425.00	450.00	
1879	(30) 207,630	400.00	410.00	425.00	450.00	9,000
1879CC	10,708	550.00	650.00	800.00	1,900	
1879O	2,325	1,100	1,500	2,500	5,000	
1879S	1,223,800	400.00	410.00	425.00	450.00	
1880	(36) 51,456	400.00	410.00	425.00	500.00	9,000
1880S	836,000	400.00	410.00	425.00	450.00	
1881	(61) 2,260	1,100	2,250	3,500	5,000	14,000
1881S	727,000	400.00	410.00	425.00	450.00	

Values of common gold coins are based on the prevailing price of gold bullion and will vary according to current market price. See Bullion Chart.

DOUBLE EAGLES

	Quan. Minted	VF-20	EF-40	AU-50	MS-60	Proof-63
1882 .... (59)	630	$1,600	$4,000	$7,500	$14,000	—
1882CC	39,140	400.00	450.00	500.00	800.00	
1882S	1,125,000	400.00	410.00	425.00	450.00	
1883 Proofs only .... (92)	92					—
1883CC	59,962	400.00	410.00	500.00	700.00	
1883S	1,189,000	400.00	410.00	425.00	450.00	
1884 Proofs only .... (71)	71					—
1884CC	81,139	400.00	410.00	500.00	700.00	
1884S	916,000	400.00	410.00	425.00	450.00	
1885 .... (77)	828	1,200	3,000	6,000	11,000	—
1885CC	9,450	500.00	600.00	750.00	1,200	
1885S	683,500	400.00	410.00	425.00	450.00	
1886 .... (106)	1,106	2,000	4,000	7,500	13,000	$22,500
1887 Proofs only .... (121)	121					27,500
1887S	283,000	400.00	410.00	425.00	450.00	
1888 .... (105)	226,266	400.00	410.00	425.00	450.00	8,000
1888S	859,600	400.00	410.00	425.00	450.00	
1889 .... (41)	44,111	400.00	410.00	425.00	450.00	8,000
1889CC	30,945	400.00	410.00	450.00	800.00	
1889S	774,700	400.00	410.00	425.00	450.00	
1890 .... (55)	75,995	400.00	410.00	425.00	450.00	8,000
1890CC	91,209	400.00	410.00	450.00	700.00	
1890S	802,750	400.00	410.00	425.00	450.00	
1891 .... (52)	1,442	550.00	1,200	2,000	3,500	9,000
1891CC	5,000	500.00	800.00	1,200	2,250	
1891S	1,288,125	400.00	410.00	425.00	450.00	
1892 .... (93)	4,523	500.00	650.00	900.00	2,500	8,500
1892CC	27,265	350.00	400.00	550.00	1,100	
1892S	930,150	400.00	410.00	425.00	450.00	
1893 .... (59)	344,339	400.00	410.00	425.00	450.00	6,000
1893CC	18,402	400.00	475.00	650.00	1,300	
1893S	996,175	400.00	410.00	425.00	450.00	
1894 .... (50)	1,368,990	400.00	410.00	425.00	450.00	6,000
1894S	1,048,550	400.00	410.00	425.00	450.00	
1895 .... (51)	1,114,656	400.00	410.00	425.00	450.00	6,000
1895S	1,143,500	400.00	410.00	425.00	450.00	
1896 .... (128)	792,663	400.00	410.00	425.00	450.00	5,500
1896S	1,403,925	400.00	410.00	425.00	450.00	
1897 .... (86)	1,383,261	400.00	410.00	425.00	450.00	5,500
1897S	1,470,250	400.00	410.00	425.00	450.00	
1898 .... (75)	170,470	400.00	410.00	425.00	450.00	5,500
1898S	2,575,175	400.00	410.00	425.00	450.00	
1899 .... (84)	1,669,384	400.00	410.00	425.00	450.00	5,500
1899S	2,010,300	400.00	410.00	425.00	450.00	
1900 .... (124)	1,874,584	400.00	410.00	425.00	450.00	5,500
1900S	2,459,500	400.00	410.00	425.00	450.00	
1901 .... (96)	111,526	400.00	410.00	425.00	450.00	5,500
1901S	1,596,000	400.00	410.00	425.00	450.00	
1902 .... (114)	31,254	400.00	410.00	425.00	450.00	5,500
1902S	1,753,625	400.00	410.00	425.00	450.00	
1903 .... (158)	287,428	400.00	410.00	425.00	450.00	5,500
1903S	954,000	400.00	410.00	425.00	450.00	
1904 .... (98)	6,256,797	400.00	410.00	425.00	450.00	5,500
1904S	5,134,175	400.00	410.00	425.00	450.00	

Values of common gold coins are based on the prevailing price of gold bullion, and will vary according to current market price. See Bullion Chart.

DOUBLE EAGLES

	Quan. Minted	VF-20	EF-20	AU-50	MS-60	Proof-63
1905 .... (92)	59,011	$400.00	$410.00	$425.00	$450.00	$5,500
1905S	1,813,000	400.00	410.00	425.00	450.00	
1906 .... (94)	69,690	400.00	410.00	425.00	450.00	5,500
1906D	620,250	400.00	410.00	425.00	450.00	
1906S	2,065,750	400.00	410.00	425.00	450.00	
1907 .... (78)	1,451,864	400.00	410.00	425.00	450.00	5,500
1907D	842,250	400.00	410.00	425.00	450.00	
1907S	2,165,800	400.00	410.00	425.00	450.00	

SAINT-GAUDENS TYPE 1907-1933

The $20 gold piece designed by Augustus Saint-Gaudens is considered to be the most beautiful United States coin. The first coins issued were 11,250 high relief pieces struck for general circulation. The relief is much higher than later issues and the date 1907 is in Roman numerals. A few of these coins were made using the lettered edge collar from the extremely high relief version. These can be distinguished by a pronounced bottom left serif on the N in UNUM, and other minor differences. Flat-relief double eagles were issued later in 1907 with Arabic numerals, and continued through 1933.

The field of the rare extremely high relief experimental pieces is excessively concave and connects directly with the edge without any border, giving it a sharp knifelike appearance; Liberty's skirt shows two folds on the side of her right leg; the Capitol building in the background at left is very small; the sun, on the reverse side, has 14 rays, as opposed to the regular high relief coins that have only 13 rays extending from the sun. High relief proofs are trial or experimental pieces.

VF-20 VERY FINE—*Minor wear on legs and toes. Eagle's left wing and breast feathers worn.*
EF-40 EXTREMELY FINE—*Drapery lines on chest visible. Wear on left breast, knee and below. Eagle's feathers on breast and right wing are bold.*
MS-60 UNCIRCULATED—*No trace of wear. Light marks or blemishes.*

	Proof
1907 Ex. high relief, plain edge (Unique)	—
1907 Ex. high relief, lettered edge	—

	Quan. Minted	VF-20	EF-40	MS-60	Proof
1907 high relief, Roman numerals (MCMVII), ...	11,250	$1,500	$2,200	$4,250	—

Values of common gold coins are based on the prevailing price of gold bullion, and will vary according to current market price. See Bullion Chart.

DOUBLE EAGLES
Arabic Numerals, No Motto

	Quan. Minted	VF-20	EF-40	MS-60
1907	361,667	$425.00	$450.00	$500.00
1908	4,271,551	425.00	450.00	500.00
1908D	663,750	425.00	450.00	500.00

With Motto IN GOD WE TRUST, 1908-1933

Mint mark location is on obverse above date.

	Quan. Minted	VF-20	EF-40	MS-60	Matte Proof-63
1908	(101) 156,359	$425.00	$450.00	$500.00	$10,000
1908D	349,500	425.00	450.00	500.00	
1908S	22,000	425.00	500.00	2,000	

1909, 9 over 8

	Quan. Minted	VF-20	EF-40	MS-60	Matte Proof-63
1909	(67) 161,282	425.00	450.00	500.00	8,000
1909, 9 over 8		425.00	450.00	500.00	
1909D	52,500	450.00	550.00	1,400	
1909S	2,774,925	425.00	450.00	500.00	

Values of common gold coins are based on the prevailing price of gold bullion, and will vary according to current market price. See Bullion Chart.

DOUBLE EAGLES

	Quan. Minted	VF-20	EF-40	MS-60	Matte Proof-63
1910	(167) 482,167	$425.00	$450.00	$500.00	$8,000
1910D	429,000	425.00	450.00	500.00	
1910S	2,128,250	425.00	450.00	500.00	
1911	(100) 197,350	425.00	450.00	500.00	8,000
1911D	846,500	425.00	450.00	500.00	
1911S	775,750	425.00	450.00	500.00	
1912	(74) 149,824	425.00	450.00	500.00	8,000
1913	(58) 168,838	425.00	450.00	500.00	8,000
1913D	393,500	425.00	450.00	500.00	
1913S	34,000	425.00	450.00	550.00	
1914	(70) 95,320	425.00	450.00	500.00	8,000
1914D	453,000	425.00	450.00	500.00	
1914S	1,498,000	425.00	450.00	500.00	
1915	(50) 152,050	425.00	450.00	500.00	8,000
1915S	567,500	425.00	450.00	500.00	
1916S	796,000	425.00	450.00	500.00	
1920	228,250	425.00	450.00	500.00	
1920S	558,000	3,000	5,000	10,000	
1921	528,500	5,000	7,000	12,000	
1922	1,375,500	425.00	450.00	500.00	
1922S	2,658,000	425.00	475.00	600.00	
1923	566,000	425.00	450.00	500.00	
1923D	1,702,250	425.00	450.00	500.00	
1924	4,323,500	425.00	450.00	500.00	
1924D	3,049,500	450.00	475.00	950.00	
1924S	2,927,500	450.00	475.00	950.00	
1925	2,831,750	425.00	450.00	500.00	
1925D	2,938,500	450.00	550.00	1,000	
1925S	3,776,500	450.00	500.00	1,000	
1926	816,750	425.00	450.00	500.00	
1926D	481,000	450.00	650.00	1,600	
1926S	2,041,500	450.00	500.00	900.00	
1927	2,946,750	425.00	450.00	500.00	
1927D	180,000			—	
1927S	3,107,000	1,500	2,000	5,000	
1928	8,816,000	425.00	450.00	500.00	
1929	1,779,750	2,000	3,000	5,000	
1930S	74,000	3,500	6,000	12,000	
1931	2,938,250	2,500	4,500	10,000	
1931D	106,500	3,000	5,000	10,000	
1932	1,101,750	3,000	5,500	12,000	
1933	445,500	None placed in circulation			

Values of common gold coins are based on the prevailing price of gold bullion, and will vary according to current market price. See Bullion Chart.

COMMEMORATIVE SILVER COINS
Isabella, Lafayette, Alabama

In 1892, to commemorate the World's Columbian Exposition in Chicago, Congress authorized the coinage of a special half dollar and quarter dollar, thus starting a long line of United States commemorative coins. Nearly all commemorative coins have been distributed by private individuals or commissions; they paid the mint the face value of the coins and in turn sold the pieces at a premium to collectors. There are a few instances in which some of the very large issues were later released to circulation at face value.

		Quan. Available	AU-50	MS-60
1893	Isabella Quarter (Columbian Exposition)	24,214	$130.00	$400.00

1900	Lafayette Dollar	36,026	250.00	700.00

HALF DOLLARS
(Listed alphabetically)

2x2 in Field

1921	Alabama, "2 × 2" in field	6,006	110.00	300.00
1921	Same, no "2 × 2"	59,038	60.00	220.00

COMMEMORATIVE SILVER
Albany, Antietam, Arkansas

		Quan. Available	AU-50	MS-60
1936	Albany, New York	17,671	$140.00	$200.00

1937	Battle of Antietam 1862-1937	18,028	175.00	265.00

1935	Arkansas Centennial	13,012 ⎫		
1935D	Same	5,505 ⎬ Set		200.00
1935S	Same	5,506 ⎭		
1936	Arkansas Centennial, same as 1935 — date 1936 on reverse	9,660 ⎫		
1936D	Same	9,660 ⎬ Set		200.00
1936S	Same	9,662 ⎭		
1937	Arkansas Centennial, same as 1935	5,505 ⎫		
1937D	Same	5,505 ⎬ Set		220.00
1937S	Same	5,506 ⎭		
1938	Arkansas Centennial, same as 1935	3,156 ⎫		
1938D	Same	3,155 ⎬ Set		380.00
1938S	Same	3,156 ⎭		
1939	Arkansas, same as 1935	2,104 ⎫		
1939D	Same	2,104 ⎬ Set		775.00
1939S	Same	2,105 ⎭		
	Single type coin		40.00	65.00

COMMEMORATIVE SILVER
Bay Bridge, Boone

		Quan. Available	AU-50	MS-60
1936S	San Francisco-Oakland Bay Bridge	71,424	$55.00	$85.00

1934	Daniel Boone Bicentennial	10,007		60.00	95.00
1935	Same	10,010	⎫		
1935D	Same	5,005	⎬ Set		275.00
1935S	Same	5,005	⎭		

1935	Daniel Boone Bicentennial, same as 1934 but small 1934 added on reverse	10,008	⎫		
1935D	Same	2,003	⎬ Set		825.00
1935S	Same	2,004	⎭		
1936	D. Boone Bicentennial, same as 1934	12,012	⎫		
1936D	Same	5,005	⎬ Set		275.00
1936S	Same	5,006	⎭		
1937	D. Boone Bicentennial, same as 1934	9,810	⎫		
1937D	Same	2,506	⎬ Set		500.00
1937S	Same	2,506	⎭		
1938	Daniel Boone, same as 1934	2,100	⎫		
1938D	Same	2,100	⎬ Set		875.00
1938S	Same	2,100	⎭		
	Single type coin			65.00	85.00

COMMEMORATIVE SILVER
Bridgeport, California, Cincinnati, Cleveland

		Quan. Available	AU-50	MS-60
1936	Bridgeport, Conn., Centennial	25,015	$90.00	$110.00

| 1925S | California Diamond Jubilee | 86,594 | 45.00 | 95.00 |

1936	Cincinnati Music Center	5,005 ⎫		
1936D	Same	5,005 ⎬ Set		645.00
1936S	Same	5,006 ⎭		
	Single type coin		175.00	215.00

| 1936 | Cleveland, Great Lakes Exposition | 50,030 | 35.00 | 70.00 |

COMMEMORATIVE SILVER
Columbia, S.C., Columbian, Connecticut, Delaware

		Quan. Available	AU-50	MS-60
1936	Columbia, S.C., Sesquicentennial	9,007 ⎫		
1936D	Same	8,009 ⎬ Set		$575.00
1936S	Same	8,007 ⎭		
	Single type coin		$150.00	190.00

1892	Columbian Exposition	950,000	8.00	20.00
1893	Same	1,550,405	8.00	20.00

1935	Connecticut Tercentenary	25,018	120.00	180.00

1936	Delaware Tercentenary	20,993	120.00	170.00

COMMEMORATIVE SILVER
Elgin, Gettysburg, Grant, Hawaiian

		Quan. Available	AU-50	MS-60
1936	Elgin, Illinois, Centennial	20,015	$90.00	$150.00

1936	Battle of Gettysburg 1863-1938	26,928	110.00	185.00

1922	Grant Memorial, small star above word "Grant" in obv. field	4,256	250.00	475.00
	(Fake stars have flattened spot on reverse.)			
1922	Same, no star in obverse field	67,405	35.00	75.00

1928	Hawaiian Sesquicentennial	10,008	450.00	675.00

COMMEMORATIVE SILVER
Hudson, Huguenot, Iowa, Lexington

		Quan. Available	AU-50	MS-60
1935	Hudson N. Y. Sesquicentennial	10,008	$300.00	$425.00

1924	Huguenot-Walloon Tercentenary	142,080	40.00	75.00

1946	Iowa Centennial	100,057	45.00	70.00

1925	Lexington-Concord Sesquicentennial	162,013	25.00	42.00

COMMEMORATIVE SILVER
Lincoln, Long Island, Lynchburg, Maine

		Quan. Available	AU-50	MS-60
1918	Illinois Centennial	100,058	$40.00	$75.00

1936	Long Island Tercentenary	81,826	40.00	70.00

1936	Lynchburg, Va., Sesquicentennial	20,013	95.00	145.00

1920	Maine Centennial	50,028	50.00	85.00

COMMEMORATIVE SILVER
Maryland, Missouri, Monroe, New Rochelle

		Quan. Available	AU-50	MS-60
1934	Maryland Tercentenary	25,015	$75.00	$100.00

		Quan. Available	AU-50	MS-60
1921	Missouri Centennial "2 ★ 4" above "1821"	5,000	175.00	400.00
1921	Same, no "2 ★ 4"	15,428	165.00	390.00

1923S	Monroe Doctrine Centennial	274,077	17.50	40.00

1938	New Rochelle, N. Y. 1688-1938	15,266	220.00	340.00

COMMEMORATIVE SILVER
Norfolk, Oregon, Panama-Pacific

		Quan. Available	AU-50	MS-60
1936	Norfolk, Va., Bicentennial	16,936	$175.00	$265.00

			AU-50	MS-60
1926	Oregon Trail Memorial	47,955	50.00	85.00
1926S	Same	83,055	50.00	85.00
1928	Oregon Trail Memorial, same as 1926	6,028	80.00	190.00
1933D	Oregon Trail Memorial, same	5,008	150.00	350.00
1934D	Oregon Trail Memorial, same	7,006	65.00	150.00
1936	Oregon Trail Memorial, same as 1926	10,006	55.00	115.00
1936S	Same	5,006	70.00	180.00
1937D	Oregon Trail Mem., D mint, same as 1926	12,008	50.00	100.00
1938	Oregon Trail Mem., same as 1926	6,006 ⎫		
1938D	Same	6,005 ⎬ Set		450.00
1938S	Same	6,006 ⎭		
1939	Oregon Trail, same as 1926	3,004 ⎫		
1939D	Same	3,004 ⎬ Set		650.00
1939S	Same	3,005 ⎭		
	Single type coin		50.00	85.00

1915S Panama-Pacific Exposition	27,134	170.00	390.00

COMMEMORATIVE SILVER
Pilgrim, Rhode Island, Roanoke, Robinson

		Quan. Available	AU-50	MS-60
1920	Pilgrim Tercentenary	152,112	$30.00	$45.00
1921	Same, with 1921 date added in field	20,053	55.00	125.00

1936	Rhode Island Tercentenary	20,013		
1936D	Same	15,010 Set		300.00
1936S	Same	15,011		
	Single type coin		50.00	95.00

1937	Roanoke Island, N. C., 1587-1937	29,030	100.00	145.00

1936	Arkansas Centennial (Robinson)	25,265	65.00	110.00

COMMEMORATIVE SILVER
San Diego, Sesquicentennial, Spanish Trail, Stone Mountain

		Quan. Available	AU-50	MS-60
1935S	San Diego, California-Pacific Expo	70,132	$30.00	$70.00
1936D	Same	30,092	35.00	80.00

1926	Sesquicentennial of American Independence	141,120	20.00	40.00

1935	Old Spanish Trail 1535-1935	10,008	425.00	600.00

1925	Stone Mountain Memorial	1,314,709	15.00	30.00

COMMEMORATIVE SILVER
Texas, Vancouver, Vermont

		Quan. Available		AU-50	MS-60
1934	Texas Centennial	61,463		$65.00	$105.00
1935	Texas Centennial, same as 1934	9,996	⎫		
1935D	Same	10,007	⎬ Set		320.00
1935S	Same	10,008	⎭		
1936	Texas Centennial, same as 1934	8,911	⎫		
1936D	Same	9,039	⎬ Set		330.00
1936S	Same	9,055	⎭		
1937	Texas Centennial, same as 1934	6,571	⎫		
1937D	Same	6,605	⎬ Set		350.00
1937S	Same	6,637	⎭		
1938	Texas Centennial, same as 1934	3,780	⎫		
1938D	Same	3,775	⎬ Set		500.00
1938S	Same	3,814	⎭		
	Single type coin			65.00	105.00

1925S	Fort Vancouver Centennial	14,994	200.00	375.00

1927	Vermont Sesquicentennial (Bennington)	28,162	85.00	180.00

COMMEMORATIVE SILVER
Washington, B. T., Washington-Carver, Washington, George

	Quan. Available		MS-60
1946 Booker T. Washington Memorial	1,000,546		
1946D	200,113	Set	$35.00
1946S	500,279		
1947	100,017		
1947D	100,017	Set	55.00
1947S	100,017		
1948	8,005		
1948D	8,005	Set	100.00
1948S	8,005		

	Quan. Available		MS-60
1949	6,004		
1949D	6,004	Set	$160.00
1949S	6,004		
1950	6,004		
1950D	6,004	Set	140.00
1950S	512,091		
1951	510,082		
1951D	7,004	Set	90.00
1951S	7,004		
Single type coin			10.00

1951 Washington-Carver	110,018		
1951D	10,004	Set	80.00
1951S	10,004		
1952	2,006,292		
1952D	8,006	Set	100.00
1952S	8,006		

1953	8,003		
1953D	8,003	Set	125.00
1953S	108,020		
1954	12,006		
1954D	12,006	Set	85.00
1954S	122,024		
Single type coin			10.00

		MS-60	Proof-65
1982D	Geo. Washington-250th Anniversary	$6.00	
1982S	Same		$8.00

COMMEMORATIVE SILVER
Wisconsin, York County

		Quan. Available	AU-50	MS-60
1936	Wisconsin Centennial	25,015	$100.00	$175.00

		Quan. Available	AU-50	MS-60
1936	York County, Maine Centennial	25,015	100.00	175.00

OLYMPIC DOLLARS

		MS-60	Proof-65
1983	XXIII Olympiad, Los Angeles	$28.00*	$32.00*

*Issue Prices

COMMEMORATIVE GOLD
Grant

		Quan. Available	AU-50	MS-60
1922	Grant Memorial Dollar, star above word "Grant"	5,016	$475.00	$925.00
1922	Same, without star	5,000	475.00	875.00

Lewis & Clark

1904	Lewis and Clark Exposition Dollar	10,025	400.00	950.00
1905	Lewis and Clark Exposition Dollar	10,041	400.00	950.00

Louisiana Purchase

1903	Louisiana Purchase Jefferson Dollar	17,500	300.00	525.00
1903	Louisiana Purchase McKinley Dollar	17,500	300.00	525.00

McKinley

1916	McKinley Memorial Dollar	9,977	275.00	575.00
1917	McKinley Memorial Dollar	10,000	300.00	650.00

Panama-Pacific

1915S	Panama-Pacific Exposition Dollar	15,000	275.00	575.00

COMMEMORATIVE GOLD
Panama-Pacific

	Quan. Available	AU-50	MS-60
1915S Panama-Pacific Exposition $2.50	6,749	$575.00	$1,400

1915S Panama-Pacific $50 Round	483	15,000	25,000
1915S Panama-Pacific $50 Octagonal	645	12,000	19,000

Sesquicentennial

1926 Philadelphia Sesquicentennial $2.50	46,019	250.00	400.00

PRIVATE OR TERRITORIAL GOLD COINS

Private coins were circulated in most instances because of a shortage of regular coinage. The words "Private Gold," used with reference to coins struck outside of the United States Mint, are a general term. In the sense that no state or territory had authority to coin money, private gold simply refers to those interesting necessity pieces of various shapes, denominations and degrees of intrinsic worth which were circulated in isolated areas of our country by individuals, assayers, bankers, etc. Some will use the words "Territorial" and "State" to cover certain issues because they were coined and circulated in a territory or state. While the state of California properly sanctioned the ingots stamped by F. D. Kohler as state assayer, in no instance were any of the gold pieces struck by authority of any of the territorial governments.

The stamped ingots put out by Augustus Humbert, the United States assayer of gold, were not recognized at the United States Mint as an official issue of coins, but simply as ingots, though Humbert placed the value and fineness on the pieces as an official agent of the federal government.

TEMPLETON REID
Georgia 1830

The first private gold coinage under the Constitution was struck by Templeton Reid, a jeweler and gunsmith, in Milledgeville, Georgia in July, 1830. To be closer to the mines, he moved to Gainesville where most of his coins were made. Although weights were accurate, Reid's assays were not and his coins were slightly short of claimed value. Accordingly, he was severely attacked in the newspapers and soon lost the public's confidence.

1830 $2.50	....	E.F.	$25,000
1830 $5.00	....	E.F.	100,000

1830 TEN DOLLARS	....	V.G.	20,000
(No date) TEN DOLLARS	....	V.G.	15,000

TEMPLETON REID
"California Gold 1849"

1849 TEN DOLLAR CALIFORNIA GOLD (Smithsonian Collection) .... Unique

THE BECHTLERS
Rutherford County, N. C. 1830-1852

Two skilled German metallurgists, Christopher Bechtler and his son August, and later Christopher Bechtler, Junior, a nephew of Christopher the elder, operated a "private" mint at Rutherfordton, North Carolina. Rutherford county in which Rutherfordton is located was the principal source of the nation's gold supply from 1790 to 1840.

CHRISTOPHER BECHTLER

	V. Fine	E. Fine	Unc.
ONE DOLLAR CAROLINA, 28 gr. N reversed	$500.00	$700.00	$1,500
ONE DOLLAR N. CAROLINA, 28 gr. no star	1,000	2,000	4,250

| ONE DOLLAR N. CAROLINA, 30 gr. .... | 700.00 | 1,000 | 2,000 |
| $2.50 CAROLINA, 67 gr. 21 carats .... | 800.00 | 1,100 | 2,750 |

| $2.50 CAROLINA, 70 gr. 20 carats .... | 850.00 | 1,200 | 3,000 |
| $2.50 GEORGIA, 64 gr. 22 carats........................ | 1,000 | 1,600 | 3,500 |

THE BECHTLERS

	V. Fine	E. Fine	Unc.
$2.50 NORTH CAROLINA, 75 gr. 20 carats. RUTHERFORD in a circle. Border of lg. beads	$2,250	$3,500	$5,000
$2.50 NORTH CAROLINA, without 75 G	2,100	3,000	4,500

	V. Fine	E. Fine	Unc.
5 DOLLARS CAROLINA, RUTHERFORD, 140 gr. 20 carats. Date August 1, 1834.			
Plain edge	1,000	1,600	3,750
Reeded edge	1,600	2,200	4,000
5 DOLLARS CAROLINA, 134 gr. 21 carats, with star	900.00	1,600	3,000

	V. Fine	E. Fine	Unc.
5 DOLLARS GEORGIA, RUTHERF. 128 gr. 22 carats	1,200	2,200	3,750
5 DOLLARS GEORGIA, RTHERF. 128 gr. 22 carats	1,100	2,000	3,500
5 DOLLARS CAROLINA, RUTHERF. 140 gr. 20 carats. Date August 1, 1834 (illustrated)	1,100	2,000	3,500
Similar. 20 distant from carats	2,750	4,500	—

Without 150 G

	V. Fine	E. Fine	Unc.
5 DOLLARS NORTH CAROLINA, 150 gr. 20 carats	1,600	3,000	7,000
5 DOLLARS. Same as last variety without 150 G	2,100	3,500	6,500

THE BECHTLERS

AUGUST BECHTLER
1842-1852

	V. Fine	E. Fine	Unc.
1 DOLLAR CAROLINA, 27 gr. 21 carats....................	$450.00	$600.00	$1,250
5 DOLLARS CAROLINA, 134 gr. 21 carats..................	1,000	1,700	3,500

   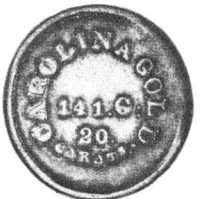

5 DOLLARS CAROLINA, 128 gr. 22 carats..................	1,600	2,500	5,500
5 DOLLARS CAROLINA, 141 gr. 20 carats..................	1,600	2,500	5,000

NORRIS, GREGG & NORRIS
San Francisco 1849

These pieces are considered the first of the California private gold coins. A newspaper account dated May 31, 1849, described a five-dollar gold coin, struck at Benicia City, though with the imprint San Francisco, and the private stamp of Norris, Gregg and Norris.

	Fine	V. Fine	E. Fine	Unc.
1849 HALF EAGLE — Plain edge	$1,200	$1,750	$4,000	$15,000
1849 HALF EAGLE — Reeded edge	1,200	1,750	4,200	16,500
1850 HALF EAGLE with STOCKTON beneath date				(Unique)

MOFFAT & CO.
San Francisco 1849-1853

The firm of Moffat and Company was perhaps the most important of the California private coiners. The assay office they conducted was semi-official in character, and successors to this firm later established the United States Branch mint of San Francisco.

In June or July, 1849, Moffat & Co. began to issue small rectangular pieces of gold in values from $9.43 to $264. The $9.43, $14.25 and $16.00 varieties are the only types known today.

$9.43 Ingot (Unique) .... —
$14.25 Ingot (Unique) .... —
$16.00 Ingot (Beware of spurious specimens cast in base metal) .... E.F. $15,000

The dies for the $10 piece were cut by Albert Kuner. The words MOFFAT & CO. appear on the coronet of Liberty instead of the word LIBERTY as in regular United States issues.

	Fine	V. Fine	E. Fine	Unc.
1849 FIVE DOL.	$450.00	$900.00	$1,300	$5,000
1850 FIVE DOL.	450.00	900.00	1,350	5,100
1849 TEN DOL.	900.00	1,300	2,600	7,200
1849 TEN D.	1,300	2,100	4,000	

United States Assay Office
AUGUSTUS HUMBERT
U. S. Assayer 1851

When Augustus Humbert was appointed United States Assayer, he placed his name and the government stamp on the ingots of gold issued by Moffat & Co. The assay office, a Provisional Government Mint, was a temporary expedient to accommodate the Californians until the establishment of a permanent branch mint.

The fifty-dollar gold piece was accepted as legal tender on a par with standard U.S. gold coins.

 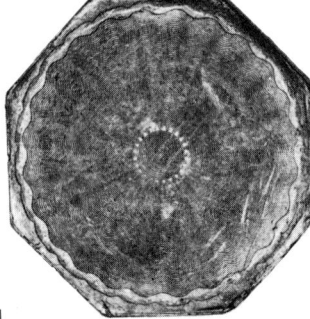

MOFFAT — HUMBERT

LETTERED EDGE VARIETIES

50 on reverse

	Fine	V. Fine	E. Fine	Unc.
1851 50 D C 880 THOUS., no 50 on Reverse. Sunk in edge: AUGUSTUS HUMBERT UNITED STATES ASSAYER OF GOLD CALIFORNIA 1851	$3,500	$5,000	$10,000	——
1851 50 D C Similar to last variety, but 50 on Reverse	4,250	5,500	12,000	——
1851 Similar to last variety, but 887 THOUS	4,000	5,250	11,000	——

REEDED EDGE VARIETIES

 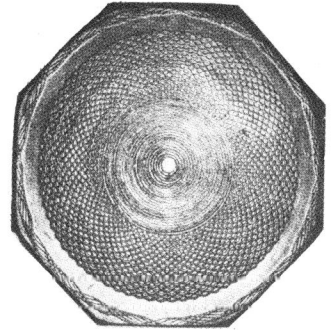

	Fine	V. Fine	E. Fine	Unc.
1851 FIFTY DOLLS 880 THOUS. "Target" Reverse	$3,500	$4,500	$8,000	$22,000
1851 FIFTY DOLLS 887 THOUS. "Target" Reverse	3,500	4,500	8,000	22,000
1852 FIFTY DOLLS 887 THOUS.	3,750	5,000	10,000	25,000

Moffat & Co. proceeded in January, 1852 to issue a new ten-dollar piece bearing the stamp MOFFAT & CO.

MOFFAT — HUMBERT

	Fine	V. Fine	E. Fine	Unc.
1852 TEN D. MOFFAT & CO.	$1,000	$2,000	$3,500	—

1852 TWENTY DOLS. 1852, 2 over 1..........	1,800	3,000	5,000	—

1852 TEN DOLS. 1852, 2 over 1..............	700.00	1,000	2,000	—
1852 TEN DOLS.	650.00	900.00	1,800	$5,000

UNITED STATES ASSAY OFFICE OF GOLD

1852

The firm of Moffat & Co. dissolved and a new reorganized company known as the United States Assay Office of Gold, composed of Curtis, Perry and Ward took over the contract.

UNITED STATES ASSAY OFFICE

 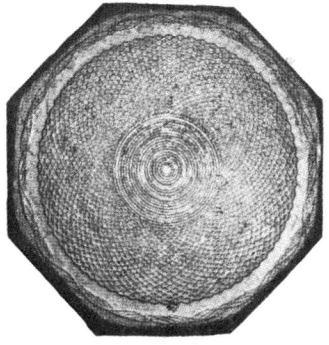

	Fine	V. Fine	E. Fine	Unc.
1852 FIFTY DOLLS. 887 THOUS.	$3,000	$5,000	$9,500	$25,000
1852 FIFTY DOLLS. 900 THOUS.	3,100	5,100	11,000	30,000

1852 TEN DOLS 884 THOUS.	600.00	1,100	1,600	5,500
1853 TEN D. 884 THOUS.	2,500	3,500	7,500	——
1853 TEN D. 900 THOUS.	1,300	2,200	3,500	——
1853 TWENTY D. 884 THOUS.	3,750	6,000	11,000	——
1853 TWENTY D. 900 THOUS.	850.00	1,500	2,500	5,500

The last Moffat issue was the 1853 twenty dollar piece which is very similar to the U.S. double eagle of that period. It was struck after the retirement of Mr. Moffat from the Assay Office.

1853 TWENTY D.	1,000	2,000	3,000	6,000

CINCINNATI MINING & TRADING CO.

The origin and location of this company are unknown.

	E. Fine	Unc.
1849 FIVE DOLLARS	—	—
1849 TEN DOLLARS	—	—

MASSACHUSETTS AND CALIFORNIA COMPANY
San Francisco 1849

This company was believed to have been organized in Northampton, Mass. in May 1849.

	Fine
1849 FIVE D.	$20,000

MINERS' BANK
San Francisco 1849

The institution of Wright & Co., exchange brokers located in Portsmouth Square, San Francisco, was known as the Miners' Bank.

A ten dollar piece was issued in the autumn of 1849, but the coins were not readily accepted because they were worth less than face value.

	V. Fine	E. Fine	Unc.
(1849) TEN. D.	$6,000	$9,000	$20,000

J.S. ORMSBY
Sacramento 1849

The initials J. S. O. which appear on certain issues of California privately coined gold pieces represent the firm of J. S. Ormsby & Co. They struck both five and ten dollar denominations, all undated.

J.S. ORMSBY

	V. Fine
(1849) 5 DOLLS. (Unique)	—
(1849) 10 DOLLS	—

PACIFIC COMPANY
San Francisco 1849

The origin of the Pacific Co. is very uncertain. All data regarding the firm is based on conjecture.

Edgar H. Adams wrote that he believed that the coins bearing the stamp of the Pacific Company were produced by the coining firm of Broderick and Kohler.

	E. Fine
1849 5 DOLLARS	—
1849 10 DOLLARS	$14,000

F. D. KOHLER
California State Assayer 1850

The State Assay Office was authorized April 12, 1850. Governor Burnett appointed F. D. Kohler that year who thereupon sold his assaying business to Baldwin & Co. He served at both San Francisco and Sacramento Offices. The State Assay Offices were discontinued at the time the U. S. Assay Office was established Feb. 1, 1851.

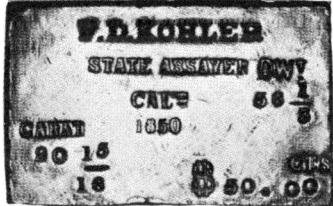

$36.55 Sacramento	—
$47.71 Sacramento	—
$37.31 San Francisco	—
$40.07 San Francisco	—
$41.68 San Francisco	—
$45.34 San Francisco	—
$50.00 San Francisco	—
$54.09 San Francisco	—

DUBOSQ & COMPANY
San Francisco 1850

Theodore Dubosq, a Philadelphia jeweler who took melting and coining machinery to San Francisco in 1849, produced the following pieces.

	V. Fine
1850 FIVE D.	$25,000
1850 TEN D.	30,000

BALDWIN & COMPANY
San Francisco 1850

George C. Baldwin and Thomas S. Holman were in the jewelry business in San Francisco and were known as Baldwin & Co. They were the successors to F. D. Kohler & Co., taking over their machinery and other equipment in May, 1850.

	Fine	V. Fine	E. Fine	Unc.
1850 FIVE DOL.	$1,600	$3,000	$5,000	$10,000
1850 TEN DOLLARS — Horseman type	8,000	14,000	22,500	—

BALDWIN & COMPANY

	Fine	V. Fine	E. Fine	Unc.
1851 TEN D.	$4,000	$6,000	$14,000	—

1851 TWENTY D.		65,000		—

[180]

SHULTZ & COMPANY
San Francisco 1851

The firm located in back of Baldwin's establishment operated a brass foundry beginning in 1851. Judge G. W. Shultz and William T. Garratt were partners in the enterprise.

	Fine	V. Fine
1851 FIVE D..........	$8,000	$13,000

DUNBAR & COMPANY
San Francisco 1851

Edward E. Dunbar operated the California Bank in San Francisco. He later returned to New York and organized the famous Continental Bank Note Co.

	E. Fine
1851 FIVE D	$40,000

WASS, MOLITOR & COMPANY
San Francisco 1852-1855

The gold smelting and assaying plant of Wass, Molitor & Co. was operated by Count S. C. Wass and A. P. Molitor. They maintained an excellent laboratory and complete apparatus for analysis and coinage of gold.

	Fine	V. Fine	E. Fine	Unc.
1852 FIVE DOLLARS.....................	$1,200	$2,000	$3,250	$8,000

Large Head			Small Head	
1852 TEN D. Large head	800.00	1,500	2,500	—
1852 TEN D. Small head	1,500	2,750	4,500	—
1855 TEN D...............................	3,000	5,000	8,000	—

WASS, MOLITOR & COMPANY

Large Head   Small Head

	Fine	V. Fine	E. Fine	Unc.
1855 TWENTY DOL. Large head	—	—	—	—
1855 TWENTY DOL. Small head	$3,250	$7,000	$9,500	—

	Fine	V. Fine	E. Fine	Unc.
1855 50 DOLLARS	7,000	10,000	18,000	—

KELLOGG & COMPANY
San Francisco 1854-1855

When the U.S. Assay Office ceased operations a period ensued during which no private firm was striking gold. The new San Francisco branch mint did not produce coins for some months after Curtis & Perry took the contract for the government. The lack of coin was again keenly felt by businessmen who petitioned Kellogg & Richter to "supply the vacuum" by issuing private coin. Their plea was answered on Feb. 9, 1854, when Kellogg & Co. placed their first twenty-dollar piece in circulation.

	Fine	V. Fine	E. Fine	Unc.
1854 TWENTY D.	$900.00	$1,300	$2,000	$6,000
1855 TWENTY D.	900.00	1,300	2,100	6,500

KELLOGG & COMPANY

1855 FIFTY DOLLS.. *Proof*

CALIFORNIA SMALL DENOMINATION GOLD

There was a scarcity of small coins during the California gold rush and starting in 1852, quarter, half and dollar pieces were privately minted from native gold to alleviate the shortage. The need and acceptability of these pieces declined after 1856 and they then became popular as souvenirs. Authentic pieces all have CENTS, DOLLAR, or an abbreviation thereof on the reverse. The tokens are much less valuable. Modern restrikes and replicas have no numismatic value.

Values are only for genuine coins with the denomination on the reverse expressed as:
CENTS, DOL., DOLL., *or* DOLLAR.

		EF-40	AU-50	MS-60
25c Octagonal:	Liberty head.........................	$40.00	$70.00	$100.00
	Indian head	50.00	80.00	125.00
	Washington head	250.00	400.00	600.00
25c Round:	Liberty head.........................	40.00	70.00	100.00
	Indian head	50.00	80.00	125.00
	Washington head	300.00	500.00	700.00
50c Octagonal:	Liberty head.........................	50.00	80.00	110.00
	Liberty head/Eagle	300.00	500.00	700.00
	Indian head	110.00	200.00	300.00
50c Round:	Liberty head.........................	50.00	80.00	110.00
	Indian head	100.00	150.00	200.00
$1.00 Octagonal:	Liberty head.........................	110.00	200.00	300.00
	Liberty head/Eagle	600.00	900.00	2,000
	Indian head	250.00	400.00	550.00
$1.00 Round:	Liberty head.........................	550.00	800.00	1,200
	Indian head	600.00	900.00	2,000

OREGON EXCHANGE COMPANY
Oregon City, 1849
THE BEAVER COINS OF OREGON

On February 16, 1849, the legislature passed an act providing for a mint and specified five and ten dollar gold coins without alloy. Oregon City, the largest city in the territory with a population of about 1,000, was designated as the location for

OREGON EXCHANGE COMPANY

the mint. At the time this act was passed Oregon had been brought into the United States as a territory by act of Congress. When the new governor arrived March 2, he declared the coinage act unconstitutional.

	Fine	V. Fine	E. Fine	Unc.
1849 5 D	$4,000	$8,000	$12,000	——

1849 TEN D	15,000	20,000	27,500	——

MORMON GOLD PIECES
Salt Lake City, Utah 1849-1860

Brigham Young was the instigator of this coinage system and personally supervised the mint which was housed in a little adobe building in Salt Lake City. The mint was inaugurated late in 1849 as a public convenience.

	Fine	V. Fine	E. Fine	Unc.
1849 TWO AND HALF DO	$1,800	$3,500	$5,000	——
1849 FIVE DOLLARS	1,200	1,900	3,000	$6,000

	Fine
1849 TEN DOLLARS	$45,000

[184]

MORMON GOLD PIECES

	Fine	V. Fine
1849 TWENTY DOLLARS	$12,000	$17,500

1850 FIVE DOLLARS
Fine	$1,300
V. Fine	1,800
Ex. Fine	3,000
Unc.	—

1860 5D
Fine	$3,000
V. Fine	4,500
Ex. Fine	7,000
Unc.	12,000

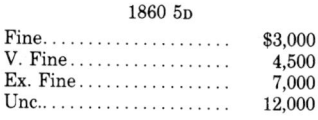

COLORADO GOLD PIECES
Clark, Gruber & Co. — Denver 1860-1861

Clark, Gruber and Co. was a well known private minting firm in Denver, Colo. in the early sixties.

	Fine	V. Fine	E. Fine	Unc.
1860 2½ D	$400.00	$700.00	$1,100	$4,500
1860 Five D	600.00	1,100	1,800	5,750

1860 TEN D	1,400	1,900	3,500	8,000
1860 TWENTY D	8,000	12,000	21,000	—

COLORADO GOLD PIECES

	Fine	V. Fine	E. Fine	Unc.
1861 2½ D	$400.00	$600.00	$1,000	$4,000
1861 FIVE D	600.00	900.00	1,800	5,000
1861 TEN D	700.00	950.00	1,900	6,250

1861 TWENTY D	2,750	5,000	10,000	—

JOHN PARSONS & COMPANY
Tarryall Mines — Colorado 1861

Very little is known about the mint of John Parsons and Co. It probably operated in Colorado, near Tarryall, in the summer of 1861.

PIKES PEAK GOLD

		V. Fine
(1861)	Undated 2½ D	$30,000
(1861)	Undated FIVE D	60,000

J. J. CONWAY & COMPANY
Georgia Gulch, Colorado, 1861

The value of gold dust caused disagreement among the merchants and the miners in all gold mining areas. The firm of J. J. Conway & Co. solved this difficulty by bringing out its gold pieces in August, 1861.

J. J. CONWAY & COMPANY

			V. Fine
(1861)	Undated 2½ DOLL'S	....	$30,000
(1861)	Undated FIVE DOLLARS	....	60,000
(1861)	Undated FIVE DOLLARS, Similar. Variety without numeral 5 on reverse	....	20,000

(1861) Undated TEN DOLLARS .... ——

CIVIL WAR TOKENS — 1861-1864

Civil War Tokens are generally divided into two groups: tradesmen's tokens, and anonymously issued pieces with political or patriotic themes. They came into existence only because of the scarcity of government coins and disappeared as soon as the bronze coins of 1864 met the public demand for small copper change.

These tokens are of great variety in composition and design. A number were more or less faithful imitations of the copper-nickel cent. A few of this type have the word "NOT" in very small letters above the words "ONE CENT."

	Fine	V. Fine	Unc.
Copper or Brass Tokens	$1.00	$2.00	$9.00
Nickel or German Silver Tokens	8.00	15.00	25.00
White Metal Tokens	8.00	15.00	25.00
Copper-Nickel Tokens	12.00	20.00	50.00
Silver Tokens	23.00	35.00	100.00

BULLION VALUE OF SILVER COINS

Common date silver coins are valued according to the price of silver bullion. In recent years the price of silver bullion has been subject to extreme fluctuation. Therefore, when you read this it is highly probable that the current bullion price may differ from the prevailing market price used in tabulating valuations of many 19th and 20th century silver coins (priced in italics) listed in this edition. The following chart will help to determine the approximate bullion value of these coins at various price levels. Or, the approximate value may be calculated by multiplying the current spot price of silver times the content for each coin as indicated below. Dealers generally purchase common silver coins at 15% below bullion value, and sell them at 15% above bullion value.

Silver Bullion	Wartime Nickel .05626 oz.	Dime .07234 oz.	Quarter .18084 oz.	Half Dollar .36169 oz.	Silver Clad Half Dollar .14792 oz.	Silver Dollar .77344 oz.
$2.00	$.11	$.14	$.36	$.72	$.29	$1.55
2.50	.14	.18	.45	.90	.37	1.93
3.00	.17	.22	.54	1.08	.44	2.32
3.50	.20	.25	.63	1.26	.52	2.71
4.00	.23	.29	.72	1.45	.59	3.09
4.50	.25	.33	.81	1.63	.67	3.48
5.00	.28	.36	.90	1.81	.74	3.87
5.50	.31	.40	1.00	1.99	.81	4.25
6.00	.34	.44	1.09	2.17	.89	4.64
6.50	.36	.47	1.18	2.35	.96	5.03
7.00	.40	.51	1.27	2.53	1.04	5.42
7.50	.42	.55	1.36	2.72	1.11	5.80
8.00	.45	.58	1.45	2.90	1.19	6.19
8.50	.48	.62	1.54	3.08	1.26	6.58
9.00	.50	.65	1.63	3.26	1.33	6.96
9.50	.53	.69	1.72	3.44	1.42	7.35
10.00	.56	.72	1.81	3.62	1.48	7.73
11.00	.62	.80	1.99	3.98	1.63	8.51
12.00	.68	.87	2.17	4.34	1.78	9.28
13.00	.73	.94	2.35	4.70	1.92	10.05
14.00	.79	1.01	2.53	5.06	2.07	10.83
15.00	.84	1.09	2.71	5.43	2.22	11.60
16.00	.90	1.16	2.89	5.79	2.37	12.38
17.00	.96	1.23	3.07	6.15	2.51	13.15
18.00	1.01	1.30	3.26	6.51	2.66	13.92
19.00	1.07	1.37	3.44	6.87	2.81	14.70
20.00	1.13	1.45	3.62	7.23	2.96	15.47
21.00	1.18	1.52	3.80	7.60	3.11	16.24
22.00	1.24	1.59	3.98	7.96	3.25	17.02
23.00	1.30	1.66	4.16	8.32	3.40	17.79
24.00	1.35	1.74	4.34	8.68	3.55	18.56
25.00	1.41	1.81	4.52	9.04	3.70	19.34
26.00	1.46	1.88	4.70	9.40	3.85	20.11
27.00	1.52	1.95	4.88	9.77	3.99	20.88
28.00	1.58	2.03	5.06	10.13	4.14	21.66
29.00	1.63	2.10	5.24	10.49	4.29	22.43

BULLION VALUE OF GOLD COINS

The value of common date gold coins listed in this book may be affected by the rise or fall in the price of gold bullion. Nearly all U.S. gold coins have an additional premium value beyond their bullion content, and thus are not subject to the minor variations described for silver coins on the preceding page. The premium amount is not necessarily tied to the bullion price of gold, but is usually determined by supply and demand levels for actual gold coins occurring in the numismatic marketplace. Because these factors can vary significantly, there is no reliable formula for calculating "percentage above bullion" prices that would remain accurate over time. For this reason the chart below lists bullion values based on gold content only. Consult your nearest coin dealer to ascertain current premium prices.

Price Per Ounce	$5.00 Liberty Head 1839-1908 Indian Head 1908-1929	$10.00 Liberty Head 1838-1907 Indian Head 1907-1933	$20.00 1849-1933
$200.00	$48.37	$96.75	$193.50
225.00	54.42	108.84	217.69
250.00	60.46	120.94	241.88
275.00	66.51	133.03	266.06
300.00	72.56	145.13	290.25
325.00	78.60	157.22	314.44
350.00	84.65	169.31	338.63
375.00	90.70	181.40	362.81
400.00	96.75	193.50	387.00
425.00	102.80	205.60	411.19
450.00	108.84	217.69	435.38
475.00	114.89	229.78	459.56
500.00	120.94	241.87	483.75
525.00	126.98	253.97	507.94
550.00	133.03	266.06	532.13
575.00	139.08	278.16	556.31
600.00	145.12	290.25	580.50
625.00	151.17	302.34	604.69
650.00	157.22	314.44	628.88
675.00	163.26	326.53	653.06
700.00	169.31	338.63	677.25
725.00	175.36	350.72	701.44
750.00	181.40	362.81	725.63
775.00	187.45	374.91	749.81
800.00	193.50	387.00	774.00

INDEX

American Plantations Token 17
Anthony, Susan B., Dollars 123
Auctori Connec Coppers (Connecticut) 28-30
Auctori Plebis Token 35

Baldwin & Co. (Private Gold) 180
Baltimore, Lord (Maryland) 16
Bar Cent 35
Barber Dimes 1892-1916 81
Barber Quarter Dollars 1892-1916 93
Barber Half Dollars 1892-1915 107
Barry, Standish, Threepence (Baltimore, Md.) .. 36
Bechtlers, The, Christopher and August 171-173
Bermuda (Sommer Islands) 14
Bicentennial Coinage 99, 113, 122
Bishop, Samuel (Connecticut) 28
Brasher, Ephraim, Doubloon 30
Brenner, Victor D. (Designer of Lincoln Cent) .. 58
Britannia (1787 Coppers) 34
Buffalo Nickels (Indian Head) 1913-1938 67
Bullion Charts -
  Silver 188
  Gold 189

California Fractional Gold 183
Carolina Elephant Tokens 20
Carolina Gold (Bechtler) 171-173
Cent, 1864, L on Ribbon 56
Cents, Large 1793-1857 47
Cents, Flying Eagle 1856-1858 55
Cents, Indian Head 1859-1909 55
Cents, Lincoln 58
Cents, Steel 1943 60
Chalmers, J., Silver Tokens (Annapolis, Md.) ... 23
Charlotte, No. Carolina Branch Mint 8
Cincinnati Mining & Trading Co. (Private Gold) 178
Civil War Tokens 187
Clad Coinage 7, 86, 98, 112, 122
Clark, Gruber & Co. (Private Gold) 185, 186
Cleaning of Coins 12
Clinton, George, Copper (New York) 31
Colorado Gold Pieces 185, 186
Commemorative Coins, General Information ... 153
Commemorative Gold 168, 169
Commemorative Silver 153-167
Condition of Coins 11
Confederatio Coppers 26
Connecticut Coppers (Auctori Connec) 28-30
Continental Dollar, 1776 24
Conway, J.J. & Co. (Private Gold) 186, 187
Cox, Albion (New Jersey) 32

Dahlonega, Ga., Branch Mint 8
Dimes 76
Dimes, Liberty Seated 1837-1891 78
Dimes, Barber 1892-1916 81
Dimes, "Mercury" Head 83
Dimes, Roosevelt 85
Distinguishing Marks 8
Dollar, Origin of 113
Dollars, Patterns (Gobrecht) 1836-1839 115
Dollars, Silver, Liberty Seated 1840-1873 116
Dollars, Trade 117
Dollars, Silver, Morgan Type 1878-1921 118
Dollars, Silver, Peace Type 1921-1935 121

Dollars, Eisenhower Type 1971-1978 122
Dollars, Susan B. Anthony Type 123
Dollars, Gold 1849-1889 124
Dollars, Gold (California) 183
Double Eagles 1849-1933 146
Dubosq & Co. (Private Gold) 180
Dunbar & Co. (Private Gold) 181

Eagles 1795-1933 140
Eisenhower Dollars 1971-1978 122
Elephant Tokens 19, 20
Excelsior Coppers (New York) 31

Five Cent, Nickel 65
Five Cent, Silver 70
Five Cent, Shield Type 1866-1883 65
Five Cent, Liberty Head 1883-1913 66
Five Cent, Indian or Buffalo Type 1913-1938 ... 67
Five Cent, Jefferson Type 70
Flying Eagle Cent 1858, LG. and SM. Letters ... 55
Fifty Dollar Gold (Private) ... 175, 177, 179, 182, 183
Five Dollar Gold Pieces 132
Four Dollar Gold Pieces 132
Franklin, Benjamin - Fugio Cents 41
Franklin Press Token 36
French Colonies 23
Fugio Cents 6, 41

George III - Immune Columbia 25
George III - Indian (New York) 31
George III - Vermont 34
Georgia Gold (Reid) 170, 171
Georgia Gold (Bechtler) 171
Gloucester Token 21
Goadsby, Thomas (New Jersey) 32
Gobrecht, Christian 115
Gold, Dollars 1849-1889 124
Gold, $2.50 126
Gold, Three Dollars 131
Gold, Stella, $4.00 Patterns 132
Gold, Five Dollars 132
Gold, Ten Dollars 140
Gold, Twenty Dollars 146
Gold, Private or Territorial 170
Goodrich, John (Connecticut) 28
Granby Coppers (John Higley) 21

Half Cents 43
Half Dime (LIBEKTY Variety 1800) 73
Half Dimes 72
Half Dimes, Liberty Seated 74
Half Dollars 99
Half Dollars, Liberty Seated 103
Half Dollars, Barber 107
Half Dollars, Liberty Walking 109
Half Dollars, Franklin 111
Half Dollars, Kennedy 112
Half Dollars, Gold 183
Half Eagles 1795-1929 132
Harmon, Rueben Jr. 33
Hibernia - Voce Populi Token 22
Hibernia Coins, William Wood 18, 19
Higley, John, Coppers (Granby, Connecticut) ... 21
Hillhouse, James (Connecticut) 28
"Hogge Money" (Sommer Islands) 14

[190]

INDEX — *Continued*

Hopkins, Joseph (Connecticut) 28
Hull, John (Mass. Colonial Silver) 14
Humbert, Augustus (U.S. Assayer) 174

Immune Columbia 25
Immunis Columbia 25, 26
Indian - George III (New York) 31
Ingots, California Gold 174, 179

Jefferson, Thomas, Nickels 70
Jenks, Joseph 14

Kellogg & Co. (Private Gold) 182, 183
Kentucky Token (Kentucky Triangle) 36
Kohler, F.D. (Calif. State Assayer) 179

LIBEKTY Variety, 1800 Half Dime 73
Liberty Head Nickels 66
Liberty Seated Half Dimes 74
Liberty Seated Dimes 78
Liberty Seated Quarter Dollars 90
Liberty Seated Half Dollars 103
Liberty Seated Dollars 116
Liberty Standing Quarter Dollars 95
Liberty Walking Half Dollars 109
LIHERTY, Cent Variety 1796 49
Liverpool Halfpenny 38
London Token (Elephant) 19, 20
Lord Baltimore (Maryland) 16

Maryland (Lord Baltimore) 16
Massachusetts & California Co. (Private Gold) . 178
Massachusetts, Colonial Silver 14
Massachusetts 1787-8 Cents and Half Cents .. 27, 28
"Mercury" Head Dimes 83
Miners' Bank (Private Gold) 178
Mint Mark "P" (Silver Five Cent Pieces) 70
Mint Sets (Regular and Special) 42
Mints and Mint Marks 7
Moffat & Co. (Private Gold) 174
Morgan Dollars (Liberty Head Type) 118
Morgan, George T 118
Mormon Gold Pieces 184, 185
Morris, Gouverneur 24
Mott Token 35
Mould, Walter (New Jersey) 32
Moulton, William (New Hampshire) 27

Newby, Mark (St. Patrick) Halfpenny 16, 17
New England (N.E.) Shillings, etc 14
New England Elephant Token 20
New Hampshire Copper 26, 27
New Jersey (Mark Newby) Halfpenny 16, 17
New Jersey Coppers 32, 33
New York (Nova Eborac - Neo Eborac) 30, 32
New Yorke Token 21
Nickel, Three Cents 65
Nickel, Five Cents 65
Non Vi Virtute Vici (New York) 30
Norris, Gregg & Norris (Private Gold) 173
North American Token 34
North Wales Halfpenny 40
Nova Caesarea Coppers (New Jersey) 32, 33
Nova Constellatio Coppers 24, 25
Nova Eborac Coppers (New York) 32

Oak Tree Shilling, etc 15
Oregon Exchange Co. (Private Gold) 183, 184
Ormsby, J.S. (Private Gold) 178, 179

Pacific Co. (Private Gold) 179
Parsons, John & Co. (Private Gold) 186
Peace Dollars 1921-1935 121
Pine Tree Shillings, etc 15, 16
Pitt Tokens 22
Pratt, Bela Lyon 130
Preserving Coins 12
Private or Territorial Gold 170
Production of Coins 6
Proof Coins 7, 42

Quarter Dollars 88
Quarter Dollars, Liberty Seated 90
Quarter Dollars, Barber Type 93
Quarter Dollars, Liberty Standing 95
Quarter Dollars, Washington Head Type 96
Quarter Dollars, Gold 183
Quarter Eagles 1796-1929 126
Quarter Eagle, "CAL." on Reverse 1848 128

Reid, Templeton (Private Gold) 170, 171
Rhode Island Ship Medal 22
Roosevelt, Franklin D., Dimes 85
Rosa Americana Coins (William Wood) 17

Saint-Gaudens, Augustus 150
St. Patrick (Mark Newby) Halfpenny 16, 17
Sanderson, Robert (Mass. Colonial) 14
Shield Nickels 65
Ship Halfpenny 39
Shultz & Co. (Private Gold) 181
Silver Composition Five Cents 70
Silver Dollars 113
Sommer Islands (Bermuda) 14
Sou Marque 23
Starting a Collection 12
Stellas, $4.00 Gold Patterns 132

Talbot, Allum & Lee Tokens 37
Templeton Reid (Private Gold) 170, 171
Ten Dollar Gold Pieces 140
Territorial or Private Gold 170
Three Cent, Nickel 65
Three Cent, Silver 64
Three Dollar Gold Pieces 131
Trade Dollars 1873-1885 117
Twenty Cent Pieces 87
Twenty Dollar Gold Pieces 146
Two and One Half Dollar Gold Pieces 126
Two Cent Pieces 63

United States Assay Office -
  Humbert 174-176
  of Gold 176, 177
United States Paper Money 13

VDB on Lincoln Cents 58, 59
Vermont Coppers 33, 34
Virginia Halfpenny 19
Voce Populi - Hibernia Token 22

INDEX — *Continued*

Washington, George........................ 37, 96	Willow Tree Shilling, etc....................... 15
Washington Head Quarter Dollars............. 96	Witherle, Joshua (Massachusetts).............. 27
Washington Pieces 1793-1795 37-40	Wood, William, Rosa Americana
Wass, Molitor & Co. (Private Gold)........ 181, 182	and Hibernia Coins 17-19

ARE YOUR COINS GENUINE...

Coin authentication and certification service is available at a fee through the following associations. Coins must not be submitted without first requesting mailing instructions and a schedule of fees charged for this service. Inquiries about coin authentication should be accompanied by a self-addressed stamped envelope and sent to:

American Numismatic Association
Certification Service
818 N. Cascade
Colorado Springs, Colo. 80903

International Numismatic Society
Authentication Bureau
P.O. Box 19386
Washington, D.C. 20036

AN INVESTMENT IN KNOWLEDGE:

The American Numismatic Association

Knowledge is the key to success in any field. Coin collecting is no exception. The American Numismatic Association, a non-profit group chartered by Congress, offers you the opportunity to share collecting experiences and to become involved with numismatists from all parts of the world. Write for complete details on membership.

**AMERICAN NUMISMATIC ASSOCIATION
P.O. BOX 2366R
COLORADO SPRINGS, CO 80901**